ARBITRATION IN HEALTH CARE

Donald J. Petersen
Julius Rezler
Keith A. Reed

AN ASPEN PUBLICATION®
Aspen Systems Corporation
Rockville, Maryland
London
1981

Library of Congress Cataloging in Publication Data

Petersen, Donald J.
Arbitration in health care.

Includes bibliographies and index.
1. Arbitration, Industrial—United States.
2. Collective labor agreements—Health facilities—United States.
I. Rezler, Julius Stephen. II. Reed, Keith A.
III. Title. [DNLM:
1. Collective bargaining.
2. Labor unions—Organization and administration. 3. Personnel
administration, Hospital. WX 159.8 P484a]
KF3450.H4P48   344.73 '0189143   81-10811
ISBN:0-89443-372-5   347.304189143   AACR2

Copyright © 1981 by Aspen Systems Corporation

Library of Congress Catalog Card Number: 81-10811
ISBN: 0-89443-372-5

Printed in the United States of America

1 2 3 4 5

Table of Contents

Preface

The health care industry represents one of the last remaining frontiers of American industrial relations. The bulk of union organizing and collective negotiations in hospitals and nursing homes was initiated during the 1970s—that is, a quarter century after employees were organized in the private sector. The principles and procedures of grievance resolution—an integral part of the collective agreement—although crystallized in the private sector long ago, are presently being formulated in the health care industry.

The purpose of this work is to help industrial relations practitioners in the health care industry function in an efficient, knowledgeable manner during arbitration, the highest level of the grievance procedure.

Although the peaceful settlement of disputes emerging between labor and management is important in any industry and sector of the economy, it is paramount in the health care industry. Here an interruption of work would cause not only loss of revenues and wages but would also endanger public health. With this in mind, the authors applied the time-honored principles and procedures of labor arbitration to the particular needs of the health care industry. It was recognized that, while in the private sector grievance arbitration prevails and interest arbitration plays a very limited role, these two basic types of arbitration are equally important in the health care industry. The authors also noted that certain issues (for example, abuse of patients, sleeping on the job) are of particular significance in the health care industry, and therefore adequate attention was given to the arbitration practice of such issues.

We realize that we tread on virgin ground. We believe this to be the first work to deal exclusively with issues and procedures of arbitration in the health care industry. In support of our research, we have relied greatly on the advice and expertise of well-known labor-management advocates. We wish to recognize here the contributions made by these eminent representatives of labor unions and management in the health care industry: Irving Kurasch, President, General

Service Employees Union, Local 73; Nancy Connolly Fibish, Health Care Coordinator at the Federal Mediation and Conciliation Service; Joel A. D'Alba, Esq., of Asher, Greenfield, Goodstein, Pavalon, Gittler, Greenfield & Segall, Ltd., Chicago, Illinois; Norman R. Burns, Vice-President, Employee Relations, Northwestern Memorial Hospital, Chicago, Illinois; John Comer, Labor Relations Director, Chicago Hospital Council; William J. Abelow, Executive Vice-President, League of Voluntary Hospitals of New York City; John Barrett, Personnel Director, Grant Hospital, Chicago, Illinois; Donald Cohen, Esq., of Asher, Greenfield, Goodstein, Pavalon, Gittler, Greenfield & Segall, Ltd., Chicago, Illinois; and Norman Metzger, Vice-President, Labor Relations, The Mount Sinai Hospital, New York, New York.

Our thanks are extended also to Helen Gayer for performing the arduous job of typing this manuscript.

Donald J. Petersen
Julius Rezler
Keith A. Reed

Part I

The Arbitration Process

The first part of this book focuses on the fundamentals necessary for a thorough understanding of the arbitration process in hospitals. In Chapter 1 the legal basis for arbitration is reviewed as is its relation to the Equal Employment Opportunity Commission (EEOC) and National Labor Relations Board (NLRB). The advantages of arbitration are also discussed. Chapter 2 deals with the preliminary stages of the grievance procedure prior to arbitration. Political and strategic reasons for presenting grievances round out the chapter. The very important process of arbitrator selection is discussed in Chapter 3. Emphasis is placed on the type of arbitrator background that may be most helpful in certain cases or issues. How to research an arbitrator's background is also discussed. Chapters 4 and 5 discuss how evidence can be effectively collected and presented. Types of evidence needed in various cases are considered and likely sources are indicated.

Finally, the authors attempt to present a framework for understanding how arbitrators make their decisions, considering both the value judgments and personal views of arbitrators (subjective factors) as well as contract construction guidelines, past practice, and precedential value of prior awards (objective factors).

Chapter 1

The Place of Arbitration in Health Care

Although arbitration is not a twentieth century invention, it has been hailed as one of the greatest social developments of the twentieth century. We will not debate whether or not arbitration deserves this accolade, but one fact cannot be ignored. Arbitration has proved to be enormously acceptable to both hospital administrators and unions. According to a recent national survey of 817 hospital collective bargaining agreements, 87.9 percent provided for binding arbitration of at least some issues, and an additional 4.4 percent had provisions for advisory arbitration.[1] This percentage is, however, not as high as that found in the private sector, where arbitration clauses are found in more than 96 percent of all contracts. Still it must be said that arbitration has achieved widespread acceptance in hospitals. Moreover, the institution of arbitration has even been adopted as an adjunct to some nonunion hospital grievance procedures.

WHY ARBITRATION IS USED SO WIDELY

There are several very good reasons why arbitration clauses appear in so many contracts, both within and outside the health care area. Three reasons are summarized here:

1. *Arbitration is a voluntary process*. In most instances, arbitration is not a compulsory process. This means that the parties have control over whether and how often they resort to arbitration. No law states that arbitration must be in a collective agreement. Such clauses are included in these agreements because the parties think they will be mutually beneficial. If arbitration does not meet the parties' expectations, they can always negotiate it out.

2. *Arbitration is a substitute for a strike*. The inclusion of an arbitration clause in a collective agreement may persuade a union to refrain from work stoppages during the term of the bargaining agreement. A national survey of hospital

contracts revealed that three-quarters of these contracts had some type of no-strike (no lockout) provision.[2] A no-strike agreement assures a hospital of relative labor peace for the duration of the contract. For a union it means that the hospital will submit to binding arbitration all grievances that cannot be resolved at lower steps in the grievance procedure.[3]

The courts have significantly enhanced the position of arbitration in this regard. In the *Lincoln Mills* case, the U.S. Supreme Court ruled that even if an arbitration clause does not exist in a collective bargaining agreement, it would read one into the contract if the union had previously negotiated a no-strike clause.[4] Obviously, if the union has given up its right to strike and is also barred from arbitration, it has no effective means for resolving grievances, beyond management's good will. The court seems to be saying that the no-strike pledge is just consideration (a *quid pro quo*) for having access to arbitration.

3. *Arbitration is a less costly and less time-consuming process than its alternatives.* Essentially there are three basic ways to resolve a grievance over which the parties are deadlocked: (a) the union can resort to a strike; (b) the matter can be submitted to the courts; or (c) the grievance can be settled through arbitration.

Obviously, a strike is not a particularly pleasant prospect for any organization, but when the organization is a hospital, strike threats are even more ominous. Imagine having to face the possibility of a strike for each grievance that came along! A hospital might have more employees outside its doors than patients inside. The threat of strikes would impose a severe cost burden on a hospital. In light of today's demands for hospital efficiency, this situation would be untenable. Nor would numerous strikes endear rank and file members to their unions. Union members would lose wages every time one of their colleagues was disciplined, discharged, or at the center of a complaint.

It is a cliché, but nevertheless true, that "justice delayed is justice denied." Submitting grievances to the courts is a more lengthy and a more costly process than taking a grievance to arbitration. For example, it costs the parties approximately $4,400 to have an arbitrator hear and decide a typical discharge case.[5] If such a claim were tried in a court of law, the costs would be at least four times greater.

In summary, it can be said that two of the greatest advantages to arbitration are speed and economy.

ARBITRATION AS CONTRASTED WITH MEDIATION AND FACTFINDING

Labor arbitration normally takes one of two forms: (1) grievance or "rights" arbitration, and (2) contract or "interest" arbitration. The former refers to the resolution of disputes that involve questions of contract interpretation and application of an *existing contract*. This is the form of arbitration most widely used. Contract or interest arbitration involves the resolution of disputes that arise over the establishment of *new* contract terms. Before contract or interest arbitration is used, the parties have already bargained to an impasse, and thus call on an arbitrator to resolve issues that still separate them. However, grievance or contract arbitration do have one thing in common—the decision of the arbitrator is final and binding.

Mediation is often confused with arbitration. The function of mediation is to bring the parties together when they cannot agree on new contract terms. In this respect, mediation is like interest arbitration. However, in mediation—unlike interest arbitration—the mediator is not empowered to make a final decision that binds the parties. Instead the mediator must depend on suggestion, persuasion, clarification, and so on, in an effort to get the parties to come to terms. However, if the parties choose not to agree, there is really nothing the mediator can do.

Factfinding also has its greatest use in contract or interest disputes. As its name implies, it involves investigation of the circumstances surrounding a dispute. The "facts" that emerge from the investigation may be publicized (through a report) or not; they may, however, form the basis for other, subsequent, compulsory actions. Like mediation, factfinding is not normally a binding process.

ARBITRATION'S TENUOUS RELATIONS WITH THE NLRB

Although the main purpose of arbitration is to resolve interest or rights disputes, a number of decisions of the National Labor Relations Board (NLRB) have markedly affected the scope of arbitrable jurisdiction. The Board has held that under certain circumstances it may defer decision making to arbitration when grievances also have unfair labor practice implications. The *Spielberg Manufacturing Company* case[6] was the first one in which the NLRB made clear comment regarding deferral. It must be emphasized that *Spielberg* dealt with an arbitration award that had already been decided prior to the filing of the unfair labor practice charge; it made no mention of prearbitral deferral.

In making its decision to defer to a prior arbitration award, the Board indicated that an unfair labor practice charge should be dismissed in favor of a prior arbitration award whenever ". . . the proceedings appear to be fair and regular, and all parties have agreed to be bound, and the decision of the arbitration panel is not clearly repugnant to the purposes and policies of the Act."[7]

The primary factor in the Board's decision to defer was that the arbitration award also disposed of the unfair labor practice.

In the *Collyer Wire* case[8] the Board further expanded the circumstances under which it would defer to arbitration. During its contract talks, the employer proposed a wage increase over and above that negotiated for a production and maintenance unit. The union rejected the proposals and the parties continued to discuss the raises. Finally the company unilaterally instituted a 20 cent increase. The union filed unfair labor practice charges, citing section 8(a)(5) of the National Labor Relations Act.[9]

Unlike the *Spielberg* case, in which the arbitrator's award had already been made, *Collyer* involved the question of whether or not the Board should defer to arbitration in the first place. The Board realized that the unfair labor practice issue would be resolved upon an appropriate interpretation of the collective agreement. While strictly speaking, the Board's decision in *Collyer* was limited to prearbitral deferral involving Section 8(a)(5) cases ("Collyer Doctrine"), concurring opinions of the Board decision suggested that deferral to arbitration could spread beyond 8(a)(5) cases alone.

This suggestion proved prophetic, because in the *National Radio* case[10] the NLRB expanded the scope of prearbitral deferral to include 8(a)(3) cases.[11] *National Radio* involved the discharge of an employee-union representative who refused to comply with a company rule that required such union representatives to report and record their whereabouts in the plant area while on union business. As a consequence of the discharge, the union filed a grievance and charged unfair labor practice. The grievance was pending resolution by an arbitrator when the unfair labor practice charge was received by the NLRB. Although the Board was somewhat divided over whether or not to defer, it finally decided that the arbitrator's interpretation of the collective agreement would also resolve the charge of unfair labor practice.

After *National Radio* the Board deferred in numerous cases that involved not only Section 8(a)(5) but also 8(a)(3). The issue in many of these subsequent cases centered on whether or not a grievant was discharged for engaging in union activity (in addition to the usual "just cause" issue).[12] In these cases the Board has held that the issue of discrimination for union activity cannot be artificially separated from the issue of just cause.[13]

EEO ISSUES AND ARBITRATION

Deferral to arbitration is not an accepted method for resolving disputes among all federal agencies, however. In the *Gardner-Denver* case[14] the U.S. Supreme Court made a landmark ruling regarding deferral to arbitration of a case that involved Title VII of the 1964 Civil Rights Act.

Harrell Alexander, Sr. was discharged as an employee of the Gardner-Denver Company. He filed a grievance that he had been released unjustly on the basis of racial discrimination (he was black). The union demanded arbitration on the matter, but before the hearing could be held, Alexander filed a complaint with the Equal Employment Opportunity Commission (EEOC). Subsequently, an arbitrator upheld the discharge. The EEOC also reviewed the case and determined that no reasonable cause existed to believe the employer had violated the prohibitions against racial discrimination found in Title VII of the 1964 Civil Rights Act. Alexander then appealed the decision to federal court. However, the court dismissed his suit, saying that the arbitrator's decision was binding, and further that Alexander was barred from court action, based on the prior arbitration award. In other words, once a complainant has chosen arbitration, he or she cannot opt for additional avenues of relief.

Alexander appealed this decision, and the case eventually reached the U.S. Supreme Court. The high court rejected the lower court's application of the doctrine of election of remedies. That doctrine bars a person from pursuing two legally consistent remedies and requires that person to choose only one. However, the court reasoned that the election of remedies doctrine does not operate where statutory rights under Title VII are distinctly separate from an employee's contractual rights through the grievance and arbitration machinery. Likewise, the court dismissed the proposition that an employee waives his or her Title VII rights by submitting a race bias claim to arbitration. Title VII statutory rights are separate from those granted in the collective bargaining agreement, and even if an arbitrator bases a decision on the legislation and not on the agreement, that arbitrator would be exceeding the scope of his or her authority. The Supreme Court did, however, note that the arbitration decision could be used as evidence and accorded appropriate weight.

ENFORCEMENT OF ARBITRATION AWARDS

The Wagner Act (1935) did not provide for enforcement of collective bargaining contracts because the common law of contracts did not recognize collective agreements as legal documents. This was because unions did not offer employers the required considerations for their contractual concessions. It was left up to the states to apply their common law in the enforcement of contracts.

This situation was changed markedly by the passage of the Taft-Hartley Act. Section 301 of that law provides in part that: "Suits for violations of contract between an employer and a labor organization . . . may be brought in any district court of the United States having jurisdiction of the parties, without respect to the amount in controversy or without regard to the citizenship of the parties."

Inclusion of Section 301 did not immediately resolve the common law problem of contract enforcement, but a number of subsequent court decisions did much to clear up the situation. In *Lincoln Mills*[15] the U.S. Supreme Court determined that federal substantive law should apply in suits under Section 301(a). Thus the arbitration provision, because it attempted to enforce the contract, fell under federal law and was thus enforceable in federal court. This, however, does not mean that state courts are barred from deciding Section 301 suits. But when such cases are heard in state courts, they must apply federal law.

The decision by the Supreme Court in *Lincoln Mills* did much to encourage the use of arbitration. Subsequent Supreme Court decisions have given even broader power to arbitrators and have major implications for the enforcement of collective bargaining agreements. On June 20, 1960, the U.S. Supreme Court handed down three decisions that have come to be known as the "Steelworkers Trilogy." The effect of these three decisions—by the highest court in the land—has been to increase greatly the prestige, importance, and authority of labor arbitration.

In the *Warrior & Gulf Navigation* case[16] the Supreme Court held that courts cannot decree that a grievance is not arbitrable *unless* clear-cut language in the collective agreement specifically excludes that grievance from the arbitration process. Of course, an arbitrator is still empowered to determine whether or not a dispute is arbitrable.[17]

The second case, *American Manufacturing*,[18] dealt with the question of whether recourse to arbitration could be barred because a grievance lacked merit. A lower court upheld that a particular grievance was not arbitrable on the grounds that it was "a frivolous, patently baseless one, not subject to arbitration." However, the Supreme Court reversed this ruling. It said in effect that it is up to the arbitrator and not the judge to determine whether or not a grievance has merit.

In the last case of the "Trilogy," *Enterprise Wheel & Car Corp.*,[19] the Supreme Court delineated the limited circumstances where an arbitrator's award could be set aside: (1) where the arbitrator exceeded his or her jurisdiction or authority (in other words, made a decision at variance with the express terms of the contract); (2) where the arbitrator failed to provide a full and fair hearing; or (3) where the arbitrator was guilty of taking a bribe or failing to disclose a conflict of interest relationship to one of the parties.

To summarize, one can say that most grievances are substantively arbitrable. Only the most forceful and specific language in the collective agreement will bar a grievance from arbitrable review. Arbitration awards are enforceable in federal district court. The chances of having an award upset or set aside in court, however, are very slim indeed. One must prove that the arbitrator exceeded his or her authority, did not provide a full or fair hearing, or took a bribe. With respect to the latter point, there are no known cases where an arbitrator has been accused of taking money to "throw a case." Moreover, most arbitrators go out of their way to permit the parties to introduce into the record all types of evidence and material that would probably not be permitted in a court of law. Thus, the only real circumstance under which the parties may overturn an arbitration award is where the arbitrator has exceeded his or her authority.

A recent ruling by the U.S. Court of Appeals (Sixth Circuit) illustrates such a situation:

> The arbitrator found the grievance arbitrable on the grounds that the parties had not used the time limits in the past as a reason to deny a grievance and that to deny the arbitrability of the grievance would bring about a "deterioration of the good company-union relationship."
>
> Reversing a lower court, the Sixth Circuit says an arbitrator is "without authority to disregard or modify plain and unambiguous provisions" in a contract. The contract requirement calling for the union to notify the company of its intent to pursue a grievance within eight days was clearly stated, the court says, finding no evidence that the parties had waived the timeliness rule in the past. The arbitrator's action amounted to dispensing "his own brand of industrial justice," the court said, approving the bid of the Detroit Coil Company to vacate the award in favor of Machinists Lodge 82.[20]

In most hospitals enforcement or vacation of award proceedings should be a very rare circumstance. When a hospital or health care union takes an arbitration award into court, even if the case is well-founded, it undermines the effectiveness of the arbitration process. If this practice becomes a regular one, the other side may also be tempted to take a case to court when it loses an arbitration. Once the parties establish a pattern of attempting to vacate the opposition's award, the benefits, as well as the meaning and effectiveness of arbitration, are lost.

THE GROWING IMPORTANCE OF THE INDIVIDUAL GRIEVANT IN ARBITRATION—THE TREND OF THE 1980s

After the Steelworkers' Trilogy, there was a feeling that the institution of arbitration would continue to grow and develop without interruption. The Supreme Court's endorsement of arbitration in the Trilogy strongly indicated that labor and management could expect very little interference with the arbitration process, especially from the courts.

However, since 1960 there have been a number of cases that may indicate a reversal of that posture. The first of these cases occurred in 1967 with the Supreme Court's decision in *Vaca* v. *Sipes*.[21] In that case an employee demanded his grievance be taken to arbitration when both an employer's doctor and a union's doctor independently concurred that his poor health justified his discharge. The union, however, refused to arbitrate. The employee brought suit under Section 301 of the Labor Management Relations Act (LMRA), charging that the union failed to represent him fairly. Eventually the Supreme Court decided that when a union showed "arbitrary, discriminatory, or bad faith" conduct in the handling of a grievance, a disgruntled employee would be allowed to avoid the arbitration process and submit a dispute directly to a court for resolution.

Then in 1976 the Supreme Court handed down its decision in the *Hines* v. *Anchor Motor Freight* case.[22] Some experts believe that *Hines* will revolutionize the role of labor arbitration in the collective bargaining relations of the 1980s.[23] In *Hines* some truck drivers were discharged for allegedly falsifying their expense sheets by overstating the amount they paid at a particular motel. The drivers claimed that a motel clerk was the real culprit, but the union representatives doubted their story. Subsequently, the drivers merely pled for mercy at the arbitration hearing. Their discharges were later sustained by the arbitrator. About four months after the arbitration decision was issued, the motel clerk admitted that he *alone* had embezzled the money. Thereupon the drivers sued both their union and their former employer.

The employer attempted to defend itself by arguing that its agreement to "final and binding" arbitration, and its subsequent victory in arbitration, insulated the company from further liability.

However, the Supreme Court did not agree. It held that the rights of employees to a fair hearing must be balanced against the interests of the parties and the interests of federal labor policy that are fostered by judicial recognition of arbitral finality. When a union's misconduct "seriously undermined" the integrity of the arbitration process, the process is simply not entitled to enjoy finality.[24]

Since *Hines* there have been numerous suits alleging "perfunctory" union representation in the preparation and presentation of grievances. Such suits have focused on the union's inadequate investigation of a grievance, or the union's failure to make every possible contractual argument during the course of the arbitration hearing, or the union's failure to argue the grievant's case with sufficient vigor. Moreover, employees are winning these suits with increasing frequency, thus marking a change in judicial attitude toward the finality of the arbitration process. If that trend is not enough, the Second Circuit Court of Appeals in the *Hussmann Refrigerator* case[25] recently decided that not only will individual grievants be entitled to bring such suits, but *other* employees affected by the award will also be permitted to be party to the suits.

Given these judicial trends, what can the parties do to preserve the integrity of the arbitration process? The parties must abandon the concept that labor arbitration is a dispute-resolving mechanism involving only the company and the union as separate entities. It must be recognized that the grievant has a right to participate meaningfully in that procedure and to secure meaningful protection under it.[26] Every effort should be made to ensure that the grievant understands what is happening to him or her during the course of the hearing. In every case the grievant is entitled to a speedy hearing, and to the justice afforded by arbitration—so long touted by adherents of the arbitration process.

THE LABOR RELATIONS CLIMATE OF HOSPITALS

Although unions have existed in some hospitals for over 50 years, national development of union organization has occurred only during the past 20 years.[27] Unions have made steady inroads into hospitals since 1961, when only one of every 30 American Hospital Association (AHA) member hospitals registered union contracts.[28] The AHA's 1970 survey found that 16 percent of all responding hospitals had labor union contracts; the 1976 survey indicated that this proportion had increased to 23˙ percent.[29]

Of course, perhaps the most significant factor influencing the growth of unionism in the hospital sector has been the coverage of not-for-profit (nongovernment) hospitals under the National Labor Relations Act (NLRA). This has brought nearly 2 million employees under the act's coverage.

In 1975 a number of NLRB decisions outlined six separate groups of health care employees considered to be appropriate bargaining units. These were: registered nurses; other professional employees; business office and clerical employees; technical employees; service and maintenance employees; and security employees.

Factors Influencing Unionization

Hospital Control

Frenzen's survey[30] reports that while only one in five nonfederal hospitals reported labor union contracts in 1976, four of every five federal hospitals were unionized. Employees of federal hospitals were first permitted to unionize in 1962 under Executive Order 10988; since then the move toward union organization has been rapid. In 1976 state and local government hospitals were also more highly unionized than either nongovernment not-for-profit or investor-owned hospitals. In that year, 32 percent of all government hospitals and 18 percent of all nongovernment hospitals were unionized.

Hospital Size

According to Frenzen, hospital size and unionization also seemed to be correlated, with the proportion of hospitals reporting labor union contracts increasing directly with bed capacity of the hospitals. More than half (54 percent) of all hospitals with 500 or more beds had contracts; while one of every eight hospitals with six to 99 beds (12 percent), and one of every four with 100 to 499 beds (28 percent) reported labor union contracts in 1976.[31] The average number of contracts per unionized hospital also increased with hospital size, from 1.5 in hospitals with six to 99 beds, to 3.0 in hospitals with 500 or more beds.[32]

Metropolitan Location

Hospitals in metropolitan areas frequently have more contracts than those outside Standard Metropolitan Statistical Areas (SMSAs). Nearly half of all U.S. hospitals are located in SMSAs and nearly one-third of these (31 percent) have union agreements. In contrast, only 14 percent of hospitals outside SMSAs are unionized. Thus, about three-fourths of all unionized hospitals are located in metropolitan areas.

City size also influences the degree of unionization. While 45 percent of the hospitals in SMSAs with more than 2.5 million people had union contracts, only 26 percent of hospitals located in SMSAs with less than 2.5 million inhabitants were unionized. However, large hospitals (those with 300 beds or more) in metropolitan or nonmetropolitan areas are unionized to an almost equal extent [33]

Geographic Location

There is a pronounced relationship between geographic location and the degree of unionization. Those areas of the country with the most highly unionized nonagricultural work force include the industrial northeast, the west coast, and the states contiguous to the Great Lakes. As might be expected, the lowest concentration of hospital unionization is in the south.

When these broad geographic areas were analyzed on a state-by-state basis, there were significant differences in hospital unionization patterns. One important factor impinging on these differences was state collective bargaining legislation. For example, half of all hospitals reporting contracts were located in six states (New York, California, Michigan, Pennsylvania, Minnesota, and Washington). These six states included only one-quarter of the nation's hospitals, but one-third of all beds.[34]

Future Trends

Between the years 1970 and 1976, the proportion of hospitals reporting union contracts increased at an average annual rate of 1.2 percent. Those hospitals most likely to face the greatest organizing pressure include the following:

- federal hospitals (five times more likely to be unionized than nonfederal hospitals)

- hospitals with 500 or more beds (three times more likely to be unionized than those with less than 100 beds)

- hospitals in metropolitan areas (one-third more likely than those located in nonmetropolitan areas)

- hospitals in the Middle Atlantic census division (15 times more likely to be unionized than those in the East South Central States)

- hospitals in the nongovernment, not-for-profit category (since 1973 these have become unionized faster than those in the state and local government categories)

- hospitals where some union contracts already have been successfully negotiated (33 percent of union hospitals reported labor union organizing activity, as opposed to only 15 percent of the hospitals without contracts).[35]

Hospitals—A Changing Labor Market

Hospitals and their workers have been considered as existing in a secondary labor market, characterized by low wages, high turnover, and limited upward mobility. As in other segments of the secondary labor market, low wages and benefits and lack of coverage by labor legislation made high turnover and unstructured internal labor markets inexpensive for employers, while low wages and dead-end jobs made attachment to jobs of small value to employees.[36] However, new developments seem to be moving hospitals toward a more *primary* labor market status. Nonprofit hospitals are, of course, now covered by the Fair Labor Standards Act, which has extended to hospital employees regulations covering overtime pay, hours, and minimum wages. The 1963 Equal Pay Act and the 1964 Civil Rights Act have covered hospital workers since their initial passage. Moreover, state unemployment and disability insurance legislation is being applied to more and more hospitals. In response to these government regulations and laws covering wages and other aspects of employment, hospital administrators have moved to centralized control over payroll costs, job structure, and personnel employment practices.

Increasing unionization in hospitals has also encouraged centralization of the personnel function. It makes sense for one unit to have primary charge over negotiating contracts; this ensures some uniformity in contract administration matters.

The public has been taking a close look at hospitals' policies for cost containment. At present the cost-pass-through reimbursement technique, for so long the basis for hospital finance, is being challenged because it does not provide an incentive for efficient service. There is a growing clamor for public regulation of hospital unit costs and budgets. Indeed, there are some areas where such regulation is already in effect. Hospitals, in response to public reaction, are more inclined to adopt various management techniques from the private sector to meet the cost challenges.

Thus, government regulation of wages and benefits, increased unionization pressure, and cost-containment have moved hospitals to adopt a more businesslike approach to employee relations. Employment conditions governed by stated policies, rather than determined in a personalized or arbitrary manner, are characteristic of the primary labor market; this marks a move up from the secondary labor market status traditionally accorded to hospitals.[37]

THE PLACE OF ARBITRATION IN HOSPITALS

The basic purpose of hospitals is, of course, to care for the ill. Mistakes, omissions of duty or untimely performance of duty can have serious—even lethal—consequences. This can be true in industry as well, but not as often. In hospitals, every day presents a life-and-death battle, and there is little tolerance for error.

Hospitals have responded to the needs and pressures of their mission by relying heavily on authoritarian management styles and highly formal rules and regulations. In hospitals power is traditionally centered in the board of trustees, administrators, physicians, and department directors. This dispersion of power makes for differences in the frequency and quality of communication between superiors and subordinates. Power dispersion has also been responsible for a variety of challenges to hospital authority because of disparities in the disciplinary treatment of employees. Of course, unions demand uniform treatment for all their members. This, in turn, has encouraged hospitals to establish personnel departments that may function as central units to ensure adherence to personnel policies, rules, and above all, the terms of any existing collective bargaining agreement.

A substantial portion of a hospital's supervisory force may lack proper management training. This can cause human relations problems that spill over to become grievances. Hospital unions, often relatively new on the scene, are frequently militant, and thus ready to "fight" over relatively minor problems that would be resolved quickly in the context of a more mature bargaining relationship.

Complicating the entire picture are some of the other unique features that characterize hospitals. One such feature is the extensive division of labor. Not only are there many different departments, staffs, and offices; frequently there are great disparities in skills among hospital employees. Work is often differentiated and specialized. Yet despite these skill gaps, a great deal of cooperation is needed—for example, between physician and technician, nurse and housekeeping.

Work in hospitals is often irregular. During emergencies, employees might work to the breaking point of endurance. Other times a hospital can be almost devoid of activity. Frequently supervisors take wide latitude in handling the shifting work load. For example, some hospital supervisors permit employees to sleep on the job when activity is at a lull. Others forbid such practice. Disparity of treatment may invite a grievance challenge and possibly arbitral review.

Hospitals, because they are repositories for quantities of drugs, often find that theft of controlled substances is a constant problem. Normally, when an employee is accused of pilfering such material, the punishment is discharge.

Absenteeism and tardiness are also problems common to hospitals (and to industry as well). Low-paying jobs, long hours, and unskilled work are factors that contribute to this problem, as does the relatively constant exposure to illness and contagion.

The chapters that follow explain the arbitration process and its role in hospitals. Chapters 2 through 6 deal with what might be termed the "nuts and bolts" of the arbitration process. Because grievances are the precursors of arbitration, they are examined first. Subsequent chapters focus on how the arbitration process is carried out in practice. Chapter 3 examines how a hospital and union go about selecting an arbitrator and details how to use sources of arbitrators and how to research their background. Chapter 4 deals with the problem of collecting evidence and discusses how one should go about arguing a particular case. Chapter 5 deals with strategy during the arbitration hearing itself and focuses on how best to present the evidence in order to convince the arbitrator. Chapter 6 rounds off these preceding considerations and discusses the standards by which arbitrators make their decisions.

In Part II the forms of rights and interest arbitration are explored. There is particular emphasis on the structure of grievance arbitration and the methods— such as mediation, factfinding, and interest arbitration—for resolving interest disputes in the hospital industry.

Finally, in Part III, we attempt to present the problems inherent in administering a collective bargaining agreement from the perspective of labor arbitration. The authors have made extensive reference to cases from the health care field. Particular attention has been given to differences arbitrators discern between hospitals and the private sector.

In the final section the authors have attempted to create a referral system of health care arbitration cases, a system that heretofore has not been available.

NOTES

1. H. Juris, et al., "Employee Discipline No Longer Management Prerogative Only," *Hospitals,* May 1977, p. 71.
2. *Ibid.*
3. See Chapter 2 for a fuller treatment of the grievance procedure.
4. Textile Workers v. Lincoln Mills of Alabama, 353 U.S. 448 (1957).
5. John Zalusky, an economist with the AFL-CIO's Department of Research, estimated that the union's cost for an average arbitration case (one-day hearing) was $2,220. (This estimate includes a transcript of the proceeding, legal representation, lost-time payments for the grievant and witnesses, shared payment for the hearing room, filing fee, and arbitrator's fees.) Presumably,

these costs would be similar for management. Thus Zalusky's $2,220 figure was simply doubled to arrive at the estimated $4,440 for both parties. See John Zalusky, *AFL-CIO American Federationist,* November 1976, p. 3.

6. Spielberg Manufacturing Company, 112 N.L.R.B. 1080 (1955).

7. Kenneth J. Simon-Rose, "Deferral Under Collyer by the NLRB of Section 8(a)(3) Cases," *Labor Law Journal* 27, (April 1976): 202-203.

8. Collyer Insulated Wire, 192 N.L.R.B. 150 (1971).

9. Section 8(a)(5) provides: "It shall be an unfair labor practice for an employer to refuse to bargain collectively with the representatives of his employees, subject to the provisions of section 9(a)."

10. National Radio, 198 N.L.R.B. No. 1.

11. Section 8(a)(3) provides in part that "It shall be an unfair labor practice for an employer by discrimination in regard to hire or tenure of employment or any term or condition of employment to encourage or *discourage* membership in any labor organization. . . ."

12. See Chapter 10 for a thorough treatment of just cause questions.

13. See Electronic Reproduction, 213 N.L.R.B. No. 110 (1974).

14. Alexander v. Gardner-Denver Co., 94 S.Ct. 1011. In the famous "footnote 21," to this case, the Supreme Court established the conditions under which an arbitration proceeding may be acceptable to the courts:

> 1. The issue of the arbitration should involve both an alleged violation of the contract and Title VII of the 1964 Civil Rights Act. It should, however, *exclude:* (a) grievances alleging only a breach of law; (b) grievances when both union and employer are charged with discrimination; (c) grievances seeking reformation of the contract; (d) grievances constituting a class action; or (e) grievances in areas where the law is still unsettled.
>
> 2. The employee involved should be allowed to have his/her own counsel at the arbitration hearing.
>
> 3. A transcript of the proceedings should be taken.
>
> 4. The arbitration award should be in writing and state findings of fact and conclusions of law.
>
> 5. The arbitration award should specifically consider and cite applicable court and agency decisions.

Further information regarding the relationship between arbitration and EEO legislation and court decisions is found in Chapter 11.

15. Textile Workers v. Lincoln Mills of Alabama, 353 U.S. 448 (1957).

16. Steelworkers v. Warrior & Gulf Navigation Corp., 363 U.S. 574 (1960).

17. The *Code of Professional Responsibility* for arbitrators provides that: (1) "The arbitrator's responsibility does not extend to the enforcement of an award" and (2) "In view of the professional and confidential nature of the arbitration relationship, an arbitrator should not voluntarily participate in legal enforcement proceedings." *Code of Professional Responsibility for Arbitrators of Labor Management Disputes of the National Academy of Arbitrators, AAA and FMCS,* November 30, 1974, p. 23.

18. Steelworkers v. American Manufacturing Co., 363 U.S. 564 (1960).

19. Steelworkers v. Enterprise Wheel & Car Co., 363 U.S. 593 (1960).

20. Bureau of National Affairs, *Daily Labor Report,* April 5, 1979, p. 2.

21. Vaca v. Sipes, 386 U.S. 171 (U.S. S.Ct., 1967), 55 LC ¶ 11,731.

22. Hines v. Anchor Motor Freight, 421 U.S. 928, 96 S.Ct. 28 (U.S. S.Ct., 1975), 77 LC ¶ 11,115.

23. Thomas W. Jennings, "The Crossroads of the Future," *Labor Law Journal*, August 1980, pp. 498-502.

24. *Ibid.*, p. 499.

25. Hussmann Refrigerator, 593 F.2d 83 (1979), *cert. denied* (U.S. S.Ct., 1979).

26. Jennings, *op cit.*, p. 501.

27. For a good summary of the development of union organization from 1919-1972, see Norman Metzger and Dennis D. Pointer, *Labor-Management Relations in the Health Services Industry* (Washington, D.C.: Science & Health Publications Inc., 1972), pp. 16-41.

28. Much of the following section is based upon Paul D. Frenzen, "Survey Updates Unionization Activities," *Hospitals* 52 (August 1, 1978): 93-98 ff.

29. *Ibid.*, p. 96.

30. The following, unless noted otherwise, is based on the Frenzen survey, *op. cit.*

31. *Ibid.*, p. 98.

32. *Ibid.*

33. *Ibid.*

34. *Ibid.*, pp. 98, 103.

35. *Ibid.*, p. 104.

36. Christine E. Bishop, "Hospitals: From Secondary to Primary Labor Market," *Industrial Relations* 16 (February 1977): 26.

37. *Ibid.*, p. 29.

Chapter 2

Grievances: Forerunners to Arbitration

To the average person the term "collective bargaining" is synonymous with "contract negotiations." Indeed, the two concepts are part and parcel of the same package. Collective bargaining as negotiation is, of course, the more spectacular and news-grabbing—particularly when negotiations fail, and that failure leads to a strike action involving a hospital. But once the rhetoric and table-pounding that characterize negotiations have concluded, labor and management embark on a new phase—namely, living with the sometimes tenuous agreement that has just been negotiated. Though not as spectacular as the negotiation phase (at least in terms of newspaper coverage), "contract administration," or the day-to-day running of a health care facility under its collective bargaining contracts, has profound impact on the welfare of the union, hospital administrators, and even patients.

To gain some appreciation of the task of contract administration, consider the task of developing a contract to cover all phases of one's married life! No matter how adept one might be at drafting contract language, there would still be phrases that would lead to misunderstandings. Moreover, who could be wise enough to anticipate all of the contingencies or changes that might occur over the life of the contract? Anyone who has spent time around health care facilities realizes that change is the rule rather than the exception. Yet a contract is a static thing, drafted at one point in time, but designed to cover *all* future contingencies.

Obviously, this is asking too much from a single document. There are bound to be times when an attempt is made to apply old contract language to new situations—and the fit may not be a particularly good one. For example, suppose a lab technician attempts to bid for a lower-rated job in order to eventually move to a better-paying career path. That technician's plan may be frustrated if the seniority clause of the contract calls only for bidding to a "higher-rated job." Or consider a classic confrontation between hospital management and a union: the hospital

19

attempts to subcontract some bargaining unit work; the union objects; but there is *no contract language at all,* either permitting or forbidding such action.

Grievances generally involve misunderstandings over the meaning and/or proper application of various terms of an agreement. These misunderstandings are to be expected and do not necessarily imply that a poor relationship exists between the parties. People of good will can have honest differences over what the contract means and how it should be applied.

DEFINING GRIEVANCES

Not all grievances relate to contract interpretation or application. Some grievances are based on personal or emotional issues, rather than on some alleged violation of the agreement. Consider, for example, the hospital employee who feels her supervisor is "picking on her," or worse, that she is being "ignored by her boss." A grievance can also reflect a protest about the working environment. An employee can claim a work area is too hot or too cold, or even too dangerous (for example, some radiology technicians believe they are exposed to too much radiation and demand that additional protective equipment be supplied).

Some health care institutions attempt to delimit grievances. Consider the contract provision below:

> Grievances, within the meaning of the grievance procedure, shall consist only of disputes about wages, hours of work, and working conditions, as provided in this agreement; about the meaning and application of this agreement; and about alleged violations of this agreement. . . .[1]

Normally, restrictions on the definition of grievances are designed to avoid overloading the grievance procedure with trivial complaints. Restrictions can also be aimed at limiting arbitrability.

The strategy of placing tight limits on the scope of grievances may be appealing in the short run, but over the long haul such restrictions may build employee resentment. Complaints do not go away just because they are not permitted formal processing. Unaired, unresolved problems can grow, and the pressure to resolve these issues may even lead to a wildcat strike. Moreover, what appears on the surface to be a frivolous complaint may not seem so frivolous to the aggrieved employee. As Cox puts it: "The cathartic value of arbitrating (grievances) even a frivolous grievance on which employees place value balances the inconvenience and cost."[2]

According to a recent survey of 817 hospital-union contracts, 75 percent do not restrict the type of issue that may constitute a formal grievance.[3] Given this preference for the unrestricted definition, the following example may be appropriate: "Should any difference of opinion, controversy or dispute, arise between the parties hereto, such difference of opinion, controversy or dispute shall constitute a grievance."[4] Of course, another alternative is to simply not define what constitutes a permissible or nonpermissible grievance.

PUTTING GRIEVANCES IN WRITING

Frequently an aggrieved employee will attempt to resolve a problem with her or his supervisor, even before filing a formal grievance. From the standpoint of industrial or human relations, this may be the preferred way to resolve most job-related problems. However, if discussions prove fruitless and the parties decide to resort to the grievance procedure, it is highly desirable to both parties that the grievance be stated in writing.

From the union's point of view, a written grievance provides a tangible record that formal protest has been made. This can, of course, be invaluable evidence when a hospital claims that a grievance was never filed or that it was not filed in a timely fashion. Putting a grievance in writing also forces the grievant to really "study" the complaint, because he or she must support it with reference to the contract clause that allegedly was violated. Sometimes the mere act of putting it in writing convinces the grievant he or she was wrong, and the matter is dropped.

From the hospital's standpoint, a written grievance represents a formal protest by the union/grievant—a protest that demands a reply. When the union issues a written protest over a management action or contract interpretation, the hospital must answer in writing. A written grievance and its written answer thus provides a permanent record of an issue raised and a managerial answer.

It should also be noted at this point that although a few contracts permit management to initiate grievances, the vast majority of hospital and nonhospital agreements are silent on this issue. This is because most management people take the view that their function is to act, not to grieve. They believe that "management acts—the union reacts" (through a grievance). For example, if management wishes to discipline an employee, it does not file a grievance against that employee. Rather it will give the employee a written warning, a disciplinary layoff, or even discharge the employee. If the union does not agree with the action taken, it (or the employee) can grieve. Even if the union employees allegedly violate the collective agreement—for example, by initiating or participating in a wildcat strike in violation of the no-strike, no-lockout clause—management normally will not file a grievance in protest. Instead, it will seek injunctive relief or some other applicable remedy.

NATURE OF THE GRIEVANCE PROCEDURE

In many hospitals the grievance procedure is essentially a set of appeal steps to higher and higher levels of management. Labor relations experts generally agree that prompt settlement of grievances is the preferred method. Delays in processing grievances may result in employee frustration and can lead to a breakdown in union-management relations or even to a wildcat strike. A smooth-functioning grievance procedure, on the other hand, can lower employee frustration and improve the general morale. Of course, it takes the cooperation of both parties to resolve grievances promptly and efficiently.

Obviously, the number of steps in a grievance procedure influences the amount of time it takes to process a grievance.[5] According to a recent study of a large national sample of hospital contracts, a four-step grievance procedure is most common in that industry.

There has been a trend toward compacting the grievance procedure.[6] For example, Table 2-1 shows that a sizable minority of hospital contracts specify a three-step process. Normally, when a grievance cannot be solved at the first two levels in the grievance procedure, it very well may be headed toward arbitration anyway, and another step would simply delay determination of the issue.

Table 2-1 Number of Steps in Grievance Procedure in Hospital Contracts

Number of Steps in Grievance Procedure	Percentage of Contracts Reporting (n=817 Contracts)
No provision	2.9
1	0.4
2	7.8
3	20.4
4	46.5
5	18.1
6	2.4
7	0.1
Other	1.2

Source: Juris et al., "Employee Discipline No Longer Management Prerogative Only," p. 71.

While the exact wording of the grievance procedure may vary from contract to contract, it is instructive to reproduce here a procedure found in a number of Hospital Employees Labor Program (HELP) contracts:

Grievance Procedure

Step 1. The employee involved shall orally discuss the grievance with his immediate supervisor. The employee or the supervisor may request that the area steward be present during such discussion. The supervisor shall reply to the grievance within four (4) calendar days.

Step 2. If the matter is not satisfactorily adjusted in Step 1, or an answer is not given within the time specified, the employee and/or the area steward shall orally discuss the grievance with the unit head and/or his designee within ten (10) calendar days after the initial discussion with the immediate supervisor. The union staff representative shall be permitted to meet with the department head before the grievance is reduced to writing in order to assist in adjusting the grievance. The reply to the grievance shall be given within four (4) calendar days.

Step 3. If the matter is not satisfactorily adjusted in Step 2 or an answer is not given within the time specified, the grievance shall be reduced to writing on a standard grievance form, signed by the employee involved and the area steward, dated and submitted to the hospital administrator within seven (7) calendar days after the Step 2 answer or the time specified for such answer. The written grievance shall contain a brief statement of the nature of the grievance and shall state the relief sought. The grievance shall be taken up in a meeting between the chief steward and/or staff representative and with the hospital administrator or his designee. Any area stewards involved in the grievance may be present at the meeting and participate in discussing the grievance. The hospital administrator or his designee shall reply to the grievance in writing within ten (10) calendar days after the meeting.

Step 4. If the matter is not adjusted in Step 3 or an answer is not given by the hospital administrator or his designee within the time specified, the union may, by written notice to the hospital within ten (10) calendar days after the Step 3 answer or the time specified for such answer, request that the grievance be referred to an impartial arbitrator selected in the manner hereinafter stated. The parties will attempt to select an arbitrator and if they fail to agree upon an arbitrator within seven (7) calendar days, the union shall, within fourteen (14) calendar days from the date of its notice to the hospital, request the American Arbitration Association to furnish each party with an identical panel of seven (7) arbitrators. In the event that either party is dissatisfied with the names appearing on such panel, such party may request a second panel, from which an impartial arbitrator must be chosen. Following the selection of the arbitrator, the parties shall make arrangements with him to hear and decide the grievance without unreasonable delay. The arbitrator selected shall have authority only to interpret and apply the provisions of this agreement to the extent necessary to decide the submitted grievance and shall not have authority to add to, detract from or alter in any way the provisions of the agreement. His award shall be final and binding upon the hospital, the union and all employees. The fees and expenses of the arbitration shall be borne equally by the hospital and the union.[7]

Note that the grievance procedure outlined above specifies that in Step 1 the aggrieved employee attempts to adjust the complaint with his or her immediate supervisor. The employee may or may not, under the HELP contract cited above, request that the union steward be present.[8] Discussion with the complainant's supervisor may result in the resolution of the grievance, thus eliminating the need to go through the entire procedure. Moreover, settling the problem at this level in the procedure may be most satisfying to the grievant. In the first place, he or she perceives that the problem is being handled promptly. There is also a closer identification with his or her own supervisor than with higher hospital personnel or with an arbitrator. Notice that in the HELP contract cited above, the second-step hospital representative is the unit head, while at the third step this representative is the hospital administrator.

METHODS FOR FACILITATING GRIEVANCE MOVEMENT

As noted earlier in this chapter, a contract may specify limitations on what constitutes a permissible grievance. Many hospital contracts place another restriction on grievance processing, simply to ensure that grievances are filed promptly. For example, a provision found in many HELP contracts states:

All grievances, except those hereafter specified, must be presented in the first step of the grievance procedure within twenty (20) calendar days from the date the cause for the grievance occurs or the employee or union has knowledge of the cause for grievance. Grievances involving discharge, suspension or layoff of an employee must be presented in the third step of the grievance procedure within seven (7) calendar days from the date of discharge, suspension or layoff. Unless grievances are so presented, the right to file a grievance shall be waived.[9]

Such a clause is important for both parties because it limits the time in which a complainant must file a grievance. Without its protection a grievant who realized he or she had a grievance, conceivably could fail to report that grievance in order to increase the benefits awarded when the truth of the matter finally unfolds. For example, suppose an employee is discharged for an offense he easily could prove he did not commit. However, the employee chooses not to protest his discharge. Later he returns to inform a chagrinned hospital administrator of the injustice done him, and also to collect a big back-pay settlement.

On the other hand, a time-limit clause like the one above also protects employees who do not realize they have a grievance. This is accomplished by providing time limits from the date that the employee has *"knowledge of the cause for (a) grievance."* Such a situation might occur where a hospital has laid off an employee for a period of time and then calls that employee back to work. During the time the employee was on layoff status, another employee with less seniority has been working. However, the first employee does not realize the hospital has laid him off wrongfully until he or she returns to work. Under these circumstances, it would be unfair to deny the first employee's grievance rights merely because he or she did not file in the time limits set by the contract.

Another technique designed to expedite the processing of a grievance involves setting time limits for management decision making at each step in the grievance procedure. Obviously, without such limits, a hospital administrator could delay resolution of the grievance simply by holding it without making a decision. In the HELP contract reproduced above, 4 calendar days were permitted for management decision at the first and second steps, and 10 calendar days were allowed at the third step.[10] Theoretically at least, under such a contract, a grievance should be answered in 18 days or less.[11] However, it is common practice to violate the time limits set by grievance procedures. To give some idea of the extent of these abuses, the Federal Mediation and Conciliation Service reported that for fiscal year 1978, the average period between the time a grievance was first filed and there was a demand for an arbitration panel was 83.32 days, or almost two-and-a-half months![12]

However, the failure of management to act or make a decision within the established time limits does not preclude a union from appealing the hospital's "no" or "non decision." Moreover, where both parties widely violate procedural time limits, one party cannot later contend that the other side's failure to observe the limits serves as a bar to arbitration.

PAYMENT OF UNION PERSONNEL FOR TIME SPENT IN GRIEVANCE PROCESSING

A sometimes sensitive area for hospital administrators is the union demand that employees be paid for time spent processing grievances during working hours. Hospitals occasionally look at such provisions as giving "aid and comfort to the enemy." Indeed, the National Labor Relations Act forbids employers from "contributing financial support to unions." However, the act does allow an employer to permit employees "to confer with him during working hours without loss of time or pay."[13] Thus there is no provision legally barring a hospital from paying union stewards and/or rank and file members for time spent processing grievances. One HELP contract attempts to balance hospital efficiency needs with legitimate union concerns when it provides:

> Stewards selected by the union will be permitted to discuss grievances with hospital representatives in the appropriate steps of the grievance procedure during normal working hours without loss of pay, provided that such discussion shall not exceed a reasonable period of time. The steward, however, shall request permission of his supervisor to leave the work area and designate his destination.[14]

On balance, however, the decision to pay stewards or other union personnel for work time spent in grievance sessions is a matter for policy, custom, or—most importantly—the collective bargaining agreement.[15]

ISSUES ARBITRATED MOST FREQUENTLY

When the lower steps of the grievance procedure fail to produce a voluntary settlement, the parties must decide whether the issue is serious enough or important enough to arbitrate. The Federal Mediation and Conciliation Service (FMCS) has published a list of the top 20 issues processed to arbitration during the first half of fiscal 1978.[16]

This list is reproduced in Table 2-2.

Table 2-2 indicates that discipline and discharge issues are the ones most likely to be arbitrated. There are many reasons for this. Some unions have a policy of arbitrating any discharge case, regardless of merit. Because discharge and discipline cases evoke so much interest among the rank and file, not to mention the effect of such cases on union member morale and security, unions are more prone to arbitrate these cases.[17] Hospitals are often inclined to back up disciplinary actions "to the limit" in order to maintain a strong disciplinary climate.

Table 2-2 Most Frequently Arbitrated Issues (First Half Fiscal 1978)

Rank	Issue	Rank	Issue
1	Discipline and discharge	12	Scheduling of work
2	Seniority	13	Job posting and bidding
3	Arbitrability	14	Job evaluation
4	Overtime	15	Health and welfare
5	Work assignment	16	Reporting, call-in and call-back pay
6	Job classification		
7	Pay	17	Wage issues
8	Scope of agreement	18	Working conditions, including safety
9	Management's rights	19	Incentive rate or standards
10	Holidays and holiday pay	20	Discrimination
11	Vacations and vacation pay		

Seniority issues also are arbitrated frequently. This is because seniority determines so many facets of hospital life and employees' well-being, including promotion, demotion, layoff, recall, overtime distribution, vacation preference, amount and duration of benefits, and so forth.[18]

The third most frequently arbitrated issue involves the question of whether or not a given issue is arbitrable. It does not take too much deep thinking to realize that raising this issue is virtually always a management maneuver. If a hospital can argue successfully that a grievance issue is not arbitrable, the merits of the case make no difference. It thus becomes an excellent defensive weapon.

STRATEGIC ASPECTS OF ARBITRATION

The foregoing section may lead the reader to believe that it is the nature of the issue or its merits[19] that ultimately determine whether or not a grievance is arbitrated. However, for unions as well as for hospitals, there are often many other considerations that enter into the decision to arbitrate.

The decision to arbitrate is initially a union decision. This is because a hospital has the option of denying a grievance at the last grievance step before arbitration. This gives the union three choices: (1) do nothing, which can and often is interpreted by the contract to bar the grievant/union from contesting the claim further; (2) agree to the hospital's position, which settles the grievance; or (3) appeal the grievance to arbitration. Of course, the hospital can forestall arbitration by capitulating to the union's position by compromise, or by challenging the arbitrability of the grievance.[20]

Given then that the decision to arbitrate is not always based on the merit of the case, and given that unions are usually the prime movers in pushing cases to arbitration, the question becomes not so much *if* unions use the arbitration process for political or strategic reasons, but rather *how often* they do. One answer to this question came from a study of 400 arbitration awards.[21] Petersen found that almost one arbitration case in four (23.5 percent) was brought to arbitration by unions primarily for political or strategic reasons. Some of the most important reasons for arbitrating are listed here and discussed below:

- to maintain union membership and improve morale
- to support the position and status of the union steward
- to harass supervision for strategic reasons
- impact of the Taft-Hartley Act (NLRA)
- to avoid the issue of race and/or religion
- to use the arbitrator as a scapegoat
- reaction to intraunion factional rivalries.

Unions will sometimes arbitrate to spark interest among union members. Cases taken to arbitration, even those done in a losing cause, demonstrate that the union is willing to fight on behalf of its members. Obviously this has a positive morale-boosting function, apart from the case's merit or lack of merit.

Unions sometimes bring cases for resolution by arbitration where the steward has put his or her reputation on the line by promising rank and file members he or she would fight a certain grievance. The steward's union superiors may realize that the case is weak, but process it to arbitration anyway to avoid embarrassing the steward or to make it appear as if the steward had full union backing. Hospitals will sometimes show similar support for a first-line supervisor or unit manager.

Unions may occasionally arbitrate as part of a strategy of harassment to retaliate for a supervisor's alleged mistreatment of union members. It may also put the supervisor/hospital on notice that the union is watching management-labor relations. In this way, the union attempts to exercise some control over the hospital.

As noted previously in this chapter, Section 9(a) of the National Labor Relations Act permits individual union members to process their own grievances, or with the aid of legal counsel, force the union to process grievances if they believe they have not received adequate union representation. Similarly, when minority group members are involved in a grievance—particularly in discipline or discharge cases—a union may be more inclined to arbitrate rather than face the prospect of being accused of not representing its membership properly. Even when the union realizes its case may lack merit, the union may determine it is better to arbitrate than risk adverse publicity or even court battles over nonrepresentation of membership.

Arbitrators sometimes provide convenient scapegoats for the parties. Where the union does not wish to tell a rank and file member he or she has a weak grievance, it can be expedient to permit the arbitrator to do so. Why? Perhaps the member in question is politically influential within the union, and the union's lack of support may alienate the member or cause him or her to speak ill of the union to other union members.

Of course, not all grievances are arbitrated either solely for merit reasons or solely for political/strategic reasons. The decision to arbitrate may represent a careful balancing of several considerations, not least of which is the economic cost of arbitration.

CONSEQUENCES OF THE ARBITRATION DECISION

The previous section strongly suggests that many factors enter into the decision to arbitrate. Robben Fleming, a nationally prominent labor arbitrator, has pointed out that the decision to arbitrate may hold more advantages for the union than for the employer.

> If the [hospital] prevails in the arbitration its right to do what it has already done will simply be sustained. Thus there is some encouragement to the union to challenge company actions which it has only a small chance of upsetting. If the union should be successful in the arbitration it may have gained a substantial advantage, while if it loses, it will be no worse off than it was before.[22]

Fleming's remarks notwithstanding, there may be significant impact on a union when it arbitrates and loses. For example, Petersen[23] found that slightly more than one out of every five arbitration awards prompts unions to attempt to reduce or obviate the arbitrator's adverse award by demanding changes in contract language at the next collective bargaining negotiations. The grievance issues which, when lost by the union, are most likely to produce such an attempt at contract modification include: subcontracting, seniority, wages, and overtime.[24] Petersen also found that adverse arbitration awards (to unions) only occasionally impact union leadership directly (6.7 percent of the sample cases produced an adverse impact on union leadership). Further, losing an arbitration case almost never prompts union rank and file members to desire to eliminate the arbitration clause in the agreement. They know that the alternative is the strike, and that is not an acceptable option to those who seek a peaceful means of settling grievances.

NOTES

1. U.S. Department of Labor, Bureau of Labor Statistics, *Grievance Procedures* (Washington, D.C.: U.S. Government Printing Office, Bulletin 1425-1, 1964), p. 7.

2. Archibald Cox, "Reflections Upon Labor Arbitration in the Light of the Lincoln Mills Case," in *Arbitration and the Law, Proceedings of the Twelfth Annual Meeting of the National Academy of Arbitrators* (Washington, D.C.: Bureau of National Affairs, Inc., 1959), p. 63.

3. Hervey Juris et al., "Employee Discipline No Longer Management Prerogative Only," *Hospitals, JAHA* 51 (May 1977): 71.

4. U.S. Department of Labor, *op. cit.*, p. 6.

5. The number of steps includes arbitration as the terminal step. For example, a four-step procedure means three steps at the prearbitration stage, and arbitration becomes the fourth (and final) step.

6. The Bureau of National Affairs, in a study of 400 sample agreements, found three-step procedures in 45 percent of all contracts, followed by four-step or two-step (20 percent each), and one-step (8 percent). *Daily Labor Report,* February 27, 1979, p. 2.

7. Chicago Hospital Council, *Analysis of Collective Bargaining Agreements in Chicago Area Hospitals 1975-1976* (Chicago: Chicago Hospital Council, 1975), pp. 47-48.

8. Section 9(a) of the National Labor Relations Act specifies that employees have the right to present grievances to their employer without union intervention, as long as any adjustment reached is not inconsistent with the collective agreement in effect. It should also be noted in this connection, that in NLRB v. Weingarten (485 F.2d 1135, 1975), the U.S. Supreme Court held that if an employee reasonably believes that an investigative interview may lead to disciplinary action, he or she has a right to refuse to submit to such an interview unless permitted union representation.

9. Chicago Hospital Council, *op. cit.*, p. 48.

10. Note the specification of "calendar days" rather than "work days."

11. A recent study by the Bureau of National Affairs indicates that the time limit most frequently set for appealing a case to arbitration is 30 days (24 percent of contracts), followed by 10 days (20 percent of contracts), and 15 days (16 percent of contracts). *Daily Labor Report, op. cit.*, p. 2.

12. Memo from Jewell L. Myers, Office of Arbitration Services, Federal Mediation and Conciliation Service (January 5, 1979).

13. National Labor Relations Act, Section 8(a)(2).

14. Chicago Hospital Council, *op. cit.*, p. 49.

15. H. Juris et al., *op. cit.*, p. 71, in their study of 817 hospital contracts, found that in a little less than half the agreements surveyed there were provisions for paid time for stewards and employees while discussing grievances.

16. Illinois Management Association, *Executive Memo,* February 6, 1979, p. 2.

17. Discipline and discharge issues are treated in depth in Chapter 10.

18. The arbitration of seniority issues is dealt with in more detail in Chapter 11.

19. Merit as used here refers to the degree to which the case is supported by the collective bargaining agreement.

20. The problem of arbitrability is discussed in Chapter 4.

21. Donald J. Petersen, "Why Unions Go to Arbitration: Politics and Strategy vs. Merit," *Personnel* 48 (July-August 1971): 44-49.

22. Robben W. Fleming, *The Labor Arbitration Process* (Urbana, Ill.: The University of Illinois Press, 1965), p. 35.

23. Donald J. Petersen, "Consequences of the Arbitration Award for Unions," *Labor Law Journal* 21 (September 1970): 613-617.

24. D. Petersen, *op. cit.*, p. 614.

Chapter 3

Selection of the Arbitrator

One of the greatest advantages of the arbitration procedure is that the parties (employer and union) have the opportunity to provide input into the selection of the "judge and jury." In the courts the parties have no control over the choice of judge, but in arbitration the arbitrator is the mutual choice of both parties. Naturally cases may be won or lost during the selection process. Therefore, the selection of an arbitrator deserves as much careful thought as the presentation of the case. The management or union representative who does not take time to research the suggested arbitrators is overlooking the main benefit of the arbitration process. In point of fact, employers usually take more time to analyze and research the background of arbitrators, and this may explain, in part, why employers win a significantly larger share of the arbitration decisions.

PROCEDURES FOR SELECTION

The more common selection procedures include (1) mutual agreement or (2) use of an agency.

Selection of an Arbitrator by Mutual Agreement

It used to be common for labor contracts to provide that the parties select, by mutual agreement, an arbitrator to hear grievances reaching the arbitration step. In the event the parties could not agree on the selection, some states allowed the court to appoint an arbitrator upon application of one of the parties. On the other hand, several states have statutory provisions preventing court appointment of arbitrators. Obviously, the parties should not place themselves in the position of letting a court appoint their arbitrator; neither should they permit either party to block the arbitration step by refusing to agree on an arbitrator. To avoid the risk of a deadlock the contract between the parties must provide for a final method of selecting the arbitrator.

Of course, the parties should try to agree on an arbitrator who is mutually satisfactory before resorting to the list supplied by outside agencies. Mutual agreement can be reached through informal discussion, or could take a more formal approach where the parties submit a list of four or five potential arbitrators to one another to see if one name can be selected from the list. This process has sometimes been criticized as a waste of time and energy because of the likelihood that each party, in constructing its list, is likely to select those arbitrators who are sympathetic to its side of the case. However, where there is a mature employer-union relationship, both parties often can agree on at least one name. The mutual selection process is certainly worth a try because it saves time and gives the parties an opportunity to select from a list of candidates who are probably well known to both parties.

If the parties are able to reach mutual agreement, usually one of the parties will undertake the task of writing to the arbitrator and asking for several dates when he or she might be available to hear the dispute. In this letter the parties should identify the nature of the grievance, the place of arbitration, and the approximate time the parties anticipate the hearing might last. The arbitrator will reply, specifying two or three available dates. The parties then confer to select the final date.

When this method is used, the contract should provide a backup method for selecting an arbitrator, in the event that mutual agreement is not reached within a specified period of time. Usually the parties will resort to a list furnished by an outside agency such as the American Arbitration Association (AAA) or the Federal Mediation and Conciliation Service (FMCS).

Some labor contracts provide for a permanent arbitrator[1] or for a list of arbitrators whom the parties use on a rotating basis.[2] In either case, the parties must go through the same selection process to name these arbitrators as they do when selecting an *ad hoc* arbitrator. The advantages and disadvantages of permanent versus temporary arbitration systems are discussed in Chapter 7.

Selection through Use of Agency

Another common method of selection is for the parties to use the services of either the American Arbitration Association or the Federal Mediation and Conciliation Service.[3] Some labor contracts provide that one of these agencies will appoint an arbitrator if the parties are unable to reach mutual agreement. A smaller number of contracts provide that one of these agencies can select the arbitrator initially. Neither of these selection methods permits the parties as much input as does the "striking" method, discussed herein, which permits the parties to strike unacceptable names from the list.

The AAA maintains a national panel of arbitrators whose members have been selected on the basis of experience, competency, and impartiality. The national panel contains names of lawyers, professors, management and union consultants, clergy, full-time arbitrators, and others. Panel members must meet the requirements established by the Panel Department of the AAA. They also must have four satisfactory recommendations from both management and labor representatives.

The AAA uses files kept in their regional offices to compile lists of arbitrators as requested by employers and unions. These lists are made up manually by regional office personnel, and there is an attempt to rotate the names of arbitrators mentioned on the regional list. The AAA will attempt to accommodate parties' joint requests for arbitrators with certain expertise, such as health care industry issues, incentive disputes, or job evaluation issues. It will also accommodate parties' joint requests to provide arbitrators who are located within a certain geographic area or who are members of certain arbitration associations (such as the National Academy of Arbitrators).[4] Although requests for arbitrators with special qualifications must be made jointly by the parties, the AAA does not usually require a joint request for a regular panel of arbitrators. If the parties require that such a request be joint, they should specify this in their labor contract. The contract also should specify the number of arbitrators to be featured on the AAA list, or else the AAA will send out a list of nine names, the usual number.

The AAA charges each party an initial administrative fee of $75 for a list of arbitrators, due and payable when the request is filed. There is no refund of the fee if the matter is withdrawn or settled after filing the request.

Under the AAA guidelines, it is important to distinguish between a simple request for an arbitration panel and an agreement of the parties to proceed under the agency's Voluntary Labor Arbitration Rules. Once the parties agree to be bound by these rules, greater authority resides in the AAA administrator. He or she can appoint an arbitrator if the normal procedure does not result in a satisfactory choice. The full procedure is:

1. Immediately after filing the demand or submission, the AAA submits simultaneously to each party an identical list of names of persons chosen from the labor panel.
2. Each party has seven days from the mailing date in which to cross off any names to which that party objects, number the remaining names indicating the order of preference, and return the list to the AAA.
3. If a party does not return the list within the time specified, all persons named in that list are deemed acceptable.
4. From among the persons who are approved on both lists, and in accordance with the designated order of mutual preference, the AAA invites an arbitrator to serve.

5. If the parties fail to agree on any of the persons named or if those named decline or are unable to act, or if for any other reason the appointment cannot be made from the submitted lists, the Administrator shall have the power to make the appointment from other members of the panel without the submission of any additional lists.[5]

Under the AAA rules a party cannot delay an arbitration hearing by refusing to select an arbitrator or by failing to attend the hearing. The AAA will proceed to select the arbitrator and schedule the hearing. Unless the applicable state law provides to the contrary, the arbitrator may proceed in the absence of any party who, after due notice of the hearing, fails to be present or fails to obtain an adjournment. The arbitrator is empowered to take evidence from the party present at the hearing and render an award. Most employers and unions that agree to be bound by the AAA rules are not aware of the full consequences of these rules. Such rules offer an advantage to the initiating party—namely, that it does not have to resort to court action to enforce the arbitration clause.

The Federal Mediation and Conciliation Service at one time maintained a computerized list of arbitrators in its Washington, D.C. office. It has now returned temporarily to manual selection of panels until it can make arrangements for increased computer capabilities.

The FMCS arbitration panels also have stringent requirements for a would-be arbitrator. The candidate must submit four recommendations from labor and management representatives. In addition, five awards must be submitted to FMCS for its review. Effective the first part of 1979, FMCS no longer placed the names of management or labor advocates on its national list of arbitrators. Advocates on the list prior to that date will remain on the list.

FMCS will also give consideration to requests concerning special areas of interest, geographic location, and membership in certain arbitration associations. However, FMCS prefers that the request for an arbitration panel must be filed jointly by both management and labor. (See Exhibit 3-1 for a sample request form.) Once a list is received by the parties, they are responsible for contacting the arbitrator selected and making arrangements for the hearing. FMCS does not charge a fee for its services.

Both the AAA and the FMCS usually offer the use of their regional offices for the hearing. Many times the parties prefer this neutral location over the employer's place of business or the union's office. Of course, site of the hearing depends on several factors—the availability of rooms, access to witnesses, the need to view the premises, and so forth.

In addition to the AAA and the FMCS, many states have agencies (such as the State Department of Labor or a State Employment Relations Board) that also provide lists of arbitrators. These arbitrators are usually local, less experienced, and less expensive than the arbitrators on the AAA and FMCS lists. These agencies

Exhibit 3-1 Sample Letter and Request Form

DATE

Director, Arbitration Services
Federal Mediation and Conciliation Service
United States Government
Washington, D.C. 20427

Re: Request for Arbitration
Panel. (Subject matter of
grievance)

Dear Sir:

The undersigned Local Union has a grievance filed by (Grievant's name) against the (Hospital), his Employer, dated _____.

The parties involved in this dispute have been unable to resolve this dispute; therefore, the parties are requesting that your office furnish them with a panel of arbitrators consisting of five (5) names of which one (1) shall be selected to decide the issue.

It is requested that the list of arbitrators furnished by your office reside in our general area.

A copy of Form R-43 is enclosed.

Very truly yours,

_____

(Local union representative)

_____

(Hospital representative)

Enclosure

Exhibit 3-1 continued

FMCS Form R—43
Sep 1975

FEDERAL MEDIATION AND CONCILIATION SERVICE
WASHINGTON, D.C. 20427

Form Approved
OMB NO. 23—R0007

REQUEST FOR ARBITRATION PANEL

To: Director, Arbitration Services
    Federal Mediation and Conciliation Service
    Washington, D.C. 20427

Date _____

1.   (For Company)

Name of Company _____

Name and Address
  of Representative _____
  to Receive Panel   (NAME)
                  _____
                     (STREET)

                  _____
                   (CITY, STATE, ZIP)

Telephone (include area code) _____

2.   (For Union)

Name of Union and Local No. _____

Name and Address
  of Representative _____
  to Receive Panel   (NAME)
                  _____
                     (STREET)

                  _____
                   (CITY, STATE, ZIP)

Telephone (include area code) _____

3. Site of Dispute _____
                         (CITY, STATE, ZIP)

4. Type of Issue _____
                (DISCHARGE, HOLIDAY PAY, SICK LEAVE, ETC.)

5. A panel of seven (7) names is usually provided; if you desire a different number, please indicate _____

6. Type of Industry

    ☐ Manufacturing   ☐ Federal Government   ☐ Public Utilities, Communi-
                                                           cations, Transportation
    ☐ Construction   ☐ State Government   (including trucking)
    ☐ Mining, Agriculture   ☐ Local Government   ☐ Retail, Wholesale and
       and Finance   Service Industries
    ☐ Other (Specify) _____

7. Special Requirements_____
                 (SPECIAL ARBITRATOR QUALIFICATIONS, TIME LIMITATIONS ON HEARING OR DECISION, GEOGRAPHICAL RESTRICTIONS, ETC.)

8. Signatures   _____
                                       (COMPANY)

                          _____
                                       (UNION)

Although the FMCS prefers to act upon a joint request of the parties, a submission will be made based on the request of a single party. However, any submission of a panel should not be construed as anything more than compliance with a request and does not reflect on the substance or arbitrability of the issue in dispute.

Additional forms may be obtained from the Federal Mediation and Conciliation Service or any FMCS Regional Office. See list on reverse of Copy No. 3.

Copy No. 1, Original - To Federal Mediation and Conciliation Service usually do not charge a fee for their lists. In fact, in some states, the State Employment Relations Board will provide arbitrators who do not charge the parties a fee for their services. Although this selection method seems attractive for this reason, it has two distinct disadvantages: (1) there is an increased likelihood of getting an inexperienced arbitrator, and (2) it might encourage one of the parties to let all grievances go to the arbitration step rather than try to settle grievances at a lower level.

RESEARCHING THE ARBITRATOR'S BACKGROUND

Assuming that the parties have not delegated the selection process to a court or outside agency, they will be responsible for evaluating and selecting an arbitrator to hear the dispute. As stated earlier, this is a very important part of case preparation. The parties should find out as much as possible about each candidate on the list. This investigation is carried out in a number of ways.

- The agency preparing the list (for example, the AAA or the FMCS) will provide biographical sketches detailing the arbitrator's occupation, address, professional affiliation, work experience, education, year of birth, and per diem fee.

- A service called Arbitration Qualification Report (AQR) provides biographical data on almost every person active in arbitration, plus it contains case citations of prior awards. Since the primary subscribers to AQR are management representatives, there is also data regarding management reaction to an arbitrator's performance. This is an excellent source for data on prior awards and on companies and unions that have used the arbitrator previously.

- The publishers of arbitration awards (such as the Bureau of National Affairs, Commerce Clearing House, and Prentice-Hall) index arbitration cases by arbitrator. There is no better way to evaluate an arbitrator's performance than by reading his or her opinions.

- Consultation with colleagues and trade associations will often reveal other parties who have had experience with a given arbitrator.

- Some law firms and management consultants maintain files on arbitrators' performance. Management and the union should also ask their labor attorneys or consultants to canvass their colleagues for additional feedback.

- Many personnel directors, attorneys, and union representatives who are regularly involved in the arbitration process keep a file on arbitration cases reported in the various labor services and thus offer their own evaluation service.

CRITERIA USED IN SELECTING ARBITRATORS

Although parties prefer to appoint arbitrators with whom they are familiar, the limited availability of such persons requires that parties consider arbitrators who have not handled cases for them previously. Julius Rezler and Donald Petersen, coauthors of this book, recently conducted a study of 26 labor and management representatives regularly involved in the task of selecting arbitrators.[6] On the basis of this study, the relative importance of the selection criteria ranked as follows: 1) experience; 2) issue in the case; 3) the party's familiarity with the arbitrator; 4) arbitrator's legal background; 5) arbitrator's early availability; 6) arbitrator's nonlegal background; 7) arbitrator's geographic proximity to the dispute; and 8) arbitrator's fee.

The measure of experience refers to the number of years the person has served as an arbitrator, the number of cases handled, the number of awards published in the reporting services, and membership in the National Academy of Arbitrators. For parties in the health care field, it would be helpful if the arbitrator had experience handling health care disputes, especially for such issues as job evaluation, application of skill and ability in promotion or layoff grievances, interest arbitration, and so on. The more important and/or complicated the issue, the more experience the parties require in an arbitrator.

With respect to the issue factor, the parties will generally take into consideration the nature of the issue when making their selection decision. Does the case involve discipline, incentives, contract language interpretation, or an interest dispute? Arbitrators come primarily from the professions of law, labor economics, industrial engineering, and the clergy. Approximately 60 percent of all arbitrators are lawyers.[7] There is a tendency for lawyers to be chosen for quasilegal issues such as arbitrability, subcontracting, and admissibility of evidence. Economists are often preferred for interest disputes, and industrial engineers are preferred for job evaluation, time study, and wage incentive cases. Employers usually look with favor on an arbitrator with industrial labor relations experience, whereas union advocates tend to prefer professors and members of the clergy. Both sides agree, however, that background is perhaps not as important as integrity, wisdom, and ability to reason through to a justifiable result.

Although there are approximately 1,000 arbitrators on the AAA's national panel, many of them handle only one or two cases a year. Only relatively few handle more than 30 cases annually. This means that the well-known arbitrators often cannot provide available dates earlier than three or four months in the future. This tends to defeat the basic purpose of arbitration, which is to settle disputes much quicker than they could be settled in the court system. Many parties will sacrifice the selection of a well-known arbitrator for a speedy resolution of the dispute in question, especially if the issue is a simple one and the liability involved is minimal.

With respect to the arbitrator's fee, it is unusual for either party to reject or select arbitrators on the basis of their per diem fee. An experienced arbitrator whose fee is on the high side may require less time to study the case and write the award than a new arbitrator. Of course, it is the total fee that is important, not the per diem fee.

In a recent FMCS study of 692 arbitration cases it handled during 1978, the following information was provided:[8]

Average Per Diem Rate for Arbitration	$239.05
Average Total Arbitrator's Fee Per Arbitration	$735.53
Arbitrator's Expenses	$ 95.00
Average Hearing Time	.99 days
Average Travel Time	.31 days
Average Study Time	1.78 days
Average Days Duration between Filing of Grievance and Request for FMCS Arbitration Panel	83.32 days
Average Days Duration between Panel Sent to Parties and Appointment of Arbitrator	39.52 days
Average Days Duration between Appointment of Arbitrator and Hearing	65.94 days
Average Days Duration between Panel Request and Award	156.73 days

The averages cited here are enlightening in that arbitrators took an average of only three days to hear and decide an arbitration case. However, it took the parties approximately 83 days to process the grievance through the grievance procedure, and 40 days to select the arbitrator. It is probable that the long delay (66 days) between appointment of the arbitrator and date of the hearing was due to the parties trying to agree between themselves on a satisfactory date. Assuming that it is reasonable for the parties to take no more than 30 days to process a grievance and 10 days to select the arbitrator, and assuming that the arbitration date can be set within 45 days thereafter, the total time preceding the arbitration hearing should be closer to 85 days—not the 189-day average referred to in the FMCS study. The point is, the parties themselves, and not the arbitrator or the arbitration process, usually bear responsibility for most of the delays that occur between filing the grievance and the arbitration hearing.

DETERMINANTS OF CONTINUING ACCEPTANCE

Once a particular arbitrator is used, there is the question of whether the parties will use that arbitrator again. Why do some arbitrators remain acceptable to both sides, while others fall out of favor with one party or the other? Probably the single most important factor is the reasoning the arbitrator puts forth in the award.

The parties want a fairly simple award that answers the disputed issue in full. Arbitrators who devote most of their award to repeating in detail the parties' positions or quoting extensively from one party's brief appear inept and incapable of original thinking. One particular arbitrator was so bold as to simply fill up most of the award document with excerpts photocopied from the parties' briefs.

Parties will even call again on the services of arbitrators who decided cases against them if the awards were timely, well reasoned, and to the point. The quality of the reasoning or logic is generally far more important than the disposition of the case.

The manner in which the arbitrator conducts the hearing is also important to the parties. They appreciate an arbitrator who conducts an orderly hearing without being abrasive or rude to the parties or witnesses. They want an arbitrator who understands that particular industrial relations setting, without having to ask a number of trite or fundamental questions. They appreciate an arbitrator who exhibits judicial temperament, impartiality, integrity, maturity, and common sense. An arbitrator who demonstrates a lack of interest or attentiveness, questions witnesses excessively, or tries to tell the parties how to present their cases loses points.

In summary, both labor and management need to devote considerable thought to the selection of an arbitrator. If arbitrators are fair and demonstrate their knowledge of industrial relations, there is no reason why their performance should cause a party to reject them for a subsequent case.

The arbitrator proves his or her skill in the content of the award. The arbitrator must write plainly and must make a clearcut decision. He or she must avoid compromising the award, giving gratuitous advice, or throwing the losing party a "bone" by using superfluous language that may be inconsistent with the final award.

NOTES

1. *Basic Patterns in Union Contracts,* 9th ed. (Washington, D.C.: Bureau of National Affairs, Inc., May 1979), p. 16.
2. Approximately six percent of labor contracts feature a list of rotating arbitrators according to *Basic Patterns in Union Contracts, op. cit.* The parties may strike arbitrators on such a list the same as they would with a list received from an outside agency; they may use the arbitrators in strict rotation order; they may move through the list in search of the first arbitrator who can hear the dispute within

a certain time period; or they may agree to use one arbitrator for all cases unless that person is unavailable or becomes an unsatisfactory arbitrator to one of the parties.

3. Regional offices of the American Arbitration Association are in Atlanta, Boston, Charlotte, Chicago, Cincinnati, Cleveland, Dallas, Detroit, Garden City, NY; Hartford, Los Angeles, Miami, Minneapolis, New Brunswick, NJ; New York, Philadelphia, Phoenix, Pittsburgh, San Diego, San Francisco, Seattle, Syracuse, Washington, and White Plains, NY. Requests for arbitration from Federal Mediation and Conciliation Service should be directed to Office of Arbitration Services, FMCS, Washington, D.C. 20427.

4. The National Academy of Arbitrators was founded in 1947 and presently has approximately 500 arbitrator members. Its executive headquarters are located in Washington, D.C. It sponsors activities designed to improve the general understanding of arbitration and the status of laws affecting arbitration. Its members must be nominated and approved by the academy's Board of Governors. Membership standards include moral character as demonstrated by adherence to sound ethical standards and professional activities; experience as an impartial arbitrator of labor-management disputes or recognition through scholarly publication or other activities as an impartial authority on labor-management relations; and general acceptability to both unions and management.

5. American Arbitration Association, *Voluntary Labor Arbitration Rules,* Rule 12 (1979).

6. See "Strategies of Arbitrator's Selection," *Daily Labor Report,* BNA D-1, June 26, 1978.

7. Donald J. Petersen and Julius Rezler, "Fee Setting and Other Administrative Practices of Labor Arbitrators," *Labor Arbitration Reports* 68 (Washington, D.C.: Bureau of National Affairs, 1978), p. 1384.

8. Federal Mediation and Conciliation Service, Management Information Services Report for Fiscal Year 1978.

Chapter 4

How To Collect Evidence

Arbitration cases are usually won or lost on the basis of facts. It is an advocate's job to bring out the facts and display them in their most favorable light. But the advocate cannot manufacture facts, and the odds are against even the best advocate if the facts are not there to support his or her position. Facts must be gathered and must be presented at arbitration in an orderly fashion. Neither party should view arbitration as an opportunity for factfinding. All facts should be known before the arbitration hearing so that they can be presented fully and clearly to the arbitrator.

GATHERING FACTS

With most grievances, particularly those involving employee conduct, the best time to gather facts is during the 24-hour period following the incident that gave rise to the grievance. The object is to get all the facts while they are fresh in witnesses' minds, and before witnesses have a chance to change their version of the facts. This is especially important in discipline or discharge cases. Contemporaneous sworn statements of witnesses are very helpful as cumulative evidence at an arbitration hearing. They are especially important should the witness decide to change his or her story later on, since the statements can be used to question or impeach said witness's testimony at the hearing if called by the opposing party.

In investigating an incident, many employers and unions abide by an unwritten rule that prohibits crossing hourly and management employee lines—that is, management interviews only salaried employees, and the union interviews only bargaining unit employees.

Union stewards and union representatives would probably have some difficulty interviewing a foreman. However, in some mature employer-union relationships this type of investigation would be permitted, and a union representative may find the foreman's statement very helpful in resolving a grievance.

Many times the employer is in a position to talk with bargaining unit employees in the course of investigating an incident. Certainly, it would be beneficial to the employer to take the employee's statement, if that is practical. The employee should be told that management is simply seeking the facts about the situation in question and that his or her cooperation is expected. Even if the employee simply says he or she "saw nothing" or "didn't hear," this admission could be helpful later on (especially if there is a signed statement to that effect), because that employee could not later come up with a story helpful to the other side. In interviewing employees, it is beneficial to have two people present in addition to the employee, so that there is a supporting witness in case the employee refuses to sign a statement. All of these techniques are helpful in obtaining and preserving evidence—evidence that might cause the parties to settle the matter before arbitration.

Both employers and unions will benefit from documentation of the evidence. Of course, all statements obtained from witnesses should be documented and sworn, if possible. Meetings held to discuss the grievance should be documented through notetaking. If these notes have been made available to the other party before the arbitration hearing, arbitrators will usually receive them into evidence. Otherwise the arbitrator probably will allow the witness to refresh his or her recollection by looking at the minutes, but will insist that the witness then testify in his or her own words. Thus, it is recommended that minutes of such meetings be distributed to the other party in the normal course of the grievance procedure, or at least prior to the arbitration hearing.

PREPARATION CHECKLIST

In preparing for an arbitration hearing, the parties should check the following items:

1. Copy of the labor agreement.
2. Copy of the written grievance.
3. Copy of the employer answer(s).
4. Copy of union appeal(s) from employer answer(s).
5. If the provision(s) concerned has changed in language over the years, then check the following:

    a. copy of the agreement(s) and language concerned for each prior provision that is different from the present language concerned;
    b. copy of all minutes (or notes) of negotiation sessions where the provision(s) concerned was discussed (to determine if the union or employer sought all or a part of what is sought in this arbitration);

    c. copy of all union and employer proposals over the years addressed to the provision(s) concerned or addressed to any provision(s) that has a bearing on it (to determine if the union or employer proposed all or a part of what it seeks in this arbitration);

    d. statements from the contract negotiators (and/or contract administrators) concerning the reason(s) the language was changed and/or why certain change(s) asked for by the employer and/or union were not agreed to (or were agreed to only in part, etc.).

6. If the provision(s) concerned has *not* changed in language over the years, then check the following:

    a. copy of the contract in which the language concerned first appeared, together with the contract that preceded it (in which the language did not appear);

    b. copy of the minutes (or notes) of the negotiation meetings wherein the provision(s) concerned was discussed and finally drafted for inclusion in the labor agreement (to determine if the union or employer sought there all or a part of what it seeks in this arbitration);

    c. copy of the union and employer proposals on the provision(s) concerned at the time when the provision(s) was first negotiated for inclusion in that contract (to determine if either party proposed all or a part of what it seeks in this arbitration);

    d. copy of any union or employer contract proposal drafted over the years (either at the time the contract was up for negotiation or even during the term of a contract) that involved the provision(s) concerned (to ascertain if, at *any time,* either party sought to achieve what it seeks in this arbitration).

7. Copy of any "side agreement" on the subject of the contract provision(s) concerned.

8. Copy of any employer policy statement or procedural statement or employer rule on the subject of the provision(s) concerned.

9. Documents or statements relating to economic reasons or business reasons or administrative or other reasons for the employer to have:

    a. adopted a certain policy or procedure with respect to the administration of the contract provision(s) concerned;

    b. changed the policy or procedure with respect to the administration of the contract provision(s) concerned.

10. Documentation based on employer records of some kind showing either:

a. a past practice that applies and administers the contract provision(s) concerned consistently and over a long period of time (preferably over the period of two or more labor contracts); or

b. an inconsistent pattern of past practice with respect to the administration of this labor contract provision(s) over a long period of time (preferably over a period of two or more labor contracts).

The above contemplates showing by some form of records, employees *by name* who have been involved in the administration of the provision(s). Practice (or administration) in the period following the first introduction of the contract language (or following its *change*) is most persuasive, since it demonstrates a practice while the provision was still *new*, and thus must have reflected the parties' intentions.

11. Past grievances relating to this subject and/or the labor contract provision(s) concerned, including:

a. the disposition of each such grievance;
b. the arbitration award and decision relating to each such grievance.

12. Investigation of (and search to uncover) any statements and/or promises made at *any* time by either employer or union representative relating to the subject concerned or to the contract provision(s) concerned (to ascertain if one or the other party is barred from taking a contrary position because it has led the other party to follow a course of action to its detriment, based on the promise or statement).

13. In discipline cases, review copy of the disciplinary suspension (or discharge notice) concerned, together with:

- a written statement as to what the supervisor, grievant, and/or union representative said when the suspension or notice was given;

- a chronological narrative statement of what happened giving rise to the grievance.

a. ascertain whether the following items do or do not exist:

1. copies of all written disciplinary suspension (or discharge) notices or letters relating to the same type of conduct for which this employee was suspended (or discharged);
2. copies of all written warning notices or letters relating to the same type of conduct;
3. copies of *records* of oral warnings given to this same employee relating to the same type of conduct.

With respect to any of the above, if the document does not make it clear, ascertain whether or not any alternative(s) was offered to the employee *before* the disciplinary action was taken or before the disciplinary warning was given.

Examples: (i) "Either you go back to work right now, or you will be discharged (suspended)."

(ii) "Either you do the work I have assigned you (or work the overtime hours I have assigned you), or I will have no choice but to discipline (discharge) you."

(iii) "Either you stop doing _____(or start doing _____) right now (or within _____ minutes) or I will have no choice but to discharge (or suspend) you."

4. Copies of any written grievance(s) over any of the actions taken against this employee (as noted in 1-3 above), and the disposition of such grievance(s), including arbitration awards.
5. Copies of all prior disciplinary action, disciplinary notices, supporting statements, and grievances (if any) over any prior discipline given to this employee *unrelated* to the conduct for which he or she was suspended (or discharged) in this case. (This—together with Point 6 below—will afford an overall view of this person's record as an employee.) ,
6. Copies of any and all evaluation sheets or records and commendation records—including promotions and merit wage increases—pertaining to this employee.
7. Copies of past cases of discipline (or discharge) of *other* employees for conduct identical or similar to the conduct for which this employee was disciplined (or discharged). Review these files for answers to the following questions:

   (a.) Was the extent of discipline in this other case(s) consistent with the discipline in the case going to arbitration? If not, can the discrepancy be explained?
   (b.) Were any of these other cases grieved? If so, what was the final disposition of the grievance(s)?

b. Review copies of minutes (or notes) of all meetings held to discuss the grievance going to arbitration.
c. Review list of any possible witness to any of the events or circumstances involved in the case. Review any written statements of that witness—or, if none, a statement by (preferably) two persons who heard the witness' oral statement.

   d. Review any past arbitration awards involving the employer that may in *any* way touch on any of the issues in the case going to arbitration.

   e. Review a copy of any (1) side agreement, (2) grievance settlement, (3) work rule, (4) employer policy statement or procedure, or (5) statement of any practice (no matter how old or inconsistent) that may have a bearing on the case going to arbitration.

INTERVIEWING WITNESSES

After reviewing the documents outlined above, witnesses must be interviewed. Witnesses include those persons who can identify documents and testify to the practice of the parties in administering the contract provision in question, as well as those individuals—management and bargaining unit employees alike—who were witness to a particular event. Interviews are conducted to obtain all the information available and to determine if that person will be an effective witness.

Many advocates actually type out sample questions for witnesses to review before the hearing so the witness can anticipate what questions will be asked on direct examination. If this precaution is followed, the witness should be reminded to listen carefully to the questions asked at the hearing because they may differ in content and sequence from the questions listed on the sample question sheet. The questions should be short, in chronological order, and not leading. The witness should be encouraged to use his or her own words in trying to persuade the arbitrator that his or her testimony is truthful. Every witness should be advised of questions to expect on cross-examination.

Each witness should be briefed on the history of the grievance and on the party's theory of the case. The witness also should be told what kind of procedure to expect at the arbitration hearing itself. Most witnesses have never seen an adversary proceeding except for "courtroom drama" on television; this is considerably different from arbitration.

The following suggestions should be made to each witness:

1. Wear clean clothes and dress conservatively.
2. Don't chew gum while testifying or taking the oath.
3. Stand upright when taking the oath. Pay attention, and say "I do" clearly.
4. Don't memorize what you are going to say.
5. Be serious at all times. Avoid laughing and talking about the case in the halls or restrooms.
6. Talk to the arbitrator. Look at the arbitrator most of the time and speak frankly and openly, as you would to any friend or neighbor. Do not cover your mouth with your hand; speak up clearly and loudly.

7. Listen carefully to the questions asked of you. No matter how nice the other attorney may seem on cross-examination, he may be trying to hurt you as a witness. Make sure you understand the question. Ask to have it repeated if necessary; then give a thoughtful, considered answer. Do not give a snap answer without thinking. You can't be rushed into answering. Of course, if you took so much time on each question the arbitrator might think you were making up your answers.

8. Answer each question in your own words. Explain your answer if necessary. This is better than a simple "yes" or "no." If a question can't be answered truthfully with a "yes" or "no," you have a right to explain the answer.

9. Answer directly and simply. Answer *only* the question asked, then stop. Do not volunteer information that is not asked for directly.

10. If you give a wrong answer, correct it immediately.

11. If your answer is not clear, clarify it immediately.

12. The arbitrator wants only *facts*—not hearsay or your conclusions or opinions. Usually you can't testify as to what someone else told you about the incident in question.

13. Don't say, "That's all of the conversation" or "nothing else happened"; say, "That's all I recall" or "That's all I remember happening." It may be that after more thought or another question you will remember something important.

14. Always be polite, even to the other attorney.

15. Don't be a smart aleck or a cocky witness! This will lose you the respect of the arbitrator.

16. You are sworn to tell *the truth*. Tell it. Every material truth should be admitted readily, even if not to the advantage of the party for whom you testify. Do not stop to figure out whether your answer will help or hurt your side. Just answer the question to the best of your memory.

17. Don't try to think back to exactly what you said in a previous statement for the purpose of repeating it verbatim. When you are asked to repeat an answer to a question, visualize the factual situation you are testifying about and then describe it in your own words. The arbitrator may question a witness' credibility if his or her story seems too "pat" or memorized, or if the witness answers several questions in the same language.

18. Do not exaggerate.

19. Stop *instantly* when the arbitrator interrupts you or when the other attorney objects to what you say. Do not try to sneak your answer in.

20. Give positive, definite answers whenever possible. Avoid qualifiers such as, "I think," "I believe," or "in my opinion." If you know the answer to a question, say it. Don't make up an answer. You can be positive about the important things that you naturally would remember. If you are asked about

little details which you naturally would not remember, it is best to just say that you don't remember. But don't let the cross-examiner trap you into answering question after question with "I don't know."

21. Don't act nervous. Avoid mannerisms that might make the arbitrator think you are scared, or not telling the truth, or not telling all that you know.

22. Above all—and this is *most* important—do not lose your temper. It can be tiring to testify for a length of time. Fatigue manifests itself in certain symptoms: (a) tiredness, (b) crossness, (c) nervousness, (d) anger, (e) careless answers, (f) willingness to say anything or answer any question in order to leave the witness stand. If you notice any of these symptoms, recognize them as such and strive to overcome the fatigue. Remember that some attorneys on cross-examination will try to wear you out so you will lose your temper and say things that are not correct. This will hurt you and your testimony. Do not let this happen.

23. If you do not want to answer a question, do not ask the arbitrator whether you must answer it. If the question is improper, your attorney will take it up with the arbitrator for you. Do not ask the arbitrator for advice.

24. Do not look at your attorney or at the arbitrator for help in answering a question. You are on your own. If the question is improper, your attorney will raise an objection. If the arbitrator then directs you to answer the question, do so.

25. Do not "hedge" or argue with the other attorney.

26. Do not nod your head to indicate a "yes" or "no" answer. Speak out clearly. The court reporter must hear the answer.

27. If you are questioned about distances or time and your answer is only an *estimate,* be sure that you say it is only an estimate. Be sure to think carefully about speeds, distances, and intervals of time before testifying; discuss these matters with your attorney so that your memory is reasonable.

28. As you leave the witness stand after testifying, wear a confident, not a downcast, expression.

29. There are several questions known as "trick questions." That is, if you answer them the way the other attorney hopes you will, your answer may sound bad to the arbitrator. Here are two examples:

   a. "Have you talked to anybody about this case?" If you say "no," the arbitrator knows that isn't right because good lawyers always talk to witnesses before they testify. If you say "yes," the lawyer may try to infer that you were told what to say. It is best to say very frankly that you have talked to whomever—lawyer, party to suit, police, etc.—and that you were asked only to describe the facts and to tell the truth.

   b. "Are you getting paid to testify in this case?" The lawyer asking this question hopes you will answer "yes," thereby inferring that you are being paid to say whatever your side wants you to say. Your answer should be something like "No, I am not getting paid to testify; I am only getting compensation for my time off from work and for any expense it is costing me to be here."

DEVELOPING THE THEORY OF THE CASE

The theory of the case is usually developed by asking three questions:

1. What do I need to prove to the arbitrator in order to win the case?
2. What are the best facts I have to prove it?
3. How can I best present those facts?

All the evidence will be pointed toward supporting this theory (one side) or constituting a defense of the theory (the other side). Therefore, the adversary should not only develop a theory of his or her own case, but attempt to ascertain the opponent's theory.

Many arbitration cases are so ill-prepared that the parties cannot develop a theory of the case until hearing the evidence. Many times the parties cannot even agree on the issue or even give an opening statement until after witnesses testify. This approach is unfair to the arbitrator and to the arbitration process because it turns the hearing into a factfinding proceeding. This is not the purpose of arbitration.

On the contrary, each party should have investigated the case thoroughly and discussed its findings openly with the other side, so that each side is able to give its statement of position before the hearing. The statements of position should constitute, in effect, each party's theory of the case and what it expects to show by the evidence.

USE OF PREHEARING BRIEFS

A few advocates prepare a brief which they submit at the arbitration hearing. Some labor contracts specify that such a brief should be submitted several days before the hearing so the arbitrator can become familiar with the case. The prehearing brief is intended to be a written narration of the case, a self-reminder to the advocate of all the elements necessary to the case. It also acts as a speech prompter from which the advocate can read all or portions of the case when making either the preliminary statement or summation, or both.

The prehearing brief offers several advantages:

- it improves the advocate's case preparation;
- it provides an outline of the essential facts about which testimony will be required;
- it provides the arbitrator with an instant view of the advocate's case and thereby avoids confusion as the facts are presented by one party or the other;
- in some simple cases, it can avoid the necessity of filing a posthearing brief.

On the other hand, the prehearing statement has several disadvantages:

- the advocate exposes the entire case theory before the other side puts on its witnesses;
- the statement may be too rigid, not allowing the advocate to adapt for unexpected angles that come up during the hearing;
- it may be a waste of time and effort if the case presented by the other side differs substantially from that which was expected.

The decision to use the prehearing statement depends on the employer and union involved, their past practice in arbitration, the complexity of the issue, and whether or not posthearing briefs are going to be filed. If the issues are complex and posthearing briefs are to be filed, most parties decide to use an oral opening statement rather than spend the time and effort to prepare a written prehearing brief.

If a prehearing brief is to be filed, it should include a statement of the facts (what happened, who said what, when and where); a statement of the issue; background of the issue; definition and description of terms to be used in the arbitration; citation of pertinent clauses in the contract; and arguments to be advanced by the advocate. In cases where posthearing briefs are not going to be used, the prehearing statement also should contain arbitration authority in support of the advocate's position.

Chapter 5

How To Present Evidence

One of the advocate's most important functions in the arbitration process is to present relevant evidence in a clear and orderly fashion. Whereas union and employee relations representatives usually have spent many hours or days discussing a grievance situation, an arbitrator has a relatively short period of time to hear and study the evidence before deciding the case. Too often representatives on both sides of the table take the arbitration process lightly or treat it solely as a factfinding process; this results in a poor and confusing presentation to the arbitrator. If one of the parties seems confused, or presents its side in a confusing way, the other party has an obvious advantage in receiving a favorable award.

PROCEDURE AND DECORUM DURING THE ARBITRATION HEARING

Order of Presentation

The general rule followed by arbitrators is that the grieving party—typically the union—bears the initial burden of proceeding and proof in *nondisciplinary* type cases. In such cases, management has acted. The union must demonstrate that management's action is inconsistent with some limitations, contractual or otherwise. The union is asserting a claim or right against management and thus has the burden or responsibility of proving it. As stated in *Columbus Bottlers, Inc.*, 44 LA 397 (Stouffer, 1965):

> Nothing is found in the Agreement charging the employer with the responsibility of bearing the burden of proof and showing that its closing of the Plant is or was for lack of work. The Union is the complaining party and in the absence of provisions to the contrary, it follows that the burden of proof rests with it to show that the Employ-

er's closing of the Plant constituted a violation of the Agreement or an abuse of discretion.

In *Koppers Co., Inc.,* 63-1 ARB ¶ 8376 (Hebert, 1963), it was stated:

> Since Management is responsible for running the plant and for seeing that it is operated productively, economically and efficiently, contract provisions such as here involved have been interpreted to mean that the initial determination as to the qualifications of an employee for a job must be made by Management . . . .
> After Management has made its determination on the issue of qualifications the burden of proof is on the Union to upset it by proving that the Company acted arbitrarily, capriciously, acted with discrimination or made an error in judgment.

In *discipline* cases, arbitrators usually designate that management has the burden of going first with the evidence. Arbitration authority has interpreted the collective bargaining contract as creating a contractual right of employment, unless the employee engages in misconduct justifying discharge. In other words, the management right to discharge an employee is limited under a labor contract to those situations where the employee's misconduct makes him or her an exception to this contractual right. Once the employer has introduced evidence of cause for the discharge, the burden of proceeding passes to the union. It must rebut management's showing of cause, prove mitigating circumstances, or show that management's action was discriminatory, arbitrary, or capricious. As stated in *Southern Bell Telephone and Telegraph Co.,* 26 LA 742 (McCoy, 1956):

> While we have held that the burden of first proceeding, and the burden of proof, are upon the company to prove a reasonable cause for discharge, the making of a prima facie case discharged the burden of first proceeding and cast upon the union a burden of rebutting that prima facie case.

Where the discipline is less than discharge, some arbitrators have held that the burden of proceeding rests with the union.[1] But the clear weight of authority is that management bears the initial burden of establishing cause for its action.

Opening Statements

The initiating party usually leads off in both the introductory statement and the presentation of its case. In nondisciplinary matters, the union is usually the initiating party; in disciplinary cases, the employer will give its opening statement first. If the party has prepared a written statement, it is usually read at this time.

(The advantages and disadvantages of the written prehearing brief are discussed in Chapter 4.)

The opening statement usually serves as each side's introduction to the case. It covers the background of the circumstances giving rise to the grievance, the pertinent contract language involved, what facts the parties intend to prove, their respective positions, and the issue. The advocate must be certain that the arbitrator understands all the facts, arguments, and contract references put forth in the opening statement. Because the opening statement usually constitutes the arbitrator's first exposure to the case, it is important that there be no confusion about either party's position.

In some cases, a party withholds its opening statement until after the initiating party has presented its case. The usual reasoning behind this is to not disclose one's case until after the initiating party has finished with its case in chief (initial presentation). Usually little is gained by this strategy because of the initiating party's right to call rebuttal witnesses.

The most important function of the opening statement is to help the arbitrator understand the case. The sooner this can be done, the better.

Swearing of Witnesses

The oath is not mandatory at arbitration, except in those few states that require the swearing of witnesses. When not mandatory, the swearing of witnesses is generally dictated by the desires of the parties. Unless there is state statutory authority for the swearing of witnesses, a witness cannot be prosecuted merely because the arbitrator or a notary public (usually the reporter) has administered the oath. Thus, in arbitration the oath has little legal value—and probably only limited psychological value. It is suggested that if an oath is used, it be administered immediately prior to the witness' testimony. This is preferable to a group oath taken by all the witnesses simultaneously at the start of the hearing.

Sequestration of Witnesses

Sometimes one or both of the parties will request that witnesses be excluded from the hearing room while other witnesses give testimony concerning the grievance. This practice is sanctioned by Rule 22 of the American Arbitration Association Rules, which states:

> Persons having a direct interest in the arbitration are entitled to attend hearings. The Arbitrator shall have the power to require the retirement of any witness or witnesses during the testimony of other witnesses. It shall be discretionary with the Arbitrator to determine the propriety of the attendance of any other persons.

Sequestering of witnesses is usually done in a case where a number of employees have witnessed the same event, and a party wants to hear each witness testify individually so as not to be influenced by another employee's rendition of the facts. This is especially helpful to the party cross-examining witnesses, because the other witnesses will not have an opportunity to hear all the questions asked in cross-examination before their own cross-examination.

Arbitrators will seldom exclude the grievant because of due process considerations. Further, they will usually permit one management witness, such as the employee relations manager, to hear the testimony of all witnesses. Arbitrators will usually permit the employee witnesses to remain in the hearing room after they have testified, if either party requests such procedure to be followed.

Use of Subpoenas

In states that have adopted the Uniform Arbitration Act, a party can request the arbitrator to issue a subpoena to a witness and can enforce that subpoena in state court. For example, the Illinois Uniform Act provides:

> The arbitrators may issue subpoenas for the attendance of witnesses and for the production of books, records, documents and other evidence, and shall have the power to administer oaths. Subpoenas so issued shall be served, and upon application to the court by a party or the arbitrators, enforced, in the manner provided by law for the service and enforcement of subpoenas in civil cases. (Ill. Rev. Stat. Ch. 10 §107)

One federal court—in *Local Lodge 1746, IAM & A.W.* v. *Pratt & Whitney Div. U.A.C.,* 329 F. Supp. 283 (D. Conn. 1971)—enforced a subpoena for the appearance of a witness issued under state statute on the basis of the authority vested in the court by the United States Arbitration Act.

In certain states there may be a question regarding enforcement of a subpoena. However, even in those states without a statute, parties may still ask arbitrators to issue subpoenas, and witnesses will usually attend without the need to answer the enforcement question. This is often done to protect employee witnesses from being accused by fellow employees of appearing voluntarily as a witness for the employer.

Closing Statement or Brief

Arbitrators will give each party the right to summarize its case at the end of a hearing, or to file a brief after the hearing if that is the desire of one or both of the parties. If the case is relatively simple and the testimony presents no credibility problems, both parties may decide to "sum up" at the hearing's close to avoid further delaying the arbitrator's award. If an oral closing statement is in order, the parties should take a 15- to 30-minute recess to study notes and briefly outline the closing comments. If the parties have anticipated an oral closing statement, they should have researched pertinent arbitration cases which they then can cite in the closing statement. Copies of such decisions should be submitted to the arbitrator for review.

Complicated arbitration cases should probably be summarized in a written posthearing brief. Complicated cases include those where there is conflicting testimony; where the case is complex or technical; where the arbitrator is inexperienced or is confused after the case presentation; or where the other side presented new evidence or argument and more time is needed to answer or rebut same. Most arbitrators believe that the posthearing brief is necessary, as expressed in Aaron, *Labor Arbitration and Its Critics,* 10 LABOR LAW JOURNAL 605, 608 (1959):

> Oral summation at the conclusion of the hearing is not—save in the simple cases— an adequate substitute; the parties have not had sufficient time for reflection and for organization of their arguments and the arbitrator may be too tired to derive much benefit from what is being said. One must sympathize with complaints against over-written briefs and against tedious and time-consuming procedures of rebuttals and surrebuttals, but a single, concise, written summary of position, submitted shortly after the conclusion of the hearing, is worth its weight in gold. As a matter of fact, disputes over the interpretation of specific provisions of collective agreements which do not raise issues of fact can often be resolved speedily and economically on the basis of briefs alone.

The written posthearing brief should be succinct and to the point. If such a brief is to be filed, the parties should have a transcript or recording made of the hearing so that the evidence can be reviewed and summarized by the brief writer. The brief should set forth the relevant facts of the case, with page citations to the transcript noted next to the stated facts. The brief should refer to only those facts testified to at the hearing.

After a statement of the facts, the brief should state the relevant contract provisions, the issue, and the position of the writer. Then the party's arguments should be made in an orderly, concise way. It is especially important to use the facts in the argument. Quote relevant parts of the testimony that support your case, and tell the arbitrator where that testimony can be found in the transcript. Point out the inconsistent and incredible parts of the opponent's testimony. All too often the arguments set forth in the brief simply restate the party's position statements. However, the posthearing brief is the place where each party should work with the testimony presented and show how it supports that party's position.

It can be helpful to cite arbitration cases in the argument section of the brief, but such cases should be relevant and few in number. Most arbitrators do not want to read a number of arbitration cases that all stand for the same proposition. Look for cases decided by well known arbitrators, cite the facts briefly, and quote the pertinent part of the decision. Make your brief a self-contained document, so the arbitrator does not need to do further research. Do not depend on the arbitrator to look up and read a case cited, especially if many cases are cited in the brief. Tell the arbitrator how the cases cited support your position. Use the language quoted in the opinions by relating it to the situation in question. Of course, it is especially helpful if a party can cite previous cases decided by the same arbitrator or previous cases that have involved the same parties.

The conclusion of the brief should contain a final summary statement for the arbitrator to consider before making a decision. Many brief writers overlook the value of a strong closing statement. This is the time to make an emotional appeal to the arbitrator to find in your favor and cite the dire consequences to befall you if the decision is against you. Make your statement brief but powerful.

The general practice is for the arbitrator to exchange the parties' briefs when he has received both, rather than for the parties to serve one another. Simultaneous filing prevents one party from having the advantage of seeing the opposing brief before submitting its own. A rebuttal brief is necessary only if the opposing party misstates facts from the hearing or perhaps sets forth a new argument for the first time.

RULES FOR ADMISSIBILITY OF EVIDENCE

A great body of arbitral law reflects the liberal attitude of labor arbitrators toward the admission of evidence. In essence it gives a party a free hand in presenting any type of evidence thought to strengthen and clarify its case. Indeed, as Arbitrator Shulman has pointed out, "The more serious danger is not that the arbitrator will hear too much irrelevancy, but rather that he will not hear enough of the relevant."[2]

Generally, arbitrators conclude that courtroom rules of evidence (used to keep improper evidence away from the jury) need not be applied in arbitration because of the arbitrator's own competence in weighing the relevancy and materiality of the evidence presented. Then there are those arbitrators who believe in the therapeutic value of allowing witnesses to tell their stories freely, without the interruption of technical objections. One guideline for admissibility of evidence is set forth in the *Code of Ethics and Procedural Standards for Labor-Management Arbitration*, prepared jointly by the American Arbitration Association and the National Academy of Arbitrators, and approved by the Federal Mediation and Conciliation Service. Section 4(e) of the Code states:

The arbitrator should allow a fair hearing, with full opportunity to the parties to offer all evidence which they deem material. He may, however, exclude evidence which is clearly immaterial. He may receive and consider affidavits, giving them such weight as the circumstances warrant, but in so doing, he should afford the other side an opportunity to cross-examine the persons making the affidavits or to to [sic] take their depositions or otherwise interrogate them.[3]

The *Voluntary Labor Arbitration Rules* of the American Arbitration Association offers another well-recognized guideline:

Evidence—The parties may offer such evidence as they desire and shall produce such additional evidence as the Arbitrator may deem necessary to an understanding and determination of the dispute. When the Arbitrator is authorized by law to subpoena witnesses and documents, he may do so upon his own initiative or upon the request of any party. The Arbitrator shall be the judge of the relevancy and materiality of the evidence offered and conformity to legal rules of evidence shall not be necessary. All evidence shall be taken in the presence of all of the Arbitrators and all of the parties except where any of the parties is absent in default or has waived his right to be present.[4]

Courts generally have held that arbitrators are not bound by the same rules of evidence that bind state or federal court judges. The courts generally have refused to vacate arbitration awards on the basis that the arbitrator did not adhere to the traditional rules of evidence. However, an arbitration award was set aside where the court concluded that the *exclusion* of evidence denied a party a fair hearing. In *Harvey Aluminum* v. *United Steelworkers of America,* 263 F. Supp. 488 (C.D. Cal. 1967), the Court noted that the parties had not agreed to be bound by formal rules of evidence and that the exclusion of certain evidence, because of its cumulative nature, denied the presenting party a fair hearing. That case quoted the following from Aaron, *Some Procedural Problems in Arbitration,* 10 VANDERBILT LAW REVIEW 733 (1957):

Despite the generally accepted principle that arbitration procedures are necessarily more informal than those in a court of law, objections to evidence on such grounds that it is hearsay, not the best evidence, or contrary to the parol evidence rule, are still frequently raised in ad hoc arbitration. To the extent that these and similar objections are intended to exclude proffered evidence, they generally fail. The arbitrator is interested in gathering all the relevant facts he can, his principal objective is to render a viable decision, and any information that adds to his knowledge of the total situation will almost always be admitted.

Although most arbitrators do not follow strict rules of evidence and will many times permit the introduction of evidence "for what it is worth," many of these same arbitrators will generally exclude evidence that is totally unrelated to the grievance at hand or clearly has no probative value on the basis that it is hearsay, rumor, speculative, and so forth. Most arbitrators will try to be uniform and consistent in their evidentiary rulings so that neither side has an advantage in this respect. Even where arbitrators admit improper evidence, usually they are careful not to rely on such evidence in the arbitration award. For example, if hearsay evidence is admitted, seldom will the arbitrator mention that evidence as a basis for the award.

It should be remembered that basic rules of evidence have been developed in order to provide for an orderly and clear presentation. Therefore, the rules of evidence should not be totally ignored by the arbitrator, especially where attorneys are representing both sides. As stated by Arbitrator Archibald Cox:

> When legal principles are invoked in arbitration proceedings it is well not to brush them aside impatiently but to recall, that behind them lies the weight of thought tested by experience. If the policy behind the legal rule holds true, the case should turn upon it. If a policy is unimportant, the legal law may safely be disregarded.[5]

Admission of Hearsay Evidence

Hearsay evidence has been traditionally defined as evidence given by a witness regarding a statement made by another person who is not a witness at the arbitration proceeding. There are a number of legal exceptions to the hearsay rule—such as the introduction of business records and oral reports made to a supervisor during the regular course of business, admissions made by an individual, and testimony given by one of the witnesses at a prior hearing.

One guideline for considering hearsay evidence was suggested in the New York Tripartite Committee report, as follows:

> a. Any evidence qualifying in courts of law as an exception to the hearsay rule should be admissible in arbitration.
>
> b. In addition, hearsay may be admitted by the arbitrator, at his discretion, if there are persuasive reasons for not requiring the presence of persons quoted and if there is reasonable ground to believe that the statement quoted is trustworthy and if the evidence is of a nature that can be readily refuted if contested.[6]

Most arbitrators will accept testimony from employees as to what a supervisor told them, even though the supervisor is not present as a witness to the hearing. This is done on the basis that the employer can call the supervisor to rebut that testimony. But arbitrators will not normally permit a witness to testify about rumors—that is, statements made by unidentified employees. Neither will most arbitrators accept testimony from an employee witness regarding a statement made to that witness by a fellow employee, a statement introduced to prove the truth of what is asserted. Again, the best evidence is the testimony of the "fellow employee."

Sometimes affidavits or statements of individuals not attending the hearing are introduced. Most arbitrators will attach little, if any, weight to such statements, because the affiant is not available to testify and be cross-examined at the hearing. This would be especially true in discipline cases. There arbitrators often rule that affidavits are inadmissible because they deprive the opposing party of its right to cross-examine in a situation where a careful evaluation of evidence is required. One arbitrator has held that an affidavit of a nonwitness could be introduced to corroborate other evidence that was subject to cross-examination, but that the affidavit was inadmissible if it produced new evidence not testified to by other witnesses.[7]

Many times arbitrators will permit a witness to testify about a statement made by another person if that person is present at the hearing and therefore can be called by a party to answer questions regarding the statement. For example, a supervisor will usually be permitted to testify about a statement made to him by an employee if the employee is present at the hearing and, therefore, is available to be called by the union to either confirm or deny making the statement. A good example would be where the supervisor testifies that Employee A told him that he saw Employee B leave the hospital with hospital property. If Employee A is present at the hearing and is not called by the union to testify regarding the statement, many arbitrators will infer that Employee A actually made the statement and that if Employee A were called to testify, he would in fact state that he saw Employee B leave the hospital with hospital property. This evidence would certainly be considered as corroborating other evidence regarding Employee B's misconduct, and in certain cases arbitrators may rely solely on such evidence in rendering their awards.

Best Evidence Rule

McCormick, in his treatise on evidence, has stated the best evidence rule as follows: "[I]n proving the terms of a writing, where such terms are material, the original writing must be produced, unless it is shown to be unavailable for some reason other than the serious fault of the proponent."[8] Behind every rule of evidence there is some reason justifying its existence. McCormick lists the three reasons basic to the original document rule:

(1) that precision is present . . . the exact words of the writing is of more than average importance, particularly as respect operative . . . instruments, such as . . . contracts, since a slight variation in words mean a great difference in rights, (2) that there is a substantial hazard of inaccuracy in the human process of making a copy by handwriting or typewriting, and (3) as respects oral testimony purporting to give from memory the terms of a writing, there is a special risk of error, greater than in the case of attempts at describing other situations generally.[9]

The application of the rule in labor arbitration was stated as follows:

Where objection is made to the introduction of evidence of a secondary nature on the ground that it is not the best evidence, the original document should be produced unless it is shown, for reasons satisfactory to the arbitrator, that it is not available. Reproductions of original documents shall be deemed the best evidence unless the authenticity of the purported original documents is significantly in question.[10]

The best evidence rule usually is not a problem in arbitration. The parties generally present reproductions of the original documents in presenting the grievance and the company reply. Timecards and other business records are usually reproduced and authenticated by a supervisor or clerk who, although perhaps not the person who made the record or even saw it made, can testify that the document is part of the business records kept under his or her supervision or control.

Many times a party, usually the employer, will review business records and simply prepare a summary of those records for presentation at the arbitration hearing. For example, the employer may prepare a list of employees, pay rates, and hours worked on a particular day, rather than introduce each individual employee's timecard. Such evidence is commonly used and accepted so long as the union is given an opportunity to examine the document and agree to its accuracy. If the union objects to such a summary, then the arbitrator will usually require the employer to substantiate the summarized facts with the "best evidence," which in this case would be copies of each individual's timecard.

Parol Evidence

The parol evidence rule as established by our common law system excludes all evidence of prior or contemporaneous oral statements offered to alter the effect of the written contract. This rule would exclude testimony that a contractual provision was not intended to be effective as literally written, or was subject to unilateral changes or to some unwritten understanding that it was not to be effective at all. To put it simply, clear and definite contract language should not give way to oral testimony. However, if the contract language is ambiguous, then arbitrators will receive evidence of the parties' mutual interpretation or practice under the contract.

When the contract is totally silent on an issue, the arbitrator will usually permit testimony regarding past practice, customs, and other matters outside the written agreement in order to shed light on the dispute. However, a majority of the arbitrators today still require an express contractual restraint on management rights before sustaining a union's allegation based on oral evidence outside the contract.

Actually, the concept of parol evidence is not mentioned very often in current circles. This concept has been merged into the question of whether a dispute is covered by express contract language or whether the arbitrator will imply a restriction on management in the absence of an express restriction.

Offers of Compromise

Settlement offers made in a spirit of compromise do not bind the offering party as admitting that its arguments are weak or incorrect. Labor relations are enhanced by such compromises, and many times one party will make an offer to avoid further processing of a grievance even though it does not agree with the other party's position. Obviously, if offers of compromise were introduced as evidence against one party or the other, the parties would never try to settle grievances in the earlier steps of the procedure. This rule is usually absolute in arbitration cases, as was indicated in *Stylon Southern Corp.,* 24 LA 430 (Marshall, 1955):

> [T]here may be many considerations in getting a grievance settled by negotiation rather than bringing it to arbitration. But more important than this is the fact that no agreement was reached at the time, and it would be very arbitrary for an arbitrator to decide a case by considering the offers and counter-offers of the parties in an attempt to reach a settlement.

Evidence Not Raised in Earlier Steps of Grievance Procedure

Most arbitrators will not permit evidence held by a party in the grievance steps but not raised before the arbitration hearing. Arbitrators guard zealously the efficiency of the grievance steps prior to arbitration. They recognize that there will be times when new facts are discovered during the grievance procedure—and those situations are troubling enough—but they feel that there is seldom justification for withholding such evidence entirely. As stated in Wirtz:

There are obvious interests from the standpoint of the parties' continuing relationship, in keeping such matters out. It is important to the efficient functioning of the grievance procedure that the company and the union representatives do their job below. The Industrial Relations Manager insists properly that he must, as a matter of operating efficiency, be in a position to rely on what the union committee has found out and decided at least by the third step meeting, and the committee has a commensurate interest in being fully informed by that time of what the basis is for the company's position. The grievance procedure will work better, furthermore, if any practice of saving the best ammunition for the hearing before the arbitrator is discouraged.

Arbitrators have responded to these considerations, to the extent that the "general rule" is usually stated as being that new evidence or argument will not be admitted at the arbitration hearing unless some special reason is shown for its not having been brought out before.[11]

Rather than exclude the evidence entirely, some arbitrators will accept the evidence and, upon motion from the other party, adjourn the hearing so that the moving party has an opportunity to prepare rebuttal to this new evidence. As stated in *Cadillac Gage Co.*, 66-3 ARB ¶ 8969 (Miller, 1966):

Material submitted by the Union indicates that in the steel industry agreements have been reached to reveal all evidence before arbitration, but no understanding existed between the parties in this case. Absent such an agreement between the parties, the course open to either party is to request a continuance of the hearing in order to rebut surprise evidence. The Arbitrator believes that if there is merit in such a request, it should be granted.

Often a question arises as to whether a party must disclose the precise identity of all its witnesses before arbitration. Such a situation usually develops in a disciplinary case. There is no law requiring that a party disclose to the other party the names of witnesses so long as the evidence to be presented by such witnesses has been submitted to the opposing party, giving it the opportunity to prepare a rebuttal.

Evidence of Prior Unrelated Disciplinary Incidents

Unions will usually object to management submitting past records of employee misconduct where there is no relationship to the misconduct in question or where these past incidents were not specified in the termination process as reasons for the discharge.

Arbitrators will usually receive such evidence when management claims that it is being offered only for the arbitrator's consideration, should he or she entertain the thought of modifying the penalty due to mitigating circumstances. In such a case, the arbitrator usually will consider the employee's past work record. In most cases, the union will point to the employee's past favorable work history as a reason for reducing the penalty. Thus, if the arbitrator is going to consider the favorable part of the employee's work record, the unfavorable part is also relevant evidence and should be admitted. As stated in *Harshaw Chemical Co.*, 32 LA 23 (Belkin, 1958):

> The question of the use of the employee's past work record by the company in making its determination to discharge him is one which has several ramifications. In the opinion of the undersigned it would be inconceivable that the company do anything else. We have here a matter of equity and fairness. In order to be fair and equitable the totality of an employee's record, good or bad, must be weighed. This would certainly be applicable where the record is good. It must also apply where the opposite is true. It must also apply insofar as an arbitrator is concerned.

A similar statement was made in *Treadwell Corp.*, AAA Case No. 86-3 (Seybold, 1965):

> Generally speaking, if the employee is guiltless then his past record, good or bad, is irrelevant. But if he did commit the offense which gave rise to the disciplinary action or discharge, it is entirely right and proper to look at his entire employment record . . . . To fail to look at this record would require that we judge each episode in a vacuum and would deprive an employee of the opportunity of capitalizing upon a past record of good performance and behavior which should be "cash in the bank" to him. But if we are to accept the good, in mitigation of an offense, we must also be prepared to examine that which is not so favorable.

Arbitrators are evenly split on the question of whether an employee's past misconduct should be introduced in a *nondisciplinary* case. For example, should an employee's past record of carelessness or absenteeism be considered when she or he is the senior bidder for a higher-rated job? Some arbitrators claim that to do so simply makes the promotion denial a second penalty for the prior offense.[12] Other arbitrators hold that prior disciplinary action is at least one measure of fitness for promotion and therefore admissible.[13]

In summary, arbitrators usually do not deny a party the opportunity to present evidence on the basis that it is immaterial or irrelevant, except where the presentation of such unnecessary evidence imposes on the time of both the other party and the arbitrator and interferes with the orderly progress of the hearing. Many arbitrators hold that the freedom of the parties to present a full story has a therapeutic effect, and that the telling of the full story may present helpful facts and even admissions.

BURDEN OF PROOF

Burden of proof concerns the relative duties of parties with respect to the initial production of evidence. It deals both with the question of which party should be required to go forward with the evidence and prove a prima facie case, and the quantum of proof required.

As stated earlier in this chapter, the general rule followed by arbitrators is that the union bears the initial burden of proceeding and proof in nondisciplinary cases. In disciplinary cases, management usually has the burden of going first.

A prima facie case is one in which the presentation of evidence is sufficient in quality and quantity to warrant a ruling by the arbitrator in favor of the presenting party if no contrary evidence is proffered by the opposing party. If an arbitrator chooses to apply a high standard of proof, he or she may find that a party failed to establish a prima facie case, even though that party supplied evidence on every essential point and the opposing party failed to offer any evidence at all. This, of course, is when the quantum of proof comes into play.

The minimum quantum of proof acceptable in arbitration is called the "preponderance of the evidence." This quantum simply requires the party involved to convince the arbitrator that more likely than not, its version of the facts is correct. This test is most often used by arbitrators, especially in cases where no burden of proof is mentioned in the award. For example, in cases involving the test of an employee's skill and ability in a promotion or layoff situation, arbitrators will often uphold management's judgment unless it is shown that the determination was arbitrary, capricious, or discriminatory. Because it is management's fundamental responsibility to make such determinations in its direction of the work force, most arbitrators agree that the employer need not affirmatively justify each such determination.

Many arbitrators even use the preponderance of evidence test in disciplinary cases—although there are a few arbitrators who require "proof beyond a reasonable doubt," which is the strictest quantum of proof required. Some arbitrators apply a stricter standard in disciplinary cases involving a charge of criminal or morally reprehensible conduct, and in such special cases require the more stringent quantum of proof. As stated in *Great Atlantic and Pacific Tea Co.*, 63-1 ARB ¶ 8027 (Turkus, 1962):

> The proof upon which the discharge is predicated, when grievous midconduct involving moral turpitude . . . is the basis, should establish guilt thereof beyond a reasonable doubt.
>
> In other types of overt misconduct such as (a) illegal strikes . . . (b) refusal to perform job assignments . . . (c) fighting . . . and (d) other offenses likewise constituting a breach of peace inside the plant or other challenge to the authority of management and its right to maintain morale, discipline and efficiency in the work force, the requisite quantum of proof may not fall short of a clear and convincing demonstration of the commission of the offense . . . .
>
> The dereliction relied upon for termination of employment may, of course, be predicated upon less dramatic forms of misconduct such as (a) incompetence . . . (b) absenteeism . . . (c) loafing . . . intoxication or gambling on Company time, and (d) violation of safety or other reasonable rules or regulations. In such instance the degree of proof required must likewise achieve the requisite *clear and convincing* demonstration of the commission of the misconduct, offense or dereliction of duty upon which the discharge is predicated. [Emphasis added.]

The "clear and convincing" test, referred to in the case above, falls somewhere between proof beyond a reasonable doubt and the preponderance of evidence test. Many arbitrators refer in their awards to evidence that is "clear and convincing," as demonstrated in *McLouth Steel Co.*, 11 LA 805 (Platt, 1948):

> It should be clear to all that, in order to decide a factual question such as the one above stated, an Arbitrator must be furnished with something more than protestations and mere assertions of an employee's general ability to work in a plant and that what is necessary in a case of this kind is that there be clear and convincing evidence which relates to the grievant's capacity for the specific job to which he seeks promotion . . . .

Many arbitrators actually use the clear and convincing test in both disciplinary and nondisciplinary cases. It is a test that arbitrators find easy to apply because it requires only that the arbitrator determine in his or her own mind and in accordance with his or her own sense of justice and fair play that the evidence is clear and convincing. The other two quantum tests require that the arbitrator first interpret somewhat vague concepts as developed by the courts and other arbitrators, and then attempt to apply those concepts to the facts at hand.

Nonetheless, despite all that has been written about the different quanta of proof, for the most part the arbitrator's choice of quantum does not affect the validity of the award. It may, however, affect the arbitrator's acceptability to the parties in the future. That is why arbitrators rarely state that they are applying the "beyond a reasonable doubt" standard, and some arbitrators are probably hesitant to express reliance on the preponderance of evidence quantum in serious discipline cases for fear of being unacceptable to union advocates. If a quantum is to be mentioned in an award, a safe one (from the standpoint of future acceptability) is the clear and convincing quantum. This probably explains its growing popularity.

The Polygraph Test and Its Effect on Burden of Proof

Due to the importance of security in many areas of health care institutions, there is still a widespread reliance on polygraph testing in the health care industry. As stated in *Mount Sinai Hospital Medical Center of Chicago*, 73 LA 297 (Dolnick, 1979):

> No single subject of evidence has raised so much controversy as the admissibility of lie detector tests. It has been written about extensively by researchers and advocates, it has been reported on by a committee of the American Bar Association, statutes have been enacted on the subject, courts have spoken and arbitrators have dealt with it.

How do arbitrators handle polygraph test results or an employee's refusal to take a polygraph test? If polygraph evidence is rejected it is due usually to its unreliability, rather than because such a test encroaches upon an employee's constitutional rights. Arbitrators have either rejected the introduction of polygraph evidence voluntarily obtained, or have received it but have required the proof of misconduct to be established with other evidence. For example, in *B. F. Goodrich Tire Co.*, 36 LA 552 (1961), Arbitrator Ryder stated that although polygraph evidence in itself does not constitute competent evidence, results of a lie detector test are admissible in evidence and may be considered where there is other acceptable evidence of reasonable certainty that the employee may be guilty of the charge. In finding that the test results could be corroborative evidence, it was stated:

> Thus [the polygraph] can become a factor of evidence in the broad searching for the facts that generally is possible in an arbitration hearing where rules of evidence are not controlling. However, this factor of testimony must be weighed with caution and where it comes up as the sole factor to support a proposition that knowledge is present against where knowledge is denied then it cannot stand alone to establish, without more, the former as a proven fact to support a resulting charge of lack of employee cooperation unless knowledge is admitted.

In *Grocers' Supply Co.*, 59 LA 1280 (Taylor, 1972), the independent evidence was held insufficient to support a finding of guilt, and as a result the discharge was reversed, even though the grievant had taken and failed two polygraph tests. In that case the insufficient evidence consisted of a "confession" by another employee implicating the grievant in a theft ring. According to the arbitrator, both the confession and the polygraph test lacked probative value and therefore failed to establish guilt beyond a reasonable doubt.

Arbitrator Singletary admitted the results of a polygraph test as corroborative evidence in *Westinghouse Electric Corp.*, 43 LA 450 (Singletary, 1964):

> The arbitrator does not pass upon the reliability of the report of the polygraph examination, but observes that the conclusions reached by the examiner are corroborated by the conclusions reached by this arbitrator from evidence other than those tests.

Likewise, in *Koppers Co., Inc.*, 68-1 ARB ¶ 8084 (Kates, 1967), it was held that the results of a polygraph examination could be used to corroborate the testimony of a supervisor. In this regard, Arbitrator Kates stated: "With respect to the polygraph (lie detector) test given to supervisor [H.], I consider the results of that test to be *one element* tending to support [H.'s] story."[Emphasis added.]

Arbitrators usually have not permitted management to take disciplinary action against an employee where the only evidence available is the employee's refusal to take a lie detector test. In *Lag Drug Co.*, 39 LA 1121 (Kelliher, 1962), it was held that the grievant was discharged improperly for refusal to take a polygraph test, because no formal accusation of direct involvement had been made against him and the test results standing alone did not constitute competent evidence.

The decision of Arbitrator Daniel Lewis in *Town and Country Food Co.*, 39 LA 332 (Lewis, 1962), typifies the reasoning of many arbitrators who hold that an employee's refusal to take a polygraph test is not a sound reason for discharge:

> Inasmuch as polygraph test results are generally inadmissible, it follows that refusal to take such a test cannot constitute a proper and just cause for discharge predicated upon insubordination. We cannot draw an inference of guilt against employees who refuse to take a "lie detector" test.

There are three principal reasons for rejecting or discounting the polygraph as a valid credibility test: (1) scientific unreliability (often coupled with the widespread refusal of courts to credit the tests on that basis);[14] (2) the invasion of privacy and dignity of the employee affected;[15] and (3) the imperiling of the constitutional right prohibiting self-incrimination.[16] Still other arbitrators refuse to admit polygraph evidence because it preempts the power of the arbitrator to decide issues of credibility. In *Cincinnati Bell, Inc.*, 73 LA 1148 (Curry, 1979), it was stated:

Had the polygraph report been admitted (it was not) it would have substituted the opinion of the polygraph operator on the question of witness credibility, for that of the Arbitrator. This responsibility is, of course, the Arbitrator's under the Collective Bargaining Agreement.*

Nonetheless, among some arbitrators there is a growing trend to admit polygraph evidence. As Professor Craver explains:

Concerned with the problem of perjury, and recognizing the significant improvements that have been made in lie detector technology, many courts have agreed to admit polygraph evidence.

Although the pace has been slow, labor arbitrators have moved in a similar direction. Conventional security measures have proven ineffective against modern, sophisticated methods of internal depredation. Traditional evidentiary rules are no better at resolving credibility conflicts in the arbitral forum than they are in courts of law. Increased awareness of these problems has prompted some arbitrators to consider polygraphic testimony as corroborative evidence in appropriate cases.[17]

In *Bowman Transportation, Inc.*, (Vadakin, 1974) (unreported but described at 64 LA 456), Arbitrator Vadakin reported that his study of the subject led him to conclude that the attitude of the courts and arbitrators toward the use of polygraph tests was not as settled as some authorities had assumed:

As a practical matter, arbitrators do sometimes permit compulsory polygraph testing, admit the test results as evidence, and place probative weight thereon. This whole question is one that should not be over-simplified. . . .

A careful reading of reported decisions would indicate that arbitrators uniformly regard the results of a polygraph examination, standing alone, as not being of sufficient weight to result in a finding of guilty. But these same decisions, either by inference or direct language, also affirm that, in conjunction with other evidence, polygraph tests results may be accorded probative value, as determined by the arbitrator.

Similarly, in another decision involving the same company, (Whyte, 1974) (unreported but described at 64 LA 456-457), Arbitrator Whyte admitted the results of a lie detector examination. In support of his ruling the arbitrator said:

---

*This case was reported in advance sheets but subsequently withdrawn at the request of one of the parties.

It would be an exercise in futility again to detail arbitration and court cases presenting various views on the reliability of the polygraph. In a nutshell it should either be admitted as evidence, when relevant, because it is accurate enough to be probative in context for which it is being used, or it should not be admitted because it is merely corroborative of the testimony of a witness not because it is deemed conclusive of the truth of the matter relevant to which it was introduced.

It would seem that if polygraph tests are to be usable and admissible on credibility issues, five conditions must be met to avoid running afoul of the concepts of due process and fair play: (1) the examiner should be qualified;[18] (2) the test should be administered promptly after the incident; (3) the subject of the examination should have an opportunity to contact an attorney or union; (4) the test should be voluntary; and (5) the examiner and his or her records should be present for cross-examination.[19]

A great number of states have enacted legislation either prohibiting or substantially limiting the use of lie detectors in the employment environment.[20] In addition, eighteen other states have statutes that require the licensing of polygraph operators.[21]

EXAMINATION OF WITNESSES

Direct Examination

The purpose of an arbitration hearing is to present the facts needed by the arbitrator to make a decision regarding the dispute in question. The arbitrator is going to make that decision on the basis of the testimony of witnesses and the documents they identify and testify about. Thus it is essential that the witnesses be examined in a way that will bring out all the facts in a clear and orderly fashion.

Remember that an arbitrator only needs to learn the facts *once* from a reliable witness who is in a position to know the facts. There is sometimes a temptation to overwhelm the arbitrator with the sheer weight of a parade of witnesses, all giving essentially the same testimony. However, this practice is not advisable, as pointed out by Arbitrator Harold Davey:

> In actual practice, the technique of parading witnesses testifying to a particular event or incident frequently boomerangs on the party using it. The opposing party, if he is skilled in cross-examination, can produce and then highlight conflicts in the witnesses' testimony, thus casting doubt on the credibility of all.[22]

If there are a number of witnesses to testify to the same event, the parties often stipulate that for the purpose of expediting the hearing, all witnesses would give the same answer as the first witness if they were called to testify and were asked the same questions.

The examination of witnesses is done in much the same manner as in the courtroom, although usually with a little less formality. The witness should be questioned as to the facts within her or his knowledge, and should not be used simply to answer "yes" or "no" to the advocate's leading questions. On direct examination of a witness, most arbitrators will uphold objections to leading questions or at least admonish counsel that witnesses should be reciting facts within their own knowledge. But the worst thing about leading questions is that they are not effective in convincing the arbitrator to decide the case in favor of the side asking the leading questions. Witnesses are very similar to salespeople. They must tell the truth and do it in such a way that the arbitrator will give more weight to their rendition of the facts than to the opposing party's. Witnesses who tell the facts in their own words are by far the most credible.

Asking witnesses to read lengthy quotes from documents and contracts is a total waste of time and makes the arbitrator question how much reliable evidence the witness really has to offer. The contracts and other exhibits speak for themselves; once they are introduced into evidence they can be used by the advocate to make arguments in either opening or closing statements. Witnesses waste time by resorting to argument in their testimony or by airing their grievances on unrelated matters.

The basic guidelines in questioning a witness may be summarized as follows:

1. Establish the witness' identity and, if necessary, his or her competence.

2. Bring the witness to the facts as quickly as possible.

3. Ask the witness only about that which is needed.

4. Ask the witness only about that which he or she saw, heard, or knows.

5. Don't testify for the witness. Let the witness tell as much of the story as possible in his or her own words. Have the witness speak directly to the arbitrator—the one who has to understand and believe the witness' testimony.

6. Ask the questions without undue hesitation, so the factual presentation flows smoothly. The advocate should work from a prepared list of questions, both for the purpose of preparing the witness and to make sure all pertinent questions are asked at the hearing. Questions can always be added or even deleted at the actual hearing, depending on how the case develops. But the basic questions should be listed, instead of having the advocate rely on memory.

7. Anticipate the doubtful areas that may be raised in cross-examination, and get that information out in the direct examination before the opposing party raises it on cross.

8. If your direct examination has been thorough and the opposing party sticks to the relevant facts of the case, the redirect examination should be very brief—perhaps only two or three quick questions. However, if new or confusing evidence is raised in the cross-examination, make sure the witness has ample opportunity to explain away such evidence. Feel free to call a recess after cross-examination. Use the recess to discuss with other representatives on your side (excluding the witness) the information raised on cross-examination and the approach to take in answering those questions. Regardless of whether you are inside or outside counsel, it is always advisable to ask the representatives on your side if there are any further questions they would like the witness to answer before concluding the redirect examination. The redirect examination should cover only those points raised by the opposing party in cross-examination. If you attempt to cover new material in a redirect examination, the opposing party may raise an objection. Occasionally an arbitrator will uphold that objection, although most arbitrators permit introduction of such evidence.

Cross-Examination

The basic purpose of cross-examination is to probe a witness' testimony to make sure it was complete or to show that it was false or distorted. The general rule is that cross-examination should deal principally with facts raised on direct examination. However, in general, arbitrators have been somewhat liberal in permitting new matters to be raised on cross-examination, where the questions are related directly or indirectly to the issue or to a credibility problem. Arbitrators usually attempt to constrain redundant cross-examination, abuse, or intimidation of the witnesses. They are also likely to discourage questions not susceptible to intelligent response. On the other hand, questions that display some vigor, repetition, and persistence on the part of the questioner usually are permitted.

Many cross-examiners attempt to get the witness to make inconsistent, unbelievable, and incredible statements. They hope to show that the witness is uncooperative in getting to the facts of the case. That is why many cross-examiners will take a witness through his or her entire direct examination again, question by question, to see if the witness will give the same answers. Most of the time the only thing accomplished by this approach is to demonstrate the advocate's note-taking ability. As far as the case is concerned, the witness, if properly prepared, will simply have a second chance to confirm all of the statements made on direct examination.

The cross-examiner should have a reason to ask every question directed to the witness on cross-examination. The advocate should not be asking random questions while trying to collect thoughts or plan strategy. It is better not to ask any questions during this planning process. Very seldom does an admission or inconsistent statement turn up as a result of this scatter-gun technique. In virtually all cases where an advocate is able to obtain an admission or an inconsistent statement from a witness, the advocate knows that the information given on direct examination was wrong. In other words, the advocate plans the cross-examination to achieve the desired results.

Cross-examination and the technique applied during cross-examination should not be influenced by what the advocate thinks his or her client wants to hear or see. It is a good idea for members of the advocate's team to take notes and write down possible questions for the advocate to present. But it is up to the advocate to sort out these questions and ask only those that are relevant. If case preparation is done properly, the advocate's team representatives will have already been briefed as to the relevant and irrelevant parts of the case. Usually there is a direct correlation between the adequacy of an advocate's preparation and the number of notes and questions team members present to the advocate during the proceeding.

Sometimes clients feel that an advocate proves his or her worth by totally destroying the opposing parties' witnesses on the stand. In arbitration, however, it is well to remember that the parties must continue "living with each other" after the arbitration hearing. An unjustified attack on employees or union stewards may do much more damage to the employer-employee relationship than the outcome of any arbitration case. The advocate must analyze carefully any justification for attacking an opposing party's witness, so that the reasoning can be explained or understood, at least to a substantial degree, by employees on the other side.

In regard to cross-examination it is often said, "Don't ask a question unless you know the answer the witness will give." That advice is still valid. Most advocates make the mistake of asking too many questions on cross-examination, rather than not enough. More cases are lost by aimless cross-examination than by an advocate's failure to extract admissions or inconsistent statements. Extensive cross-examination often sharpens the recollections of a hostile witness and affords that witness a second-thought opportunity to provide more damaging detail than he or she remembered on direct examination. Sometimes a blundering cross-examination may repair the other side's inadequacies and provide an explanation as to why the direct examination was weak or incomplete.

The advocate should have the questions for cross-examination checked off or listed on a note pad before cross-examination starts. The questions should be asked quickly so the witness does not have an opportunity to ponder what was said on direct examination. Plan those questions to be asked in leading up to the point where you hope to extract the witness' admission or inconsistent statement. If the witness starts to make totally unbelievable or uncooperative remarks, he or she should be encouraged to continue along with this type of testimony. Try to get the witness to testify that a certain event "could have happened" even though the witness cannot remember it happening. Do not ask any questions on matters about which you know the witness will not change his or her testimony. It is preferable to call your own witness as rebuttal rather than have the adversary witness simply confirm earlier testimony.

In short, there may be situations where lengthy cross-examination is unavoidable in order to show that a witness' testimony is actually improbable. In general, however, long, aimless questioning rarely strikes pay dirt. It is this type of questioning that occurs too often on both sides of the table.

Grievant Called as Adverse Witness

Although the practice is rather infrequent, some employers will initiate their case in a disciplinary matter by calling the grievant as an adverse witness. This approach is designed to prevent the grievant from changing his or her testimony after listening to the employer's witnesses on direct examination. Advocates taking this approach used to cite the authority of Federal Rule of Civil Procedure 43(b); however, since the 1975 Federal Rule revisions, the cite is now to Rule 611(c) of the Federal Rules of Evidence. State statutes usually have a similar provision permitting the calling of adverse witnesses on direct examination; these statutes can also be cited to the arbitrator.

Arbitrators generally permit this practice on the basis that neither party should be allowed to withhold relevant and material testimony or other evidence, and that the grievant might know best what occurred and the circumstances surrounding the incident in question.

However, some arbitrators—usually nonlawyer arbitrators—will be very reluctant to permit the calling of the grievant as an adverse witness in the face of routine objection by the opposing party. These arbitrators will usually remind the employer that the grievant will be available for cross-examination, or, if the opposing party fails to call the grievant as a witness, such grievant could be called as an adverse witness after the union's presentation.

In any event, the employer should be prepared to prove its case through its own witnesses, in case the arbitrator upholds the union's objection. Few cases are won or lost on the basis of getting the grievant to testify to the facts before the employer's witnesses are called. Again, it all depends on the circumstances involved. There may be situations when this tactic is quite effective.

TRANSCRIPTS AND TAPE RECORDERS

No *official* record is kept of arbitration proceedings. However, it is quite common for one or both parties to hire a court reporter to take a transcript of the proceedings. This is especially common in an extremely complicated or important case or in a case where there is going to be conflicting testimony from the witnesses. When the parties agree to hire a court reporter, they usually provide the arbitrator with a copy of the transcript and share equally the cost of the court reporter's services.

Arbitrators will normally allow one party to have a court reporter record the proceedings even when the other party does not want to pay its share of the cost. In this situation there is always the question of whether the nonparticipating party should have a copy of the transcript. Most employers will not provide the union with a copy of the transcript if the union is unwilling to pay for half its cost. In this situation, the union often will ask to use the arbitrator's copy, and most arbitrators permit such usage. In anticipation of the arbitrator's willingness to share his or her copy with the nonparticipating party, many employers will direct the court reporter to send the arbitrator's copy to the company. The company then will send that copy to the arbitrator as an exhibit attached to the company's posthearing brief.

The cost of the transcript may be excessive in certain cases, especially where the issue is simple and there is little monetary liability involved. In these cases, one or both parties may tape record the testimony in order to have some record in the event of any future questions. Sometimes arbitrators themselves bring tape recorders to make an accurate record of the proceedings.

Occasionally one party will object to the other party tape recording the session. In those cases, the arbitrator will normally permit the tape recording on the basis that a court reporter would be permitted to take the record if one of the parties requested it, and that a tape recorder is no less official a record than a court reporter retained by only one party.

NOTES

1. Dayton Malleable Iron Co., 27 LA 242 (Warns, 1956); Walter Butler Shipbuilders, Inc., 2 LA 633 (Gorder, 1944).

2. Shulman, *Reason, Contract, and Law in Labor Relations*, 68 Harv. L. Rev. 999, 1017 (1955), *quoted in* F. Elkouri & E. Elkouri, *How Arbitration Works*, 254 (3d Ed. 1973).

3. *Code of Ethics and Procedural Standards for Labor-Management Arbitration*, Part II, 4(e) at 6 (1962).

4. American Arbitration Association, *Voluntary Labor Arbitration Rules*, Rule 28 (1975).

5. Cox, *The Place of Law in Labor Arbitration, The Profession of Labor Arbitration, Selected Papers from the First Seven Annual Meetings, National Academy of Arbitrators* (J. McKelvey, ed.),(Washington, D.C.: Bureau of National Affairs, 1957), p. 86.

6. New York Tripartite Committee, *Problems of Proof in the Arbitration Process. Problems of Proof in Arbitration, Proceedings of the Nineteenth Annual Meeting,* National Academy of Arbitrators (D. Jones, ed., 1967),(Washington, D.C.: Bureau of National Affairs, 1967), pp. 297-298.

7. Milgram Food Stores, Inc., 68-2 ARB ¶ 8622 (Murphy, 1968).

8. C. McCormick, *Evidence* §196 (1954).

9. C. McCormick, *Evidence* §197 (1954).

10. New York Tripartite Committee, *op. cit.*, pp. 299-300.

11. Wirtz, *Due Process of Arbitration, The Arbitrator and the Parties, Proceedings of the Eleventh Annual Meeting*, National Academy of Arbitrators, (J. McKelvey, ed., 1958).

12. St. Mary's Kraft Corp., 40 LA 365 (Duncan, 1963); Waller Bros. Stone Co., 34 LA 852 (Dworkin, 1960).

13. Penn Controls, Inc., 45 LA 129 (Larkin, 1965); International Smelting and Refining Co., 65-1 ARB ¶ 8052 (Justin, 1964).

14. See, for example, Mount Sinai Hospital Medical Center of Chicago, 73 LA 297 (Dolnick, 1979); Bethlehem Steel Corp., 68 LA 581 (Seward, 1977).

15. Arbitrator Hardy in Bowman Transportation, Inc., 60 LA 837 (1973), in setting aside a discharge for refusal to submit a polygraph test, observed:

> The Arbitrator is mindful of the serious problem the Company has when employees tamper with Company equipment but in view of the overwhelming weight of impartial scientific authority that polygraph tests are not accurate, and legal authority that they do not constitute competent evidence and invade the right of privacy and self-incrimination, the Arbitrator cannot uphold such a requirement in the instant case.

16. For example, Arbitrator Ryder reasoned that punishing an employee for refusing a test and calling such an act ''insubordination'' due to lack of cooperation has overtones of compelled self-incrimination, ''a proposition repugnant to Anglo-Saxon legal codes.'' Illinois Bell Tel. Co., 39 LA 471 (1962).

17. Craver, *The Inquisitorial Process in Private Employment*, 63 Cornell L. Rev. 1, 35-36 (1977).

18. Professors Inbau and Reid would require that the following four requirements be met before the results of such an examination are admitted as evidence:

    1. That the examiner possess a college degree.
    2. That he or she has received at least six months of internship training under an experienced, competent examiner(s) with a sufficient volume of case work to afford frequent supervised testing in actual case situations.
    3. That the witness have at least five years experience as a specialist in the field of polygraph examinations.
    4. That the examiner's testimony must be based upon polygraph records that he or she produces in court and which are available for cross-examination purposes.

    F. Inbau and J. Reid, *Truth and Deception: The Polygraph (''Lie-Detector'') Technique* (1966), p. 257.

19. A major problem regarding the reliability of lie detectors is the fact that the validity of the tests is greatly dependent on the skill of the examiner. See Skolnick, *Scientific Theory and Scientific Evidence: An Analysis of Lie Detection*, 70 Yale L.J. 694, 704 (1961); Wicker, *The Polygraph Truth Test*, 22 Tenn. L. Rev. 711-712 (1953).

20. Seven states merely prohibit employers from ''requiring'' polygraph tests as a condition of employment: Hawaii Rev. Stat. §§378-21 to 22 (1968). Idaho Code §§44-903 to 904 (1977); Mich. Comp. Laws §338.1726 (1978); Mont. Rev. Codes Ann. 39-2-304 (Cum. Supp. 1979); Ore. Rev. Stat. §§659-225, .990(7) (1975); 18 Pa. Cons. Stat. Ann. §7321 (Purdon 1973); Wash. Rev. Code Ann. §49.44.120-.130 (Supp. 1979). Two other states forbid ''demanding'' or

"requiring" the test: Cal. Lab. Code §432.2 (West 1971); Md. Ann. Code Art. 100, §95 (Cum. Supp. 1976). Statutes that forbid only the "requiring" or demanding of polygraph tests have been construed as permitting employers to "request" such examinations, so long as workers who take the tests do so voluntarily. See, for example, 43 Op. Cal. Att'y Gen. 25 (1964). Four states forbid employers to subject employees or job applicants to the use of polygraphs: Me. Rev. Stat. Ann. §7151 (1979); Mass. Ann. Laws ch. 149, §19B (Michie/Law. Co-op 1976); R.I. Gen. Laws §§28-6.1-1 to .1-2 (1968); Va. Code §40.1-51.4:3. Seven states preclude "requiring" or "requesting" that an applicant take a polygraph test as a condition of employment: Alaska Stat. §23.10.037 (1972); Conn. Gen. Stat. §31.51g (1977); Del. Code Ann. tit. 19, §704 (1974); D.C. Code §2-320 (1979); Minn. Stat. Ann. §181.75 (West Supp. 1977); N.J. Stat. Ann. §2A:170-90.1 (West 1971). *See New Jersey v. Community Distribs. Inc.,* 64 N.J. 479, 317 A.2d 697 (1974) (upholding anti-polygraph statute against constitutional challenge by an employer as a proper exercise of state's authority to protect employees' right of privacy). N.Y. Lab. Law §§733-739 (McKinney)(1978).

21. Ala. Code tit. 46, §§297(22oo)-297(22nnn) (Cum. Supp. 1973); Ark. Stat. Ann. §§71-2201 to 2225 (Cum. Supp. 1975); Fla. Stat. Ann. §§493.40-.56 (West Supp. 1977); Ga. Code Ann. §§84-5001 to 5016 (1975); Ill. Ann. Stat. ch. 38, §§202-1 to 31 (Smith-Hurd 1973 & Cum. Supp. 1977) (It has been held that the Illinois statute allows such testing only by agreement. See 39 Op. Ill. Att'y Gen. 122 (1961)). Ky. Rev. Stat. Ann. §§329.010-.990 (Bladwin 1973); Mich. Comp. Laws §§338.1701-.729 (Supp. 1975)(Mich. Stat. Ann. §§18.186(1)-.186(29) (Callaghan Cum. Supp. 1977) ; Miss. Code Ann. §§73-29-1 to 47 (1973); Nev. Rev. Stat. §§648.005-.210 (1973); N.M. Stat. Ann. §§67-31A-1 to 11 (1974); N.C. Gen. Stat. §§66-49.1 to .8 (1975); N.D. Cent. Code §§43-31-01 to 17 (Supp. 1975); Okla. Stat. Ann. tit. 59, §§1451-1476 (West Supp. 1975); S.C. Code §§56-1543.51 to .75 (Cum. Supp. 1975); Tex. Rev. Civ. Stat. Ann. tit. 26, §§2901-2910 (Cum. Supp. 1977); Va. Code §§54-916 to 922 (Cum. Supp. 1977); Vt. Stat. Ann. tit. 26 §§2901 to 2910 (Cum. Supp. 1979); Utah Code Ann. §§34-37-1 to 14 (Cum. Supp. 1979).

22. Davey, *The Arbitrator Speaks on Discharge and Discipline,* 17 Arb. J. (n.s.) 97,102 (1962).

Chapter 6

How Arbitrators Make Their Decisions

How will the arbitrator decide? This question is always on the minds of union and hospital representatives. Many writers, including labor arbitrators, have attempted to answer this question.[1] However, there are numerous obstacles to any definitive statement. Gabriel Alexander explains some of the difficulty:

> Arbitrators cannot decide concrete cases without relying in part upon principles, rules and logic, but neither can they make decisions solely by reliance upon, or automatic application of them. To decide a concrete case, arbitrators like judges must do more than call to mind the one proper principle. They must at times make choices among conflicting principles and at times proceed to resolution with little or no help from authoritative principles. Every decision involves the exercise of volition or initiative in order to cross the ground which lies between the outpost of general principle and the objective of concrete and specific choice.[2]

Alexander seems to imply that for the arbitrator, decision making is far from a clear cut process. Indeed he suggests that conflict of principles, and even some subjectivity, enter into the process. The task of describing how arbitrators make their decisions is so difficult that one nationally prominent arbitrator was moved to call the project "A Study in Black Magic."[3]

Nevertheless, it is possible to characterize arbitration decision making, in general terms at least. It must be remembered, however, that the general observations made here may not hold in each specific case.

As Gabriel Alexander observed, there are two major influences in arbitration decision making: (1) subjective factors; and (2) the more tangible principles of contract interpretation and rules of law. The subjective factors are considered first.

SUBJECTIVE FACTORS IN ARBITRATION DECISION MAKING

Arbitrators, no less than any other people, have biases and predispositions that they cannot help but bring to the arbitration forum. Yet all arbitrators believe that they are fair and impartial, that they do not favor management over labor, or vice versa. Nevertheless, years ago Judge Cardozo made the following observation: "Deep below consciousness are the other forces, the likes and dislikes, the predilections and the prejudices, the complex of instincts and emotions and habits and convictions which make the man, whether he be litigant or judge."[4] These predispositions and predilections are known as "values." Values are not prejudices in the narrow sense of the word. They are the prevailing ideas that form the basis of the contemporary social order: they serve.as guiding principles for each individual.[5] Human beings are not born with values; these are acquired over the years through parents, church, schooling, books, television, friends, and so on. Once values are internalized, they become a strong influence on decision making.

Studies of Arbitrator Values

Actually very little is known about the impact of values on arbitration decision making. However, one early study by Arbitrator John Teele examined 295 discharge decisions, with the following results:

- in 90 cases, arbitrators relied primarily on contract language;

- in 112 cases, arbitrators relied either on local or general practices, or on arbitral or court precedent;

- in 93 cases, arbitrators relied on personal standards and judgments.[6]

A more recent study of the role of value judgments in arbitration decision making was conducted by James A. Gross.[7] Professor Gross studied cases involving subcontracting and out-of-unit transfers of work, primarily because he felt these cases would be most likely to contain value expressions since they often revolve around management rights and job protection issues. His primary case source was the Bureau of National Affairs (BNA) *Labor Arbitration Reports*. Gross concludes that: "Labor arbitration is a complex interaction of values, fact, and power."[8] He found that where companies decided to subcontract in "good faith" (a value judgment), "economy" and "efficiency" (both value judgments) were at the root of the decision. He observed: "The argument has come to rest on the value judgment that free competition is worth more to society than its costs—a philosophy of progress wherein efficiency is endorsed as socially desirable."[9] Such value judgments are extracontractual—often finding no source in the collective bargaining agreement.

A review of the writings of the late Saul Wallen, a nationally prominent arbitrator, indicates that his goals as an arbitrator were the promotion of:

1. equity and justice for all members of industrial society;
2. efficiency, productivity, and technological innovation; and
3. stable collective bargaining.[10]

With respect to Wallen's first value, he believed in fair dealing on both sides—not on caprice, favoritism, prejudice, or power. Wallen thought that arbitration was basic to this concept of justice. Efficiency and technological change were also important to him, because he felt that both management and labor gained in the long run by the prosperity such efficiency brings—not to mention the fact that efficiency and technological change also ensure the continuous production of goods and services. Finally, Wallen believed in stable collective bargaining, for he felt that unions and management were capable of creating a system of self-government that met the needs and basic rights of all governed by it.[11]

Are Subjective Factors Inappropriate in Arbitration?

The foregoing studies demonstrate with some force that values are part of the arbitration process. Is this necessarily bad? Our answer is that disparate values are not only not deleterious to arbitration, but also inevitable. As long as arbitrators continue to be human beings, differing value systems will play a part in arbitration. Moreover, some arbitrator values—such as the requirement for "just cause" in discipline or discharge matters, the concept of "progressive" discipline, the notion of "good faith" in the parties' dealings, to name just a few—have become so well accepted and embedded in the fabric of arbitration, they constitute almost a "common law" of the work place.

Arbitrator Values Expressed in Hospital Cases

Earlier in this chapter we cited a study that explored values expressed by arbitrators in subcontracting cases.[12] In such cases, efficiency and productivity were two values mentioned frequently. Are the same values held in high regard in hospital arbitrations? In *Kaiser Foundation Hospitals and Institutional Workers' Union, Local 250,*[13] Arbitrator Arthur Jacobs stated:

> . . . It must be recognized that we are dealing with a hospital which is, in the final analysis, charged with the responsibility of the care and

well-being of its patients. The well-being and care of patients is, obviously of overriding importance . . . [value judgment]. In the event the problem [too much work to be done] cannot be solved or alleviated by full utilization of its bargaining unit employees, including the offer and assignments of reasonable overtime, and it is not possible to give thirty day notice of intent to subcontract work [as required in the contract], then the hospital would be justified in subcontracting work without having given such notice even though in technical violation of the contract.

In the above case, Jacobs is taking into account the special nature of a hospital, an institution "charged with the responsibility of the care and well-being of its patients." Based on this concern or value judgment, he even permits the hospital to subcontract, in emergency situations, "though [it is] in technical violation of the contract."

Another arbitrator value widely accepted in health care is the requirement for a higher standard of performance among hospital employees, whatever their level, than in comparable industrial situations. The reason for this is expressed in a comment from an arbitrator in the *Elizabeth Horton Medical Hospital* case.[14] He stated: "A hospital isn't a factory. Its product is human life—recovery from illness and patient comfort."[15] A similar opinion was indicated in still another discharge case:[16] "Fighting on the job, and irrespective of whether the antagonists are of the male or female species is a serious offense in an industrial plant. In the judgment of this Arbitrator it is even more serious in a hospital."[17]

The above illustrations serve to drive home the point that standards for performance as well as conduct are higher in health care. Hospitals are dealing constantly with life and death struggles. Incompetence, negligence, or misconduct does not result only in a loss of efficiency, as it can in an industrial plant, but may endanger the very lives of patients. Of course, such behavior may also endanger lives in a factory, but the problem is one of degree. In a hospital, improper or incorrect dispensing of drugs and/or treatment by a nurse can lead to the death of a patient. Theft of medical supplies can result in their being unavailable in an emergency situation. Even improper housekeeping can lead to spreading of contagion, and

because no institution can have two standards for dealing with employees, most health care employers apply the single, more rigorous standard across the board, even to those employees whose duties are not directly related to patient care. Moreover, arbitrators cannot sustain double standards for employees within one institution. Therefore, they tend to apply these more stringent standards to typists, accountants, social workers, and the like.[18]

Other Subjective Factors in Arbitration Decisions

Conventional wisdom has taught that arbitrators, in order to increase their acceptability to both parties, tend to "split their awards," giving "something" to each side or dividing wins and losses among management and union.

How true is this conjecture? The practice of splitting awards is not only unhelpful to the parties, it is a practice that can explode in an arbitrator's face. Harry Dworkin, a noted arbitrator, has observed: "Similarly, no arbitrator of any integrity is concerned with repeat business in arriving at his decision."[19] We concur. Normally the parties do not want an arbitrator to split a decision, in effect mediating for them at the arbitration stage of the grievance procedure. At that point they want a decision. Surely the parties considered compromise before, and could have done this on their own without the arbitrator. Indeed, arbitrators who split awards may find that they are not called upon again.

It is sometimes said that the parties attempt to influence the arbitrator's decision by showing the arbitrator special treatment at the hearing. This treatment can run the gamut, from extreme formality and courtesy to total informality and even criticism. As Dworkin has observed, however, ". . . parties need not be concerned with either offending or flattering the arbitrator. When he retires to his ivory tower, or sits in his rocking chair, and meditates, he is oblivious of such amenities."[20]

OBJECTIVE FACTORS INFLUENCING ARBITRATOR DECISIONS

Though subjective factors cannot be overlooked in attempting to understand the arbitration decision process, there is little doubt that the bulk of arbitration cases are determined by objective criteria.[21] Most important of these criteria are the standards by which the collective bargaining agreement is interpreted. The Supreme Court underlined the importance of this criterion in the following way:

> Nevertheless, an arbitrator is confined to interpretation and application of the collective bargaining agreement; he does not sit to dispense his own brand of industrial justice. He may, of course, look for guidance from many sources, yet his award is legitimate only so long as it draws its essence from the collective bargaining agreement. When the arbitrator's words manifest an infidelity to this obligation, courts have no choice but to refuse enforcement of the award.[22]

Arbitrators have been referred to as "creatures of the contract." In other words, their power comes from the collective bargaining agreement. A provision frequently seen in hospital agreements limits an arbitrator's power in this way: "An arbitrator may not add to, subtract from, or in any way alter this agreement." There is little doubt that the parties wish arbitrators to confine their function to interpretation and/or application of the contract.

The standards by which arbitrators interpret collective agreements provide the reader with most of the objective criteria arbitrators use in making decisions. These criteria are summarized below:

1. Specific language prevails over general language.
2. Clear and unambiguous language prevails over past practice or any other standards.
3. Role of past practice.
4. Role of precedent.
5. Role of precontract negotiations.
6. The *de minimis* rule.

Each of these six criteria is discussed in the remainder of this chapter.

Specific Language Prevails Over General Language

As noted previously, in most hospital agreements arbitrators normally are bound to limit themselves to consideration of the contract language. If the contract speaks to a particular issue, the arbitrator will look first to determine whether there is *specific* language covering the problem—that is, language that is "clear, unambiguous, or exact." If such language exists in the contract, the arbitrator must go no further.

For example, in an unpublished hospital case decided by one of the authors, the following general language appeared in the contract: "Employees may be required to work a reasonable amount of overtime. The Hospital will endeavor to distribute equitably within each job classification the opportunity to work available pre-scheduled overtime insofar as practicable." This language was so broad (general), it could be considered virtually a *policy* statement. (Note the terms "reasonable amount of overtime," and "endeavor to distribute equitably.") What is a reasonable amount of overtime, and when is overtime distributed equitably? At issue was a claim by three nurse aides that the hospital had violated the collective bargaining agreement by failing to assign them overtime during a very heavy workload period for the hospital. In dismissing the grievance, the arbitrator consulted the agreement and relied on a clause that directly followed the general clause cited above. It provided:

> Overtime shall be distributed in the following manner: first, overtime
> shall be offered to the most senior employee in the bargaining unit,

qualified to perform the work; second, if the required number of employees is not achieved or if employees refuse to work overtime, then employees performing the work during the work shift shall be offered the work. If sufficient numbers of employees are not achieved, or if employees refuse to work overtime, the Hospital may fill the need with any bargaining unit employees qualified to perform the work, or use outside services.

The three nurse aides had been passed by in favor of three other bargaining unit employees who were also nurse aides but did not work on the same floor. All three of the aides who received the overtime assignment had greater seniority than any of the grievants. One can understand why the grievants were upset. On at least two other occasions, they had also been bypassed for overtime. In their minds the overtime had not been "distributed equitably," as provided in the general statement. However, the more specific, procedural statement controlled and interpreted the general language on overtime. While the arbitrator was sympathetic to the grievants' problem, his first obligation was to interpret and apply the contract *as written,* and not "dispense his own brand of [hospital] justice."

Of course, sometimes specific language can be ambiguous. In situations where this occurs, the arbitrator must look for other standards of contract interpretation, some of which are discussed in the remainder of this chapter.

Clear and Unambiguous Language Prevails Over Any Interpretation Standard

This standard of contract interpretation is undoubtedly the most persuasive of the six. It is so compelling that violation of it constitutes the primary reason for vacating arbitration awards. Arbitrators owe their fidelity to the collective agreement. They must not change the existing language, or alter or modify it in any way. To do so risks having their awards set aside by the courts.

An interesting application of this principle is found in the *Rochester Methodist Hospital* case.[23] The grievant was a cafeteria cashier during the evening shift. Her main duty, of course, was to receive money and distribute change. But she did have some other duties which included replenishing depleted food items such as desserts, sandwiches, salads, and sometimes making more coffee. Food sold at night was prepared during the day from the regular patient menu. Then the hospital discontinued the evening supper and installed vending machines. The grievant's job was thus eliminated.

The union argued that the act of subcontracting the evening supper responsibility to a vending operation violated the collective agreement as a whole— particularly the Wage Clause, Union Security Clause, and the Seniority Clause—

as well as the "general intent of the entire agreement." However, the Recognition Clause in the collective bargaining agreement provided:

> The HOSPITAL hereby recognizes THE UNION as the sole and exclusive bargaining representative of all employees of THE HOSPITAL employed in the units of THE HOSPITAL in Rochester, Minnesota, with respect to wages, hours, and all other working conditions, excluding employees in the following classifications. . . .

The recognition clause then specifically excluded the job title of "Cafeteria Cashier," the one held by the grievant. Because the job was not part of the bargaining unit represented by the union, the grievance filed was invalid. Thus, in denying it, the arbitrator made the following observation:

> The argument used by the Union, that is, finding a violation of this Contract by implication, taking into consideration all of the language in the contract, obviously flies in the face of the contract's exclusion of Cafeteria Cashier. The *implication* must obviously give way to the *expressed contract language* [emphasis added].

In short, the arbitrator dismissed the grievance because the contract language clearly excluded the job of cafeteria cashier. Other, more general language could not prevail over the unambiguous language of the recognition clause.

Role of Past Practice

The importance of past practice must be kept in proper perspective. In contract interpretation, past practice should never supersede clear and unambiguous language. For example, in one hospital case, a supervisor in the housekeeping department permitted her employees to take 20-minute breaks in disregard of the 10-minute time limit imposed by the collective bargaining agreement. One day, this practice was noticed by the hospital administrator. He told the supervisor to make sure the extension of breaks stopped at once. When the supervisor delivered "the word" to her employees, a grievance was filed immediately. The basis of the complaint was:

> Violation of Sec. 12.4. We feel that we have been given 20 minute breaks for the past year. We don't feel that Sec. 12.4 (10 minute breaks) controls any more because a 20 minute practice has been developed. Remedy sought—reinstatement of 20 minute breaks.

If the arbitrator had sided with the union, he would have, in effect, violated his duty to respect the agreement. Section 12.4 was clear; 10-minute breaks were specified. There was no reason for a past practice standard to be applied to the case; the language was clear and unambiguous. Thus it can be stated that clear language supersedes even past practice in resolving disputes over contract language.

Of course, in some situations past practice can be used as a standard of contract interpretation. It is a proper standard when: (1) the language in the agreement is too general, vague, or ambiguous to be applied to a specific issue; or (2) there is no language in the agreement covering the situation.

In the latter case, hospital management often will assert it has an unfettered right to make the final decision.[24] This contention may not be persuasive, however, where the benefit is a relatively important one and the union can demonstrate that a practice exists.

Of course, it is one thing to assert that a past practice exists and another thing to prove it. Some of the criteria for determining whether a practice is binding include the following:

- Does the practice concern a major condition of employment?
- Was it established unilaterally?
- Was it administered unilaterally?
- Did either of the parties seek to incorporate it into the body of the written agreement?
- What is the frequency of repetition of the "practice"?
- Is the "practice" a longstanding one?
- Is it specific and detailed?
- Do the employees rely on it?[25]

Mutuality is perhaps the most important factor in this list. If the employee benefit is minor, then the practice is a basic management function and the element of mutuality is irrelevant. If the practice was initiated or administered unilaterally, the party asserting its validity must establish a sufficient element of mutuality to make the practice binding.[26]

Such considerations are illustrated in the *Brookdale Hospital* case.[27] The hospital had hired part-time students from a nearby school for some of its photographic work. Later, however, the hospital decided to discontinue this practice. They hired a full-time person qualified in eye photography (ophthalmic photography). When this person was hired he was told that his position was a nonunion job. For a time his performance was satisfactory, but then he began to be "late for work," "unavailable," and generally "not dependable." He was terminated in March 1977, within one month of his six-month probationary period. He had never signed a union authorization card. The hospital claimed that this dispute was not arbitrable because the photographer was not a bargaining unit employee. Arbitrator Jerome Katz agreed with the hospital's position when he observed:

> The undisputed and credited testimony of the Hospital clearly supports the conclusion that the parties have *established a practice in the past* whereby employees in categories not listed in the collective bargaining agreement have been and are represented by the Union, following a card check when the Union submits cards signed by a majority of the employees in the category [emphasis added].[28]

Role of Precedent

In arbitration precedent may be defined as the "force or weight given to prior arbitration decisions." As a practical matter, arbitrators have no obligation to give any weight at all to prior arbitration decisions, because an arbitrator owes fidelity only to the collective bargaining agreements presently under interpretation. Thus, other cases involving *different* language and *different* circumstances are not persuasive. Of course, in the courts great weight is placed on *stare decisis* (precedent), because the courts interpret *laws* that are uniform in their application.

In an empirical study of 275 published arbitration cases, Jennings and Martin conclude: "More specifically, arbitrators give either no or negative weight to 82% of the prior arbitration awards presented by management and union officials."[29] On the basis of this evidence the investigators conclude: "It therefore appears that there is limited, if any, strategical advantage in presenting a prior arbitration award in the arbitration hearing, particularly if the prior award doesn't reflect similar circumstances including contractual language."[30]

This conclusion was confirmed in a different way by a study based on 400 arbitration cases.[31] Petersen found that the "obvious merit" of a union's case (that is, the extent to which its case was supported by clear contract language) was used three times more often than precedent as a basis for predicting the outcome of an arbitration award.[32]

It would, however, be a mistake to assume that precedent is never persuasive. In our opinion, precedent should be given a great deal of weight if a prior arbitration case exists involving the *same* company, the *same* issue, and the *same* contract language. To hold otherwise would be very disruptive to the stability of the hospital-union collective bargaining relationship. The parties have a right to expect that arbitration awards settle particular issues, and unless language changes are made through contract negotiations, prior arbitration decisions should be given considerable importance.

Role of Precontract Negotiations

When contract language is unclear or ambiguous, arbitrators will sometimes look to the history of the parties' negotiations. This standard can be very persuasive if the parties have kept careful notes of their negotiations.

Precontract negotiations played a pivotal role in the *Providence Medical Center* case.[33] At issue was the payment of accrued vacation pay for three employees who had terminated. The pertinent section (Section 5) of the agreement stated:

> After completion of one year's employment, employees shall be paid upon termination of employment for any vacation credits earned; provided, however, this provision shall not apply to those employees who .leave the employment of the Employer without giving fourteen (14) days' prior written notice, or to those employees who are discharged for cause.[34]

Under the old agreement, any terminated employee who gave two weeks' notice and had one year's employment would be given one-twelfth of scheduled vacation leave for each month worked until termination. The vacation section cited above (Section 5) replaced it. Section 5 provides that separated employees will be "paid for any vacation credits earned. . . ."

Another provision (Section 2) that was newly negotiated stated that: "All full-time and part-time employees shall be eligible to take earned vacation time off after completing 2080 hours of work. The employer may allow earned vacation time off to the extent accrued on an annual basis." Based on Section 2, the hospital claimed it would pay only that vacation that the grievants earned but did not take in the previous year of employment. Thus the grievants were not compensated for vacation benefits earned between their anniversary dates and their termination dates. All three grievants had given the required notice, pursuant to Section 5.

In making his decision in favor of the union, the arbitrator consulted the parties' negotiation history. He pointed out that Section 5 had been agreed to before Section 2. This sequence was important, because Section 5 helps determine what Section 2 means. He also found that little attention was given to negotiating Section 5, as opposed to Section 2, indicating better understanding of the former. He summarized his findings in this way:

> I must conclude from my earlier discussion of contract language and from my understanding of negotiations history that the parties did not negotiate Agreement language in Section 5 or elsewhere that intends that terminated employees shall not receive pay for vacation time

accrued between their anniversary date, or last completion of 2,080 hours, and their dates of termination.[35]

De Minimis Rule

Occasionally an arbitrator may invoke a principle of contract interpretation called the *"de minimis* rule." Actually the complete term is *"De minimis non curat lex,"* which means the "law does not concern itself with trifles." This does not mean that arbitration issues do not involve trifling sums of money. Indeed, major principles may be at stake, though monetary damages may be miniscule.

Arbitrators must be judicious when invoking the *de minimis* rule. Work assignment disputes, in particular, may seem trifling to the uninitiated, and seem to beg for the invocation of the *de minimis* rule. An arbitrator may wish to follow this guideline: if neither of the parties mention the rule, the arbitrator should not invoke it.

One hospital discovered the hazards of attempting to argue for the application of the *de minimis* rule.[36] The collective bargaining agreement had a section dealing with subcontracting, which read: "If the Employer intends to subcontract any work within the listed classifications, he shall give thirty (30) days prior notification to the Union."[37] Kaiser Hospital subcontracted medical transcription work to an outside transcription service on eight different occasions without notifying the union. The Hospital claimed that these situations were emergencies that could not be anticipated, so 30-day notice was impossible. Moreover, it claimed that employees were not entitled to overtime pay for work they did not perform. Furthermore, the hospital argued, no work was taken away from the medical transcriptionists, and under the *de minimis* doctrine, there can be no remedy without harm.

However, the arbitrator brushed aside the *de minimis* argument, pointing out that the hospital had breached the contract on eight separate occasions. And although the arbitrator concurred that emergency needs might justify a technical violation of the agreement, the hospital had abused the privilege. He found that over eight eight-hour workdays were lost through the hospital's subcontracting without notice—hardly an insignificant amount of time.

Thus, it can be readily seen that the arbitrator's decision-making process is far from clear cut. Two primary factors ultimately affect the arbitrator's decision: (1) subjective factors such as values, biases, and predilections; and (2) objective factors such as the basic rules of contract interpretation. Normally the subjective factors are subordinated to the objective ones, but when there is a conflict in objective standards of contract interpretation, arbitrators' values may determine which arbitration standards they prefer over others.

NOTES

1. See, for example, Gabriel N. Alexander, "Reflections on Decision Making," in *Collective Bargaining and the Arbitrator's Role,* Proceedings of the Fifteenth Annual Meeting of the National Academy of Arbitrators (Washington, D.C.: Bureau of National Affairs, Inc., 1962), pp. 1-7; Harold W. Davey, "Situation Ethics and the Arbitrator's Role," in *Arbitration of Interest Disputes,* Proceedings of the Twenty-sixth Annual Meeting of the National Academy of Arbitrators (Washington, D.C.: Bureau of National Affairs, Inc., 1974), pp. 162-175; and Harry J. Dworkin, "How Arbitrators Decide Cases," *Labor Law Journal* 25 (April 1974): 200-210.

2. Alexander, *op. cit.,* p. 2.

3. Peter Seitz, "How Arbitrators Decide Cases: A Study in Black Magic," in *Collective Bargaining and the Arbitrator's Role,* Proceedings of the Fifteenth Annual Meeting of the National Academy of Arbitrators (Washington, D.C.: Bureau of National Affairs, Inc., 1962), pp. 159-164.

4. Judge Cardozo, *The Nature of the Judicial Process,* Lecture IV, page 167, in Alexander, *op. cit.,* p. 4.

5. James A. Gross, "Value Judgments in the Decisions of Labor Arbitrators, *Industrial and Labor Relations Review* 21(October 1967): 55.

6. John Teele, "The Thought Processes of the Arbitrator," *Arbitration Journal* 17, no. 2 (1962): 92, 95.

7. Gross, *op. cit.*

8. *Ibid.,* pp. 71-72.

9. *Ibid.,* p. 60.

10. Brook I. Landis, *Value Judgments in Arbitration–A Case Study of Saul Wallen,* (Ithaca, New York: New York State School of Industrial and Labor Relations, Cornell University, 1977), p. 22.

11. *Ibid.,* pp. 22-25.

12. Gross, *op. cit.*

13. 61 LA 1008-1014 (1973).

14. 64 LA 96 (1974).

15. *Ibid.,* p. 100.

16. Affiliated Hospitals of San Francisco and Service Employees, Local 250, 64 LA 29 (1975).

17. *Ibid.,* p. 32.

18. Jesse Simons, Introduction to Earl R. Baderschneider and Paul F. Miller, *Labor Arbitration in Health Care* (New York: Spectrum Publications, 1976), p. xxiii.

19. Dworkin, *op. cit.,* p. 203.

20. *Ibid.,* p. 203.

21. Objective criteria discussed in this chapter relate to standards of contract interpretation. Other such criteria used in resolving "interest disputes" are discussed in Chapter 8.

22. United Steelworkers v. Enterprise Wheel and Car Corp., 363 U.S. 593 (1960).

23. 67 LA 927 (1976).

24. See Chapter 9 for a more complete discussion of management's rights.

25. Jacob Ruppert v. Office Employees International Union, Local 153, 35 LA 503, 504, October 19, 1960. Arbitrator Burton B. Turkus, cited in Paul Prasow and Edward Peters, *Arbitration and Collective Bargaining* (New York: McGraw-Hill Book Co., 1970), p. 108.

26. *Ibid.,* pp. 108-109.

27. 68 LA 908 (1977).

28. *Ibid.*, p. 911.

29. Ken Jennings and Cindy Martin, "The Role of Prior Arbitration Awards in Arbitral Decisions," *Labor Law Journal,* 29 (February 1978): 101.

30. *Ibid.*, p. 103.

31. Donald J. Petersen, "Union Prediction in Arbitration," *Labor Law Journal* 21 (December 1970): 787-793.

32. *Ibid.*, pp. 789-790.

33. 68 LA 663 (1977).

34. *Ibid.*, p. 665.

35. *Ibid.*, p. 668.

36. Kaiser Foundation Hospital, 61 LA 1008 (1973).

37. *Ibid.*, p. 1009.

Part II

Arbitration Systems

This country has no uniform organizational framework for the efficient perform-ance of the arbitration function. Modern arbitration traces its beginnings back some 35 years, to the World War II era. Since that time we have seen a growing utilization of arbitration in our industrial society. Because of this growing use and the wide variety of users, several systems of arbitration have developed. Each arbitration system has been fashioned to satisfy the particular needs of labor and management organizations operating in various sectors and industries. The health care industry is but one sector whose unique characteristics require an arbitration system that satisfies its particular needs.

In Part II of this book we examine in detail the organizational forms or systems of arbitration used in the health care industry. We evaluate them in terms of their advantages and disadvantages for the labor and management groups that make up that industry. Chapter 7 examines the arbitration systems involved in the settle-ment of so-called rights disputes, while Chapter 8 discusses systems primarily applied to the settlement of interest disputes.

Forms of Grievance Arbitration

Two periods mark the development of grievance arbitration systems in this country. During the first period, from the beginnings of U.S. labor arbitration until the late 1960s, one basic form of grievance arbitration prevailed: "conventional" or "regular" grievance arbitration. In the past decade, for various reasons to be discussed later, the parties have experimented with two novel forms of grievance arbitration: expedited arbitration and arbitration for nonunionized employees. Chapter 7 examines these three forms of grievance arbitration, with special emphasis on their utilization in the health care industry.

CONVENTIONAL GRIEVANCE ARBITRATION

Conventional or regular grievance arbitration is the oldest and most widely used form of grievance arbitration in American labor relations in general, and in the health care industry in particular. It is called conventional arbitration because its basic form, developed during the World War II years of the War Labor Board, has changed hardly at all since its inception. Approximately 95 percent of all collective bargaining agreements in the private sector, and almost 90 percent of all contracts in the health care industry, provide for binding grievance arbitration. According to a recent survey of 126 hospital contracts in Illinois, Wisconsin, and Minnesota, only 2.4 percent of the contracts did not encompass a formal grievance procedure, and 98 percent of the contracts specifying a grievance procedure provided for binding arbitration.[1]

Despite claims to the contrary, conventional grievance arbitration is heavily burdened with legalistic features and tendencies. Although most students of arbitration insist that arbitrators only loosely apply the rules of evidence to such proceedings, conventional grievance arbitration is still heavily loaded with such legalistic features as the filing of briefs in both the prehearing and posthearing phases, representation by attorneys, recordkeeping by court reporters, swearing of witnesses, and the issuance of subpoenas by arbitrators. Some of these practices are required and strengthened by recent court decisions[2] relating to arbitration. These practices also gain support in situations where administrative agencies, such as the National Labor Relations Board (NLRB), may defer a matter to arbitration under certain conditions that demand a more legalistic approach from the parties and the arbitrator involved.

Although binding arbitration is included in almost 90 percent of all contracts existing in the health care industry, arbitration is not used as widely in the health care industry as in other industries. Fifty nonprofit hospitals and nursing homes located in New York City were involved in approximately 80 grievance arbitration cases in 1977, and 70 cases in 1978—that is, less than 1.5 cases per hospital per year.[3] A recent survey of grievance procedures in Midwest hospitals concluded that "despite their availability, use of the grievance machinery is infrequent . . . and resort to arbitration is almost non-existent. On the average, less than one case was taken to arbitration, reflecting perhaps either an absence of significant problems at the work place in all but the largest hospitals, or of vigorous contract enforcement by the unions involved, or both."[4]

An informal survey among Chicago hospitals revealed that even the largest hospitals had only minimal exposure to grievance arbitration. Of the three largest Chicago hospitals, one hospital has averaged three grievance arbitration cases per year, with this number representing five percent of the total grievances. The second hospital has been involved in only one case per year, and the third did not have a single grievance arbitration case in the past two years.

The basic organization of conventional grievance arbitration usually depends on two factors: (1) the permanency of the arbitration, and (2) the size of the tribunal. In the following sections, these arbitration forms will be defined and evaluated.

Ad Hoc and Permanent Systems

On this measure, there are two alternatives. In the first, the arbitral function is performed by a temporary or *ad hoc* arbitrator; in the second, a permanent arbitrator may officiate. A temporary arbitrator may be defined as "a third party who is selected for a single case or for a specific group of cases. He is also called an *ad hoc* arbitrator, that is an arbitrator 'for this grievance.' The majority of labor agreements providing for arbitration specify this type."[5] On the other hand, a permanent arbitrator is a neutral party who is selected, usually for the duration of the agreement, to decide cases that the parties submit to arbitration. The parties may appoint a single permanent arbitrator to handle all disputes that may arise during or in the absence of a contract, or they may select a panel of arbitrators who are called to decide cases on a rotating basis.

Each alternative has its advantages and disadvantages. The relative usefulness of each system depends on the particular circumstances that characterize the industrial relations of an industry or a business organization.

In the event that the parties are dissatisfied with the performance of a temporary arbitrator, it is easy enough to simply not select that person for the next dispute. On the other hand, the parties are stuck with a permanent arbitrator for the duration of the contract, unless they reach mutual agreement to the contrary.

The use of an *ad hoc* arbitrator may provide the parties with greater flexibility. They may select different arbitrators for each kind of issue that requires special expertise. The permanent arbitrator must, of course, be an experienced "generalist" as he or she will be called on to decide all types of issues.

The volume of arbitration cases is another factor parties should consider in choosing an *ad hoc* arbitrator versus a permanent one. Parties with only a few cases per year would achieve considerable savings by using *ad hoc* arbitrators, because permanent arbitrators usually request a minimum retainer fee regardless of the number of grievances submitted to them. However, parties with a considerable volume of arbitration cases may save time by employing a permanent arbitrator, since selecting a temporary arbitrator for each case can be rather time consuming. A permanent arbitrator stands ready to handle disputes as they arise.

Another drawback in selecting an *ad hoc* arbitrator is his or her lack of specific knowledge about the parties. Because an *ad hoc* arbitrator has only infrequent contact with the parties, he or she may not be familiar enough with the circumstances and background of a particular collective bargaining relationship. Consequently, the arbitrator's need for "education" may lengthen the hearing and the delivery of the award. On the other hand, temporary arbitrators will not have enough time to develop a bias toward either party and will be less impelled to split their awards to please the parties. Of course, a permanent arbitrator will sooner or later acquire an intimate knowledge of a particular industrial relations setting, making possible a reduction in the time required to conduct hearings and prepare awards. Also, the fact that related issues are decided by the same arbitrator will ensure consistency in the awards—a consistency that will give direction and guidance to parties who wish to settle disputes at lower levels of the grievance procedure. This kind of direction might not be forthcoming if disputes of the same type are decided by several *ad hoc* arbitrators, sometimes in a conflicting manner.

For all these reasons, students of arbitration have concluded that the appointment of a permanent arbitrator may promote greater stability in labor-management relations. However, they also concede that in the majority of industrial relations settings, the circumstances (volume of grievances, diversity of issues) do not justify the appointment of a permanent arbitrator.

Solitary and Board Systems

The number of arbitrators participating in a single decision may also affect both the form of arbitration and the procedures used therein. In general, two types of tribunals are available to the parties for the purpose of arbitration: (1) the single arbitrator who decides a case alone, and (2) the arbitration board, which usually consists of three members.

Essentially, arbitration boards are usually set up in one of two ways. In one type the board is made up entirely of neutral members. In the other type, there is one neutral chairman or umpire, and the other two members each represent one of the parties. Since the two members delegated by the parties usually act as advocates rather than neutrals, it is obvious that the decisions handed down by tripartite boards are seldom unanimous. In fact, because of the expected disagreement between the partisan members of the board, the decision is usually made by the neutral member, though he or she may take advantage of the input furnished by the other two.

The particular circumstances and needs of the parties should be considered when deciding between a single arbitrator or an arbitration board. The following survey of the merits and drawbacks of arbitration boards may help parties reach such a decision. Although the evaluation focuses on arbitration boards, the weak points of the boards furnish arguments for the use of single arbitrators, and the advantages of the boards speak against the appointment of a single tribunal.

Advocates of the arbitration board list the following arguments in its favor:

1. Neutral members may get valuable advice and assistance from the partisan members.
2. Use of tripartite boards gives the parties a better opportunity to keep the neutral member informed as to their real position, which might not be the same as their formal position presented during the hearing. This is especially important in interest arbitration cases, where the partisan members may convey to the neutral member the underlying needs of the parties.
3. Awards of tripartite boards, when unanimous, tend to be more acceptable to the parties than awards of single arbitrators rendered without the input from arbitrators representing those parties.[6]
4. In interest arbitration, the use of tripartite boards reduces the risk of obtaining an unworkable award.[7]

On the other hand, the critics point out the time-consuming nature of arbitration by tripartite boards. Sometimes considerable delay results because the partisan members insist on re-arguing the case after the hearing is completed. Also, tripartite boards require extensive consultation between the neutral member and the partisan members, and this may cause further postponement of the award.

Another drawback is the possibility that the presence of partisan members may prevent the neutral chairman from reaching the best decision. The neutral member may be forced to compromise his or her own best judgment in order to secure a majority vote.[8]

Since 1945 the use of tripartite boards has declined steadily, while that of single arbitrators has grown.

EXPEDITED ARBITRATION

In the 1960s it became painfully obvious to participants in the arbitration process that the conventional arbitration system had become overburdened. On the one hand, the number of grievance arbitration cases had risen at an annual rate of 15 to 20 percent. However, the supply of experienced arbitrators acceptable to the parties remained rather limited; it certainly did not keep up with the growing demand. In addition, the parties witnessed a steady rise in the cost of arbitration. As a result of these trends, it became increasingly difficult to achieve the basic purpose of arbitration: to settle industrial disputes expeditiously and at moderate cost. One student of labor arbitration aptly remarked: "Grievance arbitration as it is structured in over 100,000 union contracts has lost many of its virtues being neither economical nor quick, neither flexible nor informal."[9]

In reaction to the problems of conventional grievance arbitration, arbitration agencies and practitioners have experimented with and developed a new system of grievance arbitration, called expedited arbitration.

Some of the ideas and features incorporated into this system were suggested by Arbitrator Davey in the late 1960s.[10] However, the actual beginnings of the system date back to 1971 when two major organizations, independent of each other, introduced two versions of expedited arbitration.

The first system was designed by the American Arbitration Association (AAA). In response to the concern of its clients over rising costs and delays in grievance arbitration, AAA's Labor-Management Committee worked out procedures under which cases could be scheduled promptly and awards delivered within a few days of the hearing. Under the AAA expedited system, once the parties submit their dispute to expedited arbitration, the AAA appoints a single arbitrator from its regular panel and fixes a mutually convenient time and place for the hearing. There is no stenographic record of the proceedings and no posthearing briefs, but the parties may be represented by attorneys. The award is delivered by the arbitrator not later than five business days from the date of a closed hearing. For his or her services the arbitrator receives a per diem fee for one day; this fee also includes the preparation of the award and a short opinion.

Some early critics, particularly on the management side, suggested two short-comings of the AAA expedited procedure. First, the parties could not choose their own arbitrator and might get someone inexperienced and unfamiliar with their particular industry. Second, the parties were not allowed to file briefs.[11]

The other pioneering system of expedited arbitration was established in the basic steel industry in 1971, under a special three-year supplementary agreement between the ten largest steel companies and the United Steelworkers of America. After the experimental period, the expedited arbitration or "mini-arb" became a permanent feature of their collective agreement.[12]

The expedited system, adopted by the basic steel industry, eliminated one of the AAA features criticized by some management representatives. In the basic steel plan the arbitrators on the panel are selected by the parties for the duration of the contract and are assigned to hear cases on a rotating basis. However, this plan retained the ban on filing briefs and went even further in simplification by excluding attorneys from expedited cases. In its seven-year existence, the expedited arbitration system in basic steel has resulted in 5,500 decisions by 330 arbitrators operating on 86 regional panels around the country.[13]

Obviously, the last few years have seen a high level of acceptance of expedited arbitration by management and labor. In 1977 expedited arbitration was used in more than 500 bargaining situations.[14] In fact, the proliferation of expedited arbitration systems introduced variations in the prototypes created in 1971. In the more than 100 situations where the parties relied on the AAA plan, arbitrators were still appointed by the Association. However, in the majority of expedited arbitration cases, the arbitrators were selected by the parties themselves. In fact, most of the expedited systems operated with permanent arbitrators. Depending on the case load, either a permanent panel or a single permanent arbitrator is appointed. *Ad hoc* arbitrators are conspicuously absent from expedited arbitration (again, the AAA plan being the major exception) because the time delay involved in selecting an *ad hoc* arbitrator is contrary to the basic idea behind expedited arbitration—that is, to settle grievances without any delay.

What about setting the date for the hearing? In some situations the parties fix the date themselves. If the arbitrator due in the rotation is not available on that date, the next arbitrator is called to hear the scheduled case. In the majority of the expedited systems, the arbitrator is allowed to schedule the hearing within a certain time limit, usually within 30 days from the date of his or her appointment.

Most expedited arbitration systems facilitate expediency by not permitting use of outside attorneys, posthearing briefs, or stenographic records of the proceedings. Another difference appears in the number of cases scheduled for one hearing day. In basic steel, as many as four grievances may be scheduled for one single hearing day. In the great majority of expedited systems, the parties are satisfied to schedule one grievance for a single hearing day.

Some variations also occur in terms of the fees and expenses paid to the arbitrator. Basic steel appears to be the most spartan of the systems. Arbitrators are not allowed to charge any expense except the cost of their transportation at 15 cents per mile. Other expedited systems are more liberal, covering arbitrators' expenses in connection with typing and mailing the award.

Following the growing acceptance of expedited grievance arbitration in the private sector, the system has been adopted by employers and unions in the health care industry—at least on paper. In the Chicago metropolitan area, a clause providing for expedited arbitration has been incorporated in the contracts between health care organizations and Hospital Employees Labor Program (HELP). However, a telephone survey covering HELP and some of the large Chicago hospitals revealed that the expedited arbitration procedure has received little use. One of the large hospitals in the sample did not have a single expedited arbitration case. The hospital officer in charge of employee relations attributed this to the small number of grievances that ended up in arbitration (only three or four cases per year). The only cases that go to arbitration are those that the parties feel very strongly about; therefore, they want full discussion of the issues involved. This spokesperson added that if there were more arbitration cases, some of them undoubtedly would be submitted to expedited arbitration.

The other large hospital surveyed had two expedited cases until November 1978, when the system was discontinued by mutual agreement. In this case the failure of the system was perhaps caused by a lack of understanding of the basic concepts underlying expedited arbitration. The parties made their first mistake when they appointed as permanent umpire one of the busiest arbitrators in Chicago. He was unable to schedule the expedited hearings within the 30-day period. Second, the parties were represented by attorneys who insisted on filing posthearing briefs. Third, the grievances submitted to expedited arbitration were of a complex nature. In one case, the union filed an unfair labor practice complaint with the NLRB. Under these circumstances, expedited arbitration could not possibly function properly.

The attitude of health care labor and management toward expedited arbitration is more favorable in the New York metropolitan area. The 1978-1978 Master Agreement between District 1199 of the Retail, Wholesale, and Department Store Union (RWDSU) and the League of Voluntary Hospitals and Homes, representing 50 health care institutions, provides for the use of expedited arbitration in discharge cases. Such cases are heard by an arbitrator appointed by the AAA from a preselected rotating panel of 20 permanent arbitrators. Approximately half of the 70 cases submitted to arbitration in the New York area during 1978 were decided through expedited arbitration.[15]

Despite the health care industry's mixed reaction to expedited arbitration, management and labor should give serious consideration to this form of grievance arbitration. In situations where such a system can be utilized, there can be substantial savings both in time and money. First, expedited arbitration dramatically shortens the length of time required to complete the arbitration process.

According to the data of the Federal Mediation and Conciliation Service (FMCS) for fiscal year 1978, in a typical conventional grievance arbitration case the average length of time that elapsed between the date on which the panel of arbitrators was requested and the date of the award amounted to 157 days. Parties using expedited arbitration can reduce this to 30 days—approximately 20 percent of the time required to process an average case under conventional arbitration. In an expedited case, the appointment of an arbitrator and the scheduling of a hearing should not take more than 15 to 20 days, and the award should be delivered within five business days from the date of the hearing.

Expenses may also be cut drastically by using expedited arbitration. In fiscal 1979, according to the FMCS figures, an arbitrator's average fees and expenses amounted to $911.83 per award. However, in most cases the arbitrator's fee constitutes a fraction of the total bill. John Zalusky, an economist with the AFL-CIO Department of Research, discovered that in 1976 the total cost of a typical conventional arbitration case, requiring one hearing day, was $4,500 for both parties. Of this amount, the arbitrator's share was only $700. The remaining amount reflected fees paid to attorneys ($2,300), the court reporter ($650), and the cost of witnesses and hearing facilities.[16] Expedited arbitration eliminates entirely the cost of legal representation and the transcript, and approximately halves the arbitrator's fees and expenses, saving about 85 percent of the total cost incurred in an average conventional grievance arbitration case.

Despite these obvious advantages, some parties may still feel uncomfortable with the simplest, "stripped-down" form of expedited arbitration. However, even if the parties are dissatisfied with some of its features, they should not reject the whole idea of expedited arbitration. They may wish to build some of its features into their conventional system. For example, conventional arbitration could be made less costly and time-consuming by eliminating such standard features as posthearing briefs and verbatim transcripts by a court reporter. These features can be eliminated without sacrificing a full-length discussion and opinion. But eliminating these two features could shorten the length of the proceeding by as much as two months and could reduce the cost of arbitration by several thousand dollars.

While recognizing the considerable advantages of expedited arbitration, labor and management in the health care industry also should remember that this simplified form of grievance arbitration has its limitations. It is best put to use to resolve uncomplicated grievances—simple discipline cases and grievances that do not require contract interpretation. In complex cases, particularly in situations where the parties intend to obtain a guiding precedent or clarification of ambiguous and confusing contract language, expedited arbitration could be somewhat risky. Similarly, complex discipline cases probably should not be processed through expedited arbitration. For example, if the issue is whether the grievant quit or was discharged for cause, or if the grievant maintains that his *Weingarten* rights[17] were violated, conventional arbitration is required to do justice to the complexity of the case.

GRIEVANCE ARBITRATION FOR NONUNION EMPLOYEES

Another recent development in the area of grievance arbitration was the result of some nonunionized companies' attempts to satisfy their nonsupervisory employees' need for protection against arbitrary treatment in the work place. In this endeavor they turned to the institution of arbitration.

Until quite recently, labor arbitration took place exclusively in organized situations where the employees of a firm were represented by one or more labor organizations. Traditionally, the union has been one of the two parties to labor arbitration. Thus grievance arbitration became identified with unionization.

While grievance arbitration provides unionized employees with a quasi-judicial means of obtaining protection against arbitrary treatment, "the nonunion employee has no institutional advocate. . . . Internal complaint procedures usually 'dead-end' in the personnel department where justice can always be distributed as charity."[18] Mr. Coulson, the author of the previous quote, added: "Most employee benefits are shared by both union and nonunion workers. . . . Nonunion employees are deprived of one important benefit: they do not have access to grievance arbitration."[19] In 1978 less than 23 percent of the persons in the labor force were unionized, which meant that at that time the great majority of the American employees did not enjoy the benefits of a formal grievance procedure.

Lately, however, a small but growing number of companies have experimented with a formal grievance procedure for their nonunion employees. For example, Trans World Airlines has offered its nonunion employees a board of arbitration to review discharges. The board is chaired by an impartial arbitrator.

These company experiments have a twofold purpose. First, they endeavor to raise employee morale by remedying real or alleged abuses perpetrated by supervisory personnel. Second, they expect to make employee unionization unnecessary by satisfying employee needs for fair treatment of their grievances.

The absence of a labor organization, however, has required the modification of the contractual labor arbitration system—a system traditionally based on the adversary relationship. Employers in the health care industry who intend to introduce a formal grievance procedure for their nonunion employees may consider three approaches to nonunion arbitration, described below. One approach was initiated by the American Arbitration Association; the other two have been adopted by hospitals located in the Chicago and New York areas.

The first plan, an experimental system of impartial review of grievances, was developed by the AAA for nonunion employees and recently was installed in a

New York State plant employing 500 persons. Under the plan, nonsupervisory employees may submit grievances in accordance with the Expedited Labor Arbitration Rules of the AAA. The hearing is held before an *ad hoc* impartial arbitrator appointed by the AAA from its regular panel. The company provides a representative at no cost to the employee; this representative helps the employee present the case before the arbitrator. Employees do not lose pay for participating in an arbitration hearing. The proceedings are informal; no stenographic transcripts are taken and no briefs are filed after the hearing. The binding award is delivered by the arbitrator within five working days after the hearing and is posted on the bulletin board.[20]

The second plan was established by Michael Reese Hospital in Chicago. The plan, called "Formal Complaint and Appeal Procedure," encompasses a formal four-step grievance procedure, with advisory arbitration being the last step. At any step, the employee may be assisted by one other hospital employee selected by the grievant. The selected employee is permitted to be absent with pay for such time as is reasonable and necessary to prepare for an effective presentation of the complaint. The grievant is required to pay ten percent of the arbitrator's fee. The decision of the arbitrator will be reviewed by the president of the hospital who may accept or reject the decision. The hospital considers the plan to be an experimental one and reserves the right to alter or discontinue this policy at any time.

Although the Michael Reese plan was put into effect in June 1978, until July 1979 not a single case was appealed to the arbitration level, although five or six complaints got as far as the third step. The employees apparently believe that since, in the final analysis, the case will be decided by hospital management, it would be a waste of time and money to appeal to arbitration.

A third arbitration system for nonunion employees has been set up recently by Northwestern Memorial Hospital in Chicago. Its "Formal Complaint and Appeal Process" covers nonsupervisory clerical personnel. The service employees are represented by HELP, and they have had the traditional grievance procedure. The Northwestern plan is similar to the Michael Reese plan in that both procedures encompass four steps. However, there is a basic difference between the two systems: the Northwestern plan offers binding arbitration at the last step, while in the Michael Reese plan arbitration serves a purely advisory function. Also, in the Northwestern system the employee pays a part of the arbitrator's fee only if the decision goes against him or her. Finally, in the Northwestern plan the grievant can choose to be assisted either by a member of the Employee Relations Department or by a fellow employee in his or her own classification. The three arbitrators, serving on the Northwestern panel on a rotating order, have been retained by the hospital. However, all of them are on the panels of the AAA and on the FMCS roster, and therefore their impartiality can hardly be impugned. Because the arbitration system of Northwestern Memorial Hospital became effective on September 1, 1979, no data are presently available to evaluate its performance.

A system quite similar to that of Northwestern Memorial Hospital has been in existence at Mount Sinai Medical Center of New York since June 1, 1974. Grievances that remain unresolved after reaching the third step of a formal grievance procedure may be referred to an outside arbitrator for an impartial and binding decision. However, the plan does not specify the circumstances under which a grievance may be referred to arbitration, the method of selecting an arbitrator, and the arrangement for paying the arbitration costs. No information is available as to the actual operation of the Mount Sinai procedure.

Modifications of the models previously described have been adopted by two unidentified small hospitals. Their arbitration systems for nonunion employees are described briefly in a survey entitled "Policies for Unorganized Employees," conducted in 1979 by the Bureau of National Affairs among the members of its Personnel Policies Forum. In one model, an outside arbitrator is selected by an advisory committee (consisting of nonmanagement employees) to serve on a review board. In the second model, arbitration is the final step of the grievance procedure. The arbitrator is chosen by the hospital with the concurrence of the grievant; he or she is compensated by the hospital. It is noted in the survey that neither hospital reported any experience with the use of these arbitration procedures.[21]

These are just a few of the various types of nonunion grievance procedures in existence today. The employer will undoubtedly establish the type of system that best satisfies the needs of the organization and its employees. In any case, it is essential that the employer installing such an arbitration procedure publicize to employees both the procedure and the rules that control employee work behavior. Moreover, it is recommended that the penalties for violating such work rules be spelled out so that employees have full knowledge of the consequences of their acts.

NOTES

1. Richard U. Miller, Brian B. Becker, and Edward B. Krinsky, "Union Effects on Hospital Administration: Preliminary Results from a Three-State Study," *Labor Law Journal* 28 (August 1977): 515.

2. Footnote 21 in Alexander v. Gardner-Denver, 415 U.S. 36 (1974).

3. Information obtained from Mr. William J. Abelow, Executive Vice-President, League of Voluntary Hospitals of New York (August 1979).

4. Miller et al., *op. cit.*, p. 515.

5. *Labor Law Course*, 24th ed. (Chicago: Commerce Clearing House, 1979), p. 4053.

6. Frank Elkouri and Edna A. Elkouri, *How Arbitration Works*, 3rd ed. (Washington, D.C.: Bureau of National Affairs, Inc., 1973), p. 83.

7. Thomas A. Kochan, "Dynamics of Dispute Resolution in the Public Sector," in *Public-Sector Bargaining*, B. Aaron et al., eds. IRRA Research Series (Washington, D.C.: Bureau of National Affairs, Inc., 1979), p. 185.

8. Elkouri & Elkouri, *op. cit.*, p. 84.

9. Lawrence Stessin, "Expedited Arbitration: Less Grief Over Grievances," *Harvard Business Review* 55 (January-February 1977): 128.

10. Harold W. Davey, "Restructuring Grievance Arbitration Procedures: Some Modest Proposals," *Iowa Law Review* 54 (1969): 565.

11. Steven E. Kane, "Current Developments in Expedited Arbitration," *Labor Law Journal* 24 (May 1973): 73.

12. Stessin, *op. cit.*, p. 130.

13. *Daily Labor Report,* May 14, 1979, p. A-3.

14. Stessin, *op. cit.*, p. 130.

15. Abelow, *op. cit.*

16. John Zalusky, "Arbitration: Updating a Vital Process," *AFL-CIO American Federationist* 83 (November 1976): 3.

17. NLRB v. J. Weingarten, Inc., 420 U.S. 251 (1975).

18. *Daily Labor Report,* June 25, 1979, p. D-1.

19. *Ibid.*

20. *Ibid.*

21. *Policies for Unorganized Employees,* Personnel Policy Forum Survey No. 125 (Washington, D.C.: Bureau of National Affairs, Inc., 1979), p. 11.

Chapter 8

Impasse Resolution Procedures

In the private sector of the economy, when an impasse is reached at a certain point in the bargaining process, usually it is resolved by some manifestation of economic force—such as strike, lockout, picketing, or boycott. In the public sector, where strikes are considered a threat to public interest, the parties (particularly the governmental bodies) have preferred a peaceful resolution rather than resort to a show of economic force. Although the majority of health care institutions, on the basis of ownership, belong to the private sector, the nature of the services performed by the health care industry places all health care organizations under public scrutiny. For this reason, health care institutions, regardless of their ownership designation, come under the term "public interest sector."

The 1974 Health Care Amendments to the National Labor Relations Act (NLRA) do not prohibit health care workers from using the strike as a means to break impasses in collective bargaining. However, both statutory provisions and tradition tend to put restraint on the use of the strike. As a result, during the past 20 years—a period that witnessed the institutionalization of collective bargaining in the health care industry—impasse resolution procedures have played an increasing role in hospital collective bargaining. In 1969 Kheel and Kaden stated, "The overriding issue in hospital labor relations remains the question of impasse resolution."[1] Twelve years later impasse resolution remains one of the critical issues in hospital industrial relations. As a result, during the past decade, several approaches were developed and tested to bring the art and technique of impasse resolution to a manageable state.

The strongest impetus to the widespread utilization of impasse resolution procedures was employers' insistence that strikes be prohibited. Particularly before the 1974 Amendments, many health care institutions had agreed to union representation of their employees only on condition that the union and the employees waive the right to strike not only during the contract but also between two contracts. But eliminating the strike weapon required that alternative methods be developed to resolve eventual impasses. Under the present industrial relations system, a procedure involving a neutral third party appears to be the only alternative to the strike. As was noted by an attorney representing unions in the health care industry, "If there is a commitment not to strike, then there is need for some outside intervention in the event an impasse develops during the negotiations."[2]

Particularly prior to the 1974 Amendments, when the health care industry settled its labor disputes on its own, union recognition frequently had been preceded by pre-election agreements which, among other things, provided for (1) a no-strike pledge during negotiations, and (2) procedures calling for neutral parties to resolve any impasses that emerged during negotiations. In the Chicago metropolitan area, most of the 22 health care institutions whose employees are represented by the Hospital Employees Labor Program (HELP) had a pre-election agreement providing for impasse resolution procedures.[3] Other Chicago hospitals did not require a pre-election agreement as a precondition to union recognition; they preferred the possibility of a strike to the intervention of a third party in the bargaining process.

A perusal of labor contracts in the New York metropolitan area shows a pattern that is somewhat different from that in Chicago. Although, at least until recently, District 1199 had a no-strike policy, the contract between the Voluntary League of Hospitals and Homes of New York and District 1199 of RWDSU, covering the service employees of 52 health care institutions, did not provide for any impasse resolution procedures. On the other hand, approximately 40 percent of the individual contracts between the League and the New York State Nurses' Association do specify some kind of impasse resolution procedure, primarily binding interest arbitration.[4]

Presently, there are three basic procedures used in the health care industry to peacefully resolve impasses that occur in bargaining situations: (1) mediation; (2) factfinding; and (3) binding interest arbitration. Although only the last procedure falls into the category of arbitration, the other two must also be discussed here because all the three types are interrelated. Mediation and factfinding may rightly be considered phases of a process that may culminate in interest arbitration. Furthermore, all the three types are characterized by the fact that a third neutral party intervenes in the dispute between labor and management, either under the contract or under statutory provisions. Mediation is obligatory under the 1974 Amendments, while binding interest arbitration, if specified, is provided by the contract. Factfinding may take place either under the Amendments or under the contract.

The following pages will examine in detail the three basic types of impasse resolution procedures and their variations, with special emphasis on their use in the health care industry.

MEDIATION

Mediation is the first possible step leading toward the resolution of an impasse reached during collective bargaining. It is also the mildest form of third-party intervention in the bargaining process. Mediation is generally welcomed and accepted by the disputing parties because the resulting settlement, if any, is reached by the parties themselves (through the help of the mediator) and is not forced upon them by an outside neutral party. For this reason, mediation is widely used even in private industry, which traditionally has rejected other forms of outside intervention in its bargaining process.

Although, at least in principle, mediation may be performed by any person selected and trusted by the parties, in practice this function usually is performed by commissioners of the Federal Mediation and Conciliation Service (FMCS), an independent federal agency of considerable reputation, or by state agencies of similar nature. FMCS in its present form was created by Title II, Section 202 of the NLRA, as amended in 1947. Prior to the 1974 Health Care Amendments to the NLRA,[5] parties to a labor dispute in the health care industry could have used the services of FMCS on a voluntary basis. However, under the 1974 Amendments, whenever a bargaining dispute involves health care employees, mediation becomes mandatory. Section 8(d)(A) of the NLRA requires that parties to a dispute in the health care industry notify FMCS and the state mediation agency 60 days prior to the expiration date of their contract. During this 60-day period, mediation becomes *mandatory,* in contrast to other industries covered by the NLRA where mediation is *voluntary.* In an initial bargaining situation, the union that became the bargaining agent must give to FMCS and the appropriate state mediation agency a 30-day notice of the existence of a dispute. During this 60-day or 30-day period, the parties must participate in the mediation process, or be subject to charges of unfair labor practice.

Pursuant to this provision, whenever health care institutions and labor organizations report a bargaining situation, the FMCS must take immediate steps to assign a mediator to that dispute. Between August 25, 1974 (the effective date of the Health Care Amendments) and December 31, 1976, the FMCS recorded 2,585 bargaining situations in the health care industry, involving 414,000 employees. This number constitutes one-quarter of the 1.7 million persons employed by those institutions affected.[6] Of the 2,585 bargaining situations, 745, or close to 30 percent, represented initial contracts, and the remaining 70 percent involved contract renewals.[7] Seventy percent of the 2,585 bargaining situations were located in hospitals, 25 percent in nursing homes, and the remaining five percent in other types of health care facilities.[8]

Immediately after the passage of the 1974 Amendments, FMCS was very much concerned with ongoing negotiations in health care institutions and literally forced itself into the bargaining process at an early stage, even before the contract expired. More recently, FMCS has been more confident about the state of negotiations in the health care industry. Although mediators who are assigned to the dispute keep in touch with the parties, they do not intervene unless they are invited.[9] Between August 1974 and December 1976, active mediation, defined as holding meetings with both parties, occurred in 1,328 (about one-half of all) bargaining situations. Between January 1, 1977 and December 31, 1978, the total number of health care cases closed by FMCS amounted to 2,694; active mediation took place in 1,527, or 57 percent of the total.[10]

In the states that enacted special dispute resolution statutes covering the health care industry, FMCS and the respective state have joined together to provide mediation services. This, however, has been at the option of FMCS, as the 1974 Amendments did not cede jurisdiction to the states. Some of the states frequently involved in mediation services in cooperation with FMCS include the following: Connecticut, Michigan, New Hampshire, North Carolina, Rhode Island, and the Commonwealth of Puerto Rico.[11]

Although, at present, mediators are not as active in the health care field as they had been in the first few months following the passage of the 1974 Amendments, they are still more active in that industry than in other industries covered by the NLRA. On the average, 3.6 meetings are held per bargaining situation in health care bargaining, as contrasted with 3.3 sessions in all other industries. The degree of mediation activity in health care cases shows certain regional variations. In the Southeastern United States, 65 percent of the health care bargaining situations required active mediation, while in the Midwest region mediators intervened actively in only 47 percent of the cases.[12]

Mediators who actively participated in health care bargaining were impressed by the differences between bargaining in that industry versus other private industries. According to James Scearce, former Director of FMCS, "these differences include . . . the larger size of bargaining committees in the health industry, the inexperience of the bargaining parties, and more reliance on attorneys for negotiating more than in other industries."[13] Experts also referred to another characteristic peculiar to mediation in health care—namely, that mediation is interrelated to the Board of Inquiry (BOI), a factfinding body that may be appointed by FMCS following the mediation phase.[14] It was found that in health care cases a part of the efforts made by mediators was directed toward determining the need for a BOI or educating the parties about its procedure and purpose.

How effective are mediators in health care bargaining situations? Does their presence and participation promote and accelerate the settlement of issues at impasse? The President of Local 73 of the Service Employees International Union (SEIU), which represents service employees in Chicago health care institutions, believes that "from the union's viewpoint, mediation is most effective in those situations where hospitals are inexperienced in negotiations. In some cases, an agreement may not be reached without the active assistance of mediators; in other cases, although their presence may speed up negotiations, an agreement would have been reached without them.''[15]

Some conclusions about the effectiveness of mediation in the health care industry may be drawn from Thomas Kochan's evaluation of the mediation function in the public sector. Although the majority of health care institutions by virtue of ownership do not belong to the public sector, their essential service function and corresponding legal arrangements do give bargaining situations in the health care industry a great deal of affinity with those in the public sector. Kochan lists the following conditions under which mediation may prove to be most effective in resolving impasses:

> (1) the negotiators—especially the union negotiators—lacked experience; (2) the negotiations process broke down because one of the parties was overcommitted to a particular position; (3) a dispute was below average in intensity or difficulty, that is, the magnitude and number of sources of impasse were relatively small; (4) the parties were motivated to reach a settlement; and (5) an aggressive, experienced and high-quality (as perceived by the parties) mediator was involved. On the other hand, mediation was least successful in situations (1) where the underlying dispute arose because of an employer's inability to pay; (2) where the parties had a history of going to impasse and to the later stages of the dispute-resolution procedure; and (3) where the jurisdiction was among the largest.''[16]

Managers and union officers in the health care industry may promote successful mediation by furnishing the following vital information to the mediator: (1) the history of relations between the parties; (2) the stress-points existing in their present relationship; (3) the priority of the issues at impasse; and (4) the identity of each party's spokesperson(s).

Obviously mediation will be short and successful primarily in those situations where mediation was preceded by hard bargaining and, as a result, the positions of the parties became narrow enough to be reconciled through the efforts of a skillful and sensitive mediator.

FACTFINDING

Factfinding is a second method of impasse resolution in collective bargaining. In this method the alleged facts surrounding a dispute over the terms and conditions of employment are presented by the negotiators to a neutral third party for investigation and possible recommendations.

There are two schools of thought concerning the proper function of factfinding. One school considers it as supermediation—implying that factfinding is a natural continuation of mediation and, like mediators, factfinders should interfere with the process of bargaining as little as possible. Accordingly, in their reports factfinders should limit themselves to stating the facts as they see them. In the opinion of the second school, the term factfinding is a misnomer, as "the factfinding process involves more than searching-out the factual basis of the parties' positions; it also involves an effort to identify an acceptable compromise settlement."[17] Arbitrator Anthony Sinicropi adds to the above: "The purpose of the factfinder is to write a report that the parties can live with and satisfy their expectations."[18] When factfinders report their recommendations for the settlement of the terms in dispute, factfinding actually becomes advisory arbitration. This differs from binding interest arbitration only in that factfinders' recommendations may be accepted or rejected by the parties.

The underlying theory behind factfinding is "that when both parties in a dispute argue their positions before a factfinder, the facts obtained through these hearings will result in a reasonable recommendation. The parties may be forced to clarify their positions in preparing for the presentation to the factfinding board, and this may also facilitate collective bargaining."[19]

Factfinding in the Nongovernment Segment of the Health Care Industry

Before the passage of the 1974 Amendments, factfinding had been used in the nongovernment sector of the health care industry on a voluntary basis. However, the Amendments made factfinding mandatory, at the discretion of the FMCS director. First, in accordance with Section 8(d)(A) of the NLRA, the parties are required to give FMCS timely notice (60 days prior to the expiration date of their contract) of a potential dispute. Second, Section 213 of the same act empowers the Director of FMCS to appoint an impartial Board of Inquiry (BOI) if, in his or her opinion, "a threatened or actual strike or lockout affecting a health care institution will, if permitted to occur or continue, substantially interrupt the delivery of health care in the locality concerned." Such a BOI shall be appointed not more than 30 days from the date of the notice filed by the parties under Section 8(d)(A).

If and when a BOI is selected, it is required to investigate the issues involved in the dispute and make a written report containing the finding of facts and its recommendations for settling the dispute—all within 15 days after its appointment. However, the recommendations of a BOI are not binding on either party. (The full text of regulations Part 1420, dealing with the functions of the Federal Mediation and Conciliation Service in Health Care Industry Bargaining under the Labor-Management Relations Act, as promulgated effective August 1, 1979 [44 F.R. 42683], appears as Appendix A, following Chapter 13.)

Presently, the Director of the FMCS relies on two criteria in determining whether or not to appoint a BOI: (1) threat or existence of a strike that would cause a health care crisis in the community; and (2) the status of the collective bargaining involved. Initially, FMCS had considered only the effect of a strike threat and had disregarded the impact of BOI on ongoing collective bargaining. However, early experience with the administration of BOIs revealed that the 30-day requirement—that a BOI must be appointed in 30 days from the date of the notice given by the parties under Section 8(d)(A)—put undue pressure on the collective bargaining process. In numerous cases the early appointment of BOIs impaired their effectiveness and, at the same time, slowed the bargaining process. FMCS research indicated that "In some cases the parties had not even met prior to the appointment of the BOI."[20]

To remedy the situation, FMCS first attempted to gain additional time by giving liberal interpretation to the time limits set by Section 213 for the appointment of BOIs. However, in the *Affiliated Hospitals of San Francisco* v. *Scearce* case,[21] the court disagreed with FMCS's interpretation and required it to appoint a BOI within 30 days after being notified of the dispute, rather than 30 days following the date by which the notice is required.[22]

Therefore, more recently FMCS has experimented with an alternate approach to avoid the BOI's premature interference with the bargaining process. Since the statute requires FMCS to appoint a BOI within 30 days after receiving notice under Section 8(d)(A), FMCS developed the concept of a stipulation agreement in order to avoid such appointment at an early stage. This concept was promulgated by a memorandum of the FMCS Director dated January 24, 1975. The memorandum states in its introduction:

> On numerous occasions in health care industry cases, it is apparent that a board of inquiry is warranted yet negotiations have not progressed to the stage where the convening of a board by the statutory due date would benefit the overall negotiations. In such cases, the use of a stipulation from the parties allowing FMCS to subsequently appoint a factfinder is one technique which should be utilized.

Under such agreement, both parties authorize FMCS to appoint a factfinder at a date later than the last date specified under the statute. The factfinder, if eventually appointed, would operate under the same mandate as a BOI. In the meantime, FMCS can review the state of negotiations to determine if there is a need for appointing a factfinder in that particular dispute.

The success of this FMCS policy is plain. Between August 25, 1974 and March 1, 1977, in one-third of the 129 bargaining situations that required factfinding, factfinders under stipulation agreement (rather than BOIs) were appointed by

FMCS.[23] It should be noted, however, that in cases where one or both parties decline to enter a stipulation agreement, FMCS must determine whether or not to appoint a BOI 30 days prior to the date of contract expiration.

Although the term "Board of Inquiry" implies a multiperson tribunal, in the great majority of cases, FMCS appointed a single arbitrator as a BOI. Of the 120 BOIs appointed between August 25, 1974 and December 31, 1976, a multiperson board was appointed only in ten situations where the dispute was particularly complex or significant.[24] In cases where FMCS appoints factfinders under the parties' stipulation agreement, a single arbitrator is always selected.

FMCS initially considered four criteria in selecting persons for BOIs or factfinding under stipulation appointments: (1) competency in impasse resolution procedures; (2) some experience in the health care field; (3) availability on short notice; and (4) membership in FMCS's roster of private arbitrators.[25] More recently, however, FMCS added a fifth criterion: the parties' preference either for certain arbitrators or for their own factfinding procedure.

Under Section 213 of NLRA as amended in 1974, FMCS issued in September 1979 new regulations entitled: "Input of Parties to Board of Inquiry Selection." Pursuant to the new regulations, FMCS recognizes two kinds of input. First, the parties to a dispute in the health care industry may jointly submit a list of arbitrators whose service as BOI members would be acceptable to both parties. This list would be submitted at any time within 90 days prior to the contract expiration date in a contract renewal dispute, or at any time prior to the statutory notice to FMCS in an initial contract dispute. FMCS then would make "every effort" to select BOI members or factfinders from that list, although their appointment would not be guaranteed.

Second, under the new regulations, FMCS may defer to the parties' own factfinding or interest arbitration procedure, rather than appoint a BOI. This new FMCS policy is based on the fact that in a number of bargaining situations the parties have long established their own private factfinding or interest arbitration procedures, usually in their pre-election agreement. The new regulations allow FMCS to establish a written policy of deferral so long as such private impasse resolution procedures meet the following conditions:

1. The factfinding procedure must be invoked automatically at a specified time (for example, at contract expiration if no agreement is reached).
2. It must provide a fixed and determinate method for selecting the impartial factfinder.
3. It must provide that there can be no strike or lockout and no changes in conditions of employment (except by mutual agreement) prior to and during the factfinding procedure and for a period of at least seven days after the factfinding is completed.

4. It must provide that the factfinder(s) will make a written report to the parties, containing the findings of fact and any recommendations for settling the dispute, a copy of which is sent to FMCS.

In case of a deferral to interest arbitration, an additional condition is set by FMCS: that the award must be final and binding on both parties. In both private factfinding and interest arbitration, both parties should jointly submit a copy of their agreed-upon private procedure to the appropriate regional office of FMCS as early as possible.

Because more than five years have passed since the effective date of the 1974 Health Care Amendments, the available data make it possible to evaluate the extent and effectiveness of the factfinding procedures administered by FMCS for the health care industry. According to FMCS figures, between August 25, 1974 and December 31, 1978, FMCS attended a total of 6,586 bargaining situations in the health care industry. During the same period, the number of BOIs and factfinders appointed by FMCS totalled 187.[26] This means that less than three percent of all bargaining situations required the appointment of a BOI or factfinder under stipulation. One cannot escape the conclusion that FMCS has exercised considerable restraint in using its authority under the 1974 Amendments.

More detailed data on FMCS factfinding procedures are available only for the period of August 25, 1974 through December 31, 1976. During that time, 120 factfinding boards were appointed by FMCS, representing 91 BOIs and 29 stipulation factfinders. Data concerning the geographic location of the 120 boards show that 79 percent functioned in the states along the Atlantic coast. Only 1.7 percent dealt with disputes originating in the Midwest.

There are two major reasons why health care institutions on the East Coast were involved in a disproportionate number of factfinding boards: (1) the poor quality of industrial relations between management and unions; and (2) the militancy of District 1199, which represents employees in the majority of health care institutions in that region. On the other hand, the Midwest remained relatively untouched by FMCS factfinding procedures because health care institutions, particularly those in metropolitan Chicago, have been engaged in pattern bargaining. As soon as the patternmaker agreed with HELP, then the others, with slight modifications, followed suit. Therefore, in the worst, factfinding would have been limited to the pattern bargaining institution. Furthermore, in the Midwest, both management and the unions preferred contractual private factfinding to statutory factfinding and, in most cases, FMCS informally deferred to such procedures even before the promulgation of new regulations in September 1979.

As to the format of the reports issued by factfinding boards in the 120 cases, it is interesting to note that despite Section 213's requirement that such reports contain recommendations for settling the dispute, in 45 out of the 120 factfinding proceedings, no recommendations were issued. However, in 17 of those 45 cases, the dispute was settled before the factfinding board convened. In the majority of the remaining 28 cases, the factfinders felt that "bargaining had not progressed sufficiently to make recommendations possible or useful."[27]

Whether recommendations are made depends not only on the bargaining situation but also on how factfinders perceive their role. According to the findings of FMCS, about 43 percent of the appointed factfinders thought their role was to mediate the dispute. Another 43 percent saw their function as helping the parties define the issues and then proposing recommendations for settlement. The remaining 15 percent stressed either the need to force the parties into a position of agreement or direct their efforts toward avoiding a work stoppage. Only 12 percent of the factfinders indicated that they restricted their activities to mediation efforts; 43 percent said they used the tools of both mediators and factfinders.[28]

Norman Metzger examined the effect of factfinding recommendations, where such were issued, on the final settlement. His sample was limited to the 58 BOIs that were appointed by FMCS during the 12 months following the effective date of the 1974 Amendments. His questionnaire was returned by 31 institutions. Six of these reported that their dispute was settled prior to the hearing date. In eleven of the remaining 25 cases, the factfinder's recommendations were completely accepted by both parties. In four cases, both parties rejected the recommendations. In all 11 cases where negotiations continued after the issuance of the factfinding report, the institutions indicated that "the factfinder's recommendations were the basis for the final settlement."[29]

It is also of considerable interest how the BOIs and the stipulation factfinders were evaluated by the three parties who had actively participated in those proceedings—that is, the factfinders, health care management personnel, and the unions. The factfinders listed both the positive and negative aspects of the boards. On the positive side they found that (1) the parties were forced to develop supportive data for their respective positions; (2) the board served as a face-saving device; (3) at times the board functioned as a catalyst to get the parties to start negotiating or move off dead center; and (4) the threat of a board may have prompted the parties to settle before the board convened or issued its recommendations. The only negative matter they found was that the BOI procedure was instituted too early in the collective bargaining process, and the 15-day time period within which factfinders had to meet with the parties and write a report was too short. Meanwhile, the first criticism was remedied by the use of the stipulation agreement.[30]

Turning to the evaluation of the FMCS boards by the unions, they seem to be more critical than management. Their criticisms were summarized in a memorandum addressed to FMCS, dated March 7, 1977, and signed by the presidents of the five national unions that represent the large majority of employees in the health care industry. Their censure was directed both toward FMCS and the management personnel of the health care institutions. The union officers complained that FMCS did not appoint BOIs more frequently than FMCS actually did. They also exhorted

FMCS to use a more judicial approach in applying the "area-wide impact on health-care delivery" criterion. According to the unions, FMCS had not been sensitive to all the factors that determined whether or not a crisis existed. In the opinion of the union presidents, a crisis could come about even when a relatively small number of workers were involved. In addition, the unions urged FMCS to give greater exposure to the findings and recommendations of its factfinders so that the public could exert pressure on the parties to settle their disputes.[31]

In their memorandum, the union presidents also blamed management for some of the shortcomings of the boards. They complained that

> management does not provide full financial disclosure to BOI's. Fact-finders are often forced to accept hospitals' assertions about their financial conditions rather than being supplied hard data. . . . At the very least, factfinders should be provided with copies of standard financial reporting forms on file with various government agencies and this data should be appended to the factfinder's final report.[32]

The unions' memorandum also blames management for the strikes occurring in 1975, saying they were a result of management's frequent rejection of the fact-finders' awards.

While unions would have preferred the appointment of more BOIs, management representatives questioned the need for so many.

Both unions and management were generally satisfied with the qualifications and performance of the arbitrators who served on BOIs or as factfinders. Three-quarters of the chief labor and management negotiators involved in BOI proceedings between August 1974 and December 1976 agreed that the persons assigned to BOIs were qualified and knowledgeable in labor relations.

In their appraisal of the factfinding proceedings, both management and unions recognized that the pressure from outside groups played a considerable role in the negotiations that preceded and followed the factfinding proceedings. The FMCS research study shows that

> Sixty-two percent of the chief labor negotiators and 57 percent of the chief management negotiators found that outside groups were influential during the contract talks. Both agree that third-party payors and community groups were the most active in trying to impose their needs on the negotiations. (Third-party payors include both insurance companies and government reimbursement or financial assistance agencies).[33]

Although the chief negotiators did not indicate explicitly that pressure groups had influenced the findings of the BOIs under the above conditions, their acceptance and adoption of the BOI recommendations was certainly affected by outside pressure. In this manner, then, the pressure groups had some input into the factfinding procedure.

Arbitrators who served on the factfinding boards, particularly those in the New York area, believed that in order to constructively harness the influence of outside pressure groups on collective bargaining in the health care industry, "a representative of the third-party payors should be at the bargaining table."[34]

In summary, it may be stated that experience with factfinding boards operating under Section 213 of the NLRA shows considerable flexibility and innovation on the part of FMCS in modifying and adjusting the original procedures to the needs of the parties involved in the private sector of the health care industry. Those parties who wish to exert some control over the factfinding procedures, within the latitude granted by FMCS, should specify in their contracts the factfinding procedures to which FMCS may defer in the event the use of such procedures becomes necessary.

Factfinding in the Governmental Institutions

The previous discussion centered exclusively on various aspects of factfinding taking place in the nongovernment segment of the health care industry covered by the 1974 Amendments of the NLRA. However, according to a 1975 census, 37 percent of all health care institutions are found in the public sector.[35] Therefore, a brief review of federal and state statutes regulating factfinding in that sector is warranted. Although the legal basis on which factfinding procedures may be evoked in the public sector differs from that in the so-called private sector, once these procedures are evoked, their operation and effect are quite similar. In order to avoid repetition, these similar aspects will not be discussed here.

Labor relations in the federal administration are regulated by Title VII of the Civil Service Reform Act,[36] which became effective January 11, 1979. Section 7119 of the act provides for procedures in case an impasse develops in the course of collective bargaining between federal agencies and their employees. The Federal Service Impasses Panel is authorized to enter into impasse situations and, according to Section 7119, it may use an "arsenal of weapons," including factfinding, to break the impasse.[37]

Accordingly, in the federal sector of the health care industry provisions of collective bargaining agreements that deal with the resolution of interest disputes usually refer to the respective provisions of the Civil Service Reform Act. For example, in the contract between the Veterans Hospital of North Chicago and the Illinois Nurses' Association, Article IX provides that when the services of the FMCS fail to resolve the negotiations impasse, either party may request that the Federal Service Impasses Panel consider the matter. Arbitration or third-party factfinding, with recommendations to assist in the resolution of an impasse, may be used by the parties only when authorized or directed by the panel.

Among the 50 states, there is considerable variation as to their legislative efforts to regulate collective bargaining in the public sector. There is also variation as to the coverage of such statutes. According to B.V. Schneider's survey of state legislation in the area of employee relations, by 1977, 37 states had enacted collective bargaining statutes covering all or some occupational groups of public employees. Only Illinois had extended by executive order the right of state employees to bargain collectively.[38]

A breakdown of these 37 states shows that statutes in 26 states cover all public employees, including those in health care institutions maintained by the state and its municipalities. Two statutes cover state employees only, while two states legislated coverage for local public employees. The remaining states restricted their legislation over employee relations to special groups of public employees, such as teachers, firefighters, and police officers. None of these latter states included health care employees in their coverage.

The 26 states that legislated collective bargaining for all of their public employees offer a variety of methods for the peaceful resolution of disputes over the terms and conditions of employment. These methods include statutory factfinding (with the exception of North Dakota, which provides only for mediation). Because there is considerable variation both in the coverage and the impasse procedures of various state statutes, it is strongly recommended that health care unions and management in the public sector familiarize themselves with any statutes regulating the collective bargaining of public employees in their own state.

INTEREST ARBITRATION

Interest arbitration is potentially the final phase of the bargaining process in the health care industry. Furthermore, it is the impasse resolution procedure through which a third party exerts the greatest impact on the contractual relationship of the negotiating parties. Obviously in only a small fraction of the bargaining situations will the parties submit their dispute to interest arbitration, as it allows a third party to make a binding determination of those contract terms over which the parties reached an impasse. Thus, interest arbitration constitutes a "court of last resort" for the bargaining parties.

Interest arbitration has developed as a substitute for strike or lockout in those sectors and industries where such manifestations of economic force were considered an anathema. As Grodin pointed out, "Interest arbitration involving the binding determination of contract terms has some private-sector roots but is mainly a public sector phenomenon, developed in response to the legal prohibition against strikes by public employees."[39] In many states, a strike by public employees is no longer outlawed. Nevertheless, even in those states every legal effort is made to use methods other than strike to break a bargaining impasse.

Although proprietary and nonprofit health care institutions—constituting over 60 percent of the health care industry—are officially classified as being in the private sector, they too have availed themselves of interest arbitration because they provide a public service. Under pressure of government and public opinion, both management and unions try to avoid strikes as a means of breaking an impasse reached during negotiations. Aside from a strike, interest arbitration provides a good alternative for solving an impasse.

The only major similarity between interest arbitration and grievance arbitration is the binding nature of the award delivered by a neutral third party. There are, however, numerous differences between these two:

1. Grievance arbitration and interest arbitration differ in their functional role. While grievance arbitration performs a quasi-judicial function, interest arbitration is held to legislate the terms of employment.
2. An interest arbitration case is more important to the parties than a grievance arbitration case. The outcome of the former will affect the relationship between the parties for the duration of their contract—that is, for two or three years. On the other hand, in a grievance case, particularly a discipline case, the award will have only a rather isolated effect on industrial relations between the parties.
3. Arbitrators called on to decide interest arbitration cases should have qualifications that are different from those required in grievance arbitration. Interest arbitrators should be able to deal effectively with economic and financial matters. Grievance arbitrators are usually trained in the law and are equipped for contract interpretations.
4. Hearing an interest arbitration case may take longer than a typical grievance case; therefore, the former are more time-consuming and costly.

The use and requirement of interest arbitration is not uniform within the health care industry. It varies with the sectoral position of the particular health care institution. In the federal sector, impasses that cannot be resolved through mediation must be forwarded to the Federal Service Impasses Panel for resolution. Although the panel may first attempt to resolve the dispute by means of factfinding, if that approach fails it may direct the parties to accept a settlement drawn by a third party. Such resolution falls in the category of interest arbitration.

While the resolution of bargaining impasses in federally owned health care institutions is uniformly provided by Title VII of the Civil Service Reform Act of 1979, considerable differences exist between those state statutes that regulate impasse resolution in the public sector. On the basis of their statutory control over interest arbitration, the states may be divided into four groups:

1. Twenty-seven states provide some type of interest arbitration for collective bargaining in the public sector. Of these states, 18 offer compulsory or legislative arbitration for at least some categories of public employees.
2. Seven states, while allowing some or all public employees a limited right to strike (upon the failure of mediation or factfinding), make voluntary interest arbitration available to the parties.
3. In three states (Texas, North Carolina, and Tennessee) both collective bargaining and strikes by public employees are outlawed.[40]
4. In those states where the legislature *did not* enact statutes regulating the collective bargaining process or the resolution of impasses during contract negotiations in the public sector, public employees are free to bargain collectively and design voluntary impasse resolution procedures—including interest arbitration—in their contract.

Industrial relations in health care institutions in the private sector are controlled by the 1974 Amendments to the NLRA. While the amendments provide for compulsory mediation and, under certain conditions, for factfinding, they are silent on interest arbitration. Consequently, health care institutions and unions are free under the statute to include or reject the inclusion of interest arbitration provisions in their contract.

The voluntary nature of interest arbitration in the private sector is underlined by a recent decision of the NLRB that was upheld by a federal court of appeals. The board ruled that the interest arbitration clause in the collective bargaining agreement bears only a remote relationship, if any, to wages, hours, or other terms and conditions of employment and, therefore, it is not a mandatory subject of bargaining under the NLRA. Accordingly, such a clause may be included only on the basis of mutual acceptance.[41]

Nevertheless, a considerable number of contracts contain interest arbitration clauses on a voluntary basis; particularly contracts that feature perpetual no-strike clauses. However, despite the fact that interest arbitration clauses appear in many contracts in the private health care industry, such clauses are invoked only sparingly.

In private health care institutions located in the Chicago metropolitan area, only one interest arbitration took place between 1975 and 1979. In New York City, where an industry-wide pattern of bargaining prevails between the Voluntary League of Hospitals and Homes and District 1199, the two negotiating parties appealed to interest arbitration only once during their long bargaining relationship. In June 1976, 37,000 hospital employees were engaged in a 10-day strike against 57 health care institutions in New York City. Due to the intervention of Governor Hugh Carey, the issues in dispute had been submitted to binding interest arbitration. However, District 1199, representing the employees, was so disappointed in the decision of Arbitrator Margery Gootnick, that Moe Faner, executive secretary of the union, insisted that the union would never again agree to binding interest arbitration. In 1978, after federal mediation and factfinding, the parties reached a voluntary settlement of their contract without interest arbitration. In the individual negotiations between the New York City hospitals and the Nurses Association, interest arbitration was not used in any instance.[42]

The limited use of interest arbitration by parties in the nongovernment health care industry may be attributed to several factors:

1. The parties—primarily management, but in the New York situation the union as well—try to avoid third-party intervention in their bargaining process whenever possible.
2. Federal mediation and the BOIs help the parties narrow their differences to the point where final settlement may be reached without binding arbitration.
3. In the Chicago area, interest arbitration was avoided because of the pattern bargaining prevailing in that area. For almost a decade, the contract between HELP and Rush-Presbyterian-St. Luke's Hospital was the patternmaker for all other health care institutions in Chicago. During the four contract negotiations that took place since the hospital's unionization in 1967, the resolution of impasses did not require interest arbitration. At the last round of negotiations, Mercy Hospital took over the role of patternmaker without the necessity of turning to interest arbitration.[43]

In the cases where the parties do appeal to interest arbitration the success of this ultimate remedy depends to a large extent on the qualifications of the arbitrator. In the first place, the parties should realize that an interest arbitrator should demonstrate qualifications different from those of a grievance arbitrator. Most of the contractual issues submitted to interest arbitration are in the economic area, involving wages and various kinds of fringe benefits. Therefore, in order to be effective, an interest arbitrator must have training and experience in economics (possibly labor economics), accounting/finance or the equivalent, and must be familiar with the process and criteria of wage determination. He or she must also be able to foresee the long-term economic effects of any decision on the finances of the health care institutions involved in the arbitration. In the event an interest arbitrator is called on to decide cases in the public sector, he or she should be equipped to deal with budgetary and other financial matters and should know something about the factors that determine an employer's ability to pay. In short, health care institutions should not make the mistake of automatically selecting as arbitrator for their interest arbitration cases a person who proved to be satisfactory in their grievance arbitration cases.

Most parties recognize the importance of choosing an interest arbitrator with a background in economics. A recent study of the process of arbitrator selection demonstrated that the majority of the parties in the sample preferred economists to lawyers in interest disputes.[44]

What about the size and permanency of arbitration tribunals used in interest arbitration cases? No discernible pattern has emerged thus far. This may be attributed to the infrequent use of interest arbitration and the relatively recent history of industrial relations in the health care field. In the interest arbitration case between Michael Reese Hospital and HELP in Chicago, the parties selected an *ad hoc* single arbitrator from a list of seven arbitrators furnished by the American Arbitration Association. Similarly, in the bargaining impasse that took place in 1976 between the Voluntary League of Hospitals in New York and District 1199, the parties selected an *ad hoc* single arbitrator. On the other hand, the agreement between the University of Chicago and the Illinois Nurses Association provides for a board of arbitrators; the neutral chairman is to be chosen by the two partisan members from a list.

The form of interest arbitration generally adopted by health care institutions and unions is the conventional type. Conventional interest arbitration is defined in the following manner:

> In conventional arbitration, the arbitrator or a panel of arbitrators hears the evidence and renders a reasonable award. The award's format is thus fashioned by the arbitrator according to his best judgment, though it will almost always be based on express or implied statutory standards. Such an award may contain bits and pieces of the positions of both parties.[45]

Nevertheless, an "unconventional" form of interest arbitration may deserve the consideration of labor and management in the health care industry. It is known as "final offer" interest arbitration. This form has two variations. "In the 'total package' format, each bargaining party submits to the arbitrator its last bargaining offer from which the arbitrator must make a binding selection without modification." In the "issue-by-issue" format, the arbitrator is not obligated to select the final offer of either party in its totality, but may select final positions on an issue-by-issue basis.[46]

The main advantage of the "final offer" format over conventional interest arbitration is that "the parties know that they may be penalized heavily if they do not formulate realistic positions. Theoretically, the parties will reach settlement more often under this system and, in cases where agreement is not reached, they will be closer together so that the arbitrator will have less room for error."[47]

In conclusion, it should be reemphasized that interest arbitration allows a third party to set vital terms of employment for the bargaining parties. Therefore, both the qualifications of the arbitrator and the format of interest arbitration should be selected carefully by the parties in order to achieve results with which the parties can live for the duration of their contract.

MEDIATION-ARBITRATION

Mediation-arbitration or "med-arb" represents a novel approach to the resolution of impasses in the health care industry. As the term indicates, med-arb resulted from the integration of two conventional impasse resolution procedures: mediation and binding interest arbitration. Since one of the earliest applications of med-arb took place in a dispute involving the California Nurses Association and three groups representing hospitals in the San Francisco-Oakland area, this innovative labor-management relations technique may be of special interest to those in the health care industry.

As was pointed out by Werther and Lockhart,

> Under this technique, the arbitrator joins the parties well before they are to submit their disagreements to arbitration. During the pre-arbitration phase the arbitrator acts as a mediator. If negotiations do not conclude by some predetermined date or the parties feel they have reached a deadlock, the mediator then assumes the role of arbitrator and produces a decision based on inside information to which an arbitrator would not, under normal circumstances, have been privy.[48]

The necessity for combining two different procedures of impasse resolution was explained by Harry Pollard, who represented the employee side in several med-arb proceedings:

> It is an issue-oriented procedure, . . . mediation-arbitration stimulates more creative thinking and more alternatives to fixed positions than is found in conventional bargaining. . . . In conventional interest arbitration, the role of arbitrator is also limited. He is remote from the parties and the issues and is bound by formal procedures. . . . In mediation-arbitration, no precedents are set by transcripts, technical procedures or arbitrators' opinions. Through this flexibility, the process takes on more of the characteristics of bona fide negotiations than it does of conventional mediation or conventional arbitration. It incorporates the elements of both processes. . . .[49]

Pollard further emphasized that med-arb is particularly applicable to industries where a strike would cause considerable damage, not only to the owners and the clients but also to the efficiency and morale of the work force. This situation prevails in the health care industry where "delicate relationships exist between management and employees, and the teamwork in providing patient care is basic."[50]

The idea of med-arb was first advanced by the late George W. Taylor in 1957. He observed then: "An impartial chairman is first of all a mediator. But he is a very special kind of mediator. He has the reserve power to decide the case either by effectuating his own judgment or by joining with one of the partisan board members to make a majority decision."[51]

The technique involved in med-arb was aptly described by Sam Kagel, one of the architects of this innovative approach:

> When parties agree to med-arb, they have to agree in advance that all decisions, whether reached by mediation or arbitration, become part of the mediator-arbitrator's award and are final and binding. . . . In carrying out the functions of med-arb, you have in effect negotiating meetings. Most interest problems are settled by direct negotiations. . . . If certain issues are left on which the med-arbitrators will have to make the decision, by the time that point is reached, there is usually a very small difference left between the parties. The med-arbitrator has only to decide within that area.[52]

In the opinion of one of the early pioneers of med-arb, certain preconditions must be met in order to realize the full potential of this process: "(1) It is a delicate mechanism which should be undertaken primarily in situations where the issues truly are difficult or complex; (2) it should be used where an impasse in negotiations could result in a strike that would have a serious impact upon the community or on the economy."[53]

Reviewing statements made by management and union representatives who participated in med-arb, we see that trade unionists are somewhat more enthusiastic about med-arb than their management counterparts. Karen Dunlap, a spokesperson for hospitals in the San Francisco-Oakland area, acknowledges that ". . . med-arb is a viable and good option to strike particularly in the health industry where the impact of the strike can be so great." However, she warns about some potential pitfalls of this approach:

1. Employers usually do not do as well in the area of managerial rights or work-related issues as might have been   the case in traditional negotiations.
2. The more orthodox negotiations usually result in a negotiated settlement "package," while in med-arb each proposal on the long list submitted by the employees is discussed and resolved one-by-one. Therefore, in the more traditional negotiations, the hospitals might not have to agree to changes in so many areas.[54]

Some experts criticize med-arb for its functional weakness. They believe that the primary duty of an arbitrator is to arbitrate and maintain that only confusion would result if arbitrators tried to combine the functions of mediation and arbitration.[55]

The above criticisms notwithstanding, med-arb is an innovative approach, and it appears to be tailored to the particular needs of the health care industry. Therefore, it deserves the consideration of health care labor and management. However, those who wish to experiment with this new approach should keep in mind that its success depends greatly on the arbitrator who is selected to perform the dual role of mediator-arbitrator. Such a person must possess the qualities of a successful mediator *and* the experienced interest arbitrator. There are only a few such persons around, and this is one of the major obstacles to the growing use of med-arb in the health care industry or elsewhere.

CRITERIA OF WAGE AND BENEFIT DETERMINATION

Mediators, factfinders, and interest arbitrators who are called upon by parties to recommend or determine wages and benefits are not expected to make their decisions either in a vacuum or subjectively. Their recommendations and decisions are supposed to satisfy certain generally accepted criteria or standards; they must stay within the parameters set by fiscal constraints and labor market conditions.

In the following section, we will examine criteria of wage and benefit determination considered by third-party neutrals. The purpose of this review is to help health care practitioners understand the process of wage and benefit determination by third-party neutrals, and call their attention to the type of information that the neutrals may need in order to proceed expeditiously in resolving impasse situations.

First, a distinction must be made between the public sector and the private one. In the public sector, wage criteria are established by legislative fiat or intent. In the private sector, these criteria are firmly anchored in past and present practice as developed in the course of the collective bargaining process.

Robert Helsby surveyed the criteria of wage and benefit determination prescribed by statutes of six representative states for the guidance of third-party neutrals. Although the specific criteria vary somewhat from state to state, the following criteria appear in the majority of the six statutes: (1) comparison with other employees in public and private sectors doing similar work; (2) cost of living; (3) ability to pay; (4) public interest and welfare; (5) internal wage structure; (6) stipulation of the parties; and (7) overall compensation.[56]

A review of factfinding reports and interest arbitration awards reveals that the following criteria are considered by neutrals in setting wages and benefits in the private sector of the health care industry covered by the 1974 Amendments: (1) comparison; (2) cost of living; (3) ability to pay; (4) productivity; and (5) labor market conditions. A comparison of the two sectors shows that some of the factors—such as comparison, cost of living, and ability to pay—are equally important in both sectors, while the consideration of public interest and welfare is more prevalent in the public sector, and productivity and labor market conditions are rather basic to wage and benefit determination in the private sector.

A mere listing of these criteria is of little value to practitioners in the health care industry. As Helsby remarked, "The major problem with these criteria remains what do they mean and how are they used?"[57] We will attempt to answer these questions by analyzing the criteria used most frequently in the two sectors.

Public Interest

Of the major criteria of wage setting, the public interest factor and the voluntary wage guidelines are primarily political; the other criteria lie in the economic domain. The consideration of public interest is required by law only in the public sector. However, because of the special relationship that exists between public interest and health care institutions, regardless of their sectoral categorization, this criterion is given serious consideration both by the parties and the neutrals even in the so-called private sector. Reference to the public interest is frequently included in the text of collective agreements between proprietary and nonprofit health care organizations on the one hand and unions on the other. For example, Section 2.1 of the agreement between Michael Reese Hospital and HELP in Chicago states: "The parties acknowledge the interest of the general community in the medical care offered by the Medical Center and its employees."

"Public interest" is an elusive term. It is almost impossible to quantify it. Nevertheless, students of employee relations in the public sector have attempted to define it and indicate its application in impasse resolution. Morris raises the following question:

> What effect should arbitrators give to the "public interest" in formulating their awards? This is like asking whether arbitrators should dispense "equity" . . . Unless a particular award is so unrelated to specific statutory standards and to evidence in the record that a reviewing court would be compelled to set aside or modify it, the award should be deemed "in the public interest." To ask more of the arbitrator—to ask him to dispense abstract justice—would probably lead to a system of normative rather than accommodative awards.[58]

Comparison

While the public interest factor remains an aloof and abstract concept overhanging bargaining in the health care industry, the economic criteria, including comparison, lend themselves to more exact measurement. By using comparison, the parties and neutrals involved in wage and benefit determination, can set individual wage rates and a total wage structure in relation to wages prevailing in similar labor markets and institutions.

For the purpose of wage setting, wage and benefit comparisons may take place at various levels. In the health care industry, comparisons are usually made on three levels: intraindustry, local labor markets, and intracompany. The first two categories of comparison are considered external comparisons; the latter type is known as internal comparison.

In the case of intraindustry comparisons, wages and benefits prevailing in other health care institutions are measured against the wages sought by labor and management. The hiring and retention of personnel is affected to no small degree by the wages paid by other health care institutions in the area. For similar reasons, health care institutions must also consider wage rates paid by other local industries, as these institutions compete for labor not only with each other but also with private business organizations and government entities that hire the same type of labor.

In external comparisons, wage rates for the same job in different organizations are related. In internal comparisons, wage rates for various job classifications *within* an organization are compared. Internal comparison is as essential as external in order to maintain or promote equity among the various job classifications on the basis of their relative value to the institution.

Before one can make a valid comparison, one must have reliable wage and benefit data. Wage and benefit statistics, indicating wage rates and benefit levels in other health care institutions or in the local labor market, may be obtained from several sources. Such data are collected and published by the Bureau of Labor Statistics (BLS), the research division of the U.S. Department of Labor. A call or inquiry to the regional BLS office would yield a wealth of information on local labor market conditions. As to intraindustry wage comparison, wage and benefit data reflecting payments by various health care institutions within a state or metropolitan area are recorded regularly by regional associations of health care institutions. The Chicago Hospital Council and the League of Voluntary Hospitals and Homes of New York are two examples of such associations. Of course, an informal telephone survey of wage administrators in several local health care institutions may furnish the necessary data on a short notice.

Cost of Living

The importance of the cost-of-living standard varies with the rate of inflation. At a time of relative price stability, such as the first half of the 1960s, the cost-of-living consideration played only a minimal role. On the other hand, in an economy marked by rapidly escalating inflation, changes in the cost of living exert a major impact on the wage-setting process. One of labor's most persuasive arguments during contract negotiations is its demand to preserve the purchasing power of present wages. Factfinders or interest arbitrators are not immune to this argument either.

Neutral parties involved in impasse resolution procedures generally use two widely accepted statistical yardsticks to measure changes in the cost of living: the Consumer Price Index (CPI) and the Urban Family Budget (UFB). Both economic indicators were developed and are published on a regular basis by the BLS.

The CPI is a statistical measure of changes in prices of goods and services at the retail level. It compares the present cost of a constant market-basket of goods and services (approximately 400 items) against its cost in a previous month or a previous year. The point of time to which prices are compared is called the base period. The total cost of the constant market-basket in a given month or given year is expressed as a percentage of the total cost of that market-basket in the base period. The resulting index figures are published each month and furnish an easy comparison of changes in the cost of living. The base period for the current CPI is 1967.

Since its 1978 revision, CPI actually consists of two concurrent indexes: CPI for all urban consumers (CPI-U), and CPI for urban wage earners and clerical workers (CPI-W). Obviously, for the purpose of wage negotiations, the CPI-W is usually used.

The CPI is published by the BLS every month not only for the country as a whole but also for 25 major metropolitan areas. Therefore, negotiators and third-party neutrals can consider the CPI prevailing in their own local area.

The CPI may be used in the wage-setting process in a formal or informal manner. In the former, cost-of-living adjustment (COLA) clauses are included in the contract. A COLA provides for automatic wage adjustment according to a formula tied to the CPI. For example, an 0.3 percent rise in the CPI may mean an automatic 1-cent increase in the hourly wage rate. At the end of 1978, approximately six million workers were covered by agreements containing a COLA clause. In the second instance, CPI is used informally as an argument for higher wages during negotiations and factfinding hearings, but no COLA is included in the resulting contract. The majority of collective bargaining agreements in the health care industry fall in this category.

The Urban Family Budget (UFB) represents the other statistical instrument that neutral parties consider when adjusting wage rates to changes in the cost of living. The UFB actually consists of three separate family budgets, measuring the cost of consumption at three different standards of living: lower, intermediate, and higher. These budgets indicate the consumption costs of a precisely defined urban family of four at the three different income levels: a 38-year-old husband employed full-time, a nonworking wife, a boy of 13, and a girl of 8. For the sake of information, in autumn 1978 the total annual budget of this hypothetical urban family at the lower, intermediate, and higher income levels amounted to $11,546, $18,622, and $27,420, respectively. For the purpose of wage setting, third-party neutrals consider the family budget at the lower standard of living. Factfinders and interest arbitrators usually disregard the absolute amount of the UFB and take into account only the year-to-year percentage changes.

Ability to Pay

While the cost-of-living criterion is advanced primarily by the unions to support their wage demands, the ability-to-pay (or rather the inability-to-pay) argument is used by health care management as a defense against the wage demands of labor. Labor economists have correctly concluded that "one of the most important considerations affecting wage determination is the basic economic situation in the firm and industry which for convenience we can denominate as 'ability to pay.' "[59]

Although the economic well-being of a firm or industry is a complex matter that depends on numerous internal and external factors, it is easier to evaluate the ability to pay for a profit organization in the private sector than for a government or private nonprofit institution. In the former case, the institution's overall financial situation is fairly well documented by such indicators as changes in the profit margin or changes in the net return of capital or changes in the return on the stockholders' investment. Such data are readily available in the corporation's annual financial report issued to stockholders and the public, or in the K-10 report filed with the Securities and Exchange Commission. Furthermore, in the event that a business organization in the private sector pleads inability to pay higher wages to its employees, the union is entitled to check the company's financial records. The U.S. Supreme Court in its *Truit Mfg. Co.* decision ruled that "refusal by an employer to substantiate a claim of inability to pay increased wages may support a finding of failure to bargain in good faith."[60]

Although it is somewhat problematic to ascertain a profit organization's ability to pay, it is infinitely more difficult to do the same in a nonprofit or government institution, which make up the great majority of organizations in the health care industry. Neither government nor nonprofit private institutions gauge their performance on the profit scale. Their books more often show deficits than surpluses. Nevertheless, their employees request and usually receive wage and salary increases at various rates, just as their colleagues in the profit sector.

Although health care institutions in the government sector and those in the nonprofit private sector are similar in that their ability to pay increased wages is not based on the profitability standard, these two types of health care organizations must be distinguished from one another on the basis of their funding. The revenues of a government institution are received primarily from taxes and other public budgetary sources, while the revenues of a nonprofit private institution are furnished largely by so-called third-party payers. Therefore, in the course of impasse resolution procedures, the ability-to-pay standard is evaluated by different methods.

Morris rightly stated that in public sector bargaining "the most troublesome standard is that 'of ability to pay' . . . It generally means that the difference between the revenues that the public employer estimates it will receive during the contract period and the amount it is willing to spend in the area is insufficient to fund the award."[61]

To what extent was ability to pay a factor in the awards of interest arbitrators presiding over cases involving health care institutions in the public sector? Four arbitrators offered the following observations: James Stern noticed that, in Wisconsin, "inability to pay has not been pleaded seriously." Because government bodies have been generally unsuccessful in claiming inability before arbitrators, they have not relied on it heavily. According to Arbitrator Charles Rehmus, in Michigan, the inability-to-pay argument "has often been raised in an almost frivolous context." Arbitrators have generally disregarded this argument. However, when a legitimate claim of inability was presented, the arbitrator extended the period of time over which a community or organization is given to become comparable with their counterparts in the state. Arbitrator Loewenberg, on the basis of his experience in Pennsylvania, concluded that the argument of inability to pay is brought up quite frequently, but arbitrators only seldom reduce their awards on this account. Arvid Anderson, in New York State, attributes somewhat greater weight to the ability-to-pay standard than do his colleagues in the three other states. In his opinion, "collective bargaining agreements are not self-implementing. Therefore, the money to honor the arbitration award . . . has to be found." Consequently, ability to pay is involved in considering wage awards.[62]

The ability-to-pay factor carries considerably more weight in bargaining situations in the private sector. Management representatives interviewed for an FMCS research study were unanimous in believing that third-party neutrals "must consider the financial plight of the institution: To ignore the inability-to-pay issue of the hospital is to ignore life."[63] Surprisingly, almost half of the union negotiators interviewed in the same project agreed with their management counterparts that third-party neutrals should consider the financial picture of the institution in their decision, but under the following conditions:

1. To determine the institution's inability to pay, the neutral should scrutinize the hospital's books. The poverty statement of management should not be accepted at face value.
2. Whenever possible, the neutral should attempt to evaluate the efficiency of hospital operations, as inefficiencies of management should not be subsidized by wage sacrifices of the employees.[64]

The primary reason for the importance of the ability-to-pay standard for wage determination in the private sector is found in the financial structure of nonprofit health care institutions. In 1976, 90 percent of all revenues received by hospitals came from such third-party payers as private insurance carriers and government agencies (Medicare and Medicaid). Therefore in the private health care industry, third-party payers have become increasingly influential in deciding whether the institution is able to increase its labor costs. Management representatives frequently argue at negotiations and factfinding hearings that "the third-party payers would refuse to reimburse hospitals for negotiated labor cost increases as they exert pressure on the hospitals to hold down cost increases."[65]

The active role played by third-party payers in wage determination is a relatively recent development. Before 1975 increased health care costs were almost automatically passed on to clients in the form of higher premiums. However, since 1975 and due to political and economic pressures, third-party payers have become more cost-conscious. Negotiators representing hospital management and labor agree that settlements reached between late 1975 and early 1977 "would have been more costly without having to consider the reimbursement posture of the payers."[66]

A sample of third-party neutrals involved in BOIs maintained that, in the majority of cases, the hospital's inability to increase labor costs was the central issue in their cases. The neutrals realized that the resolution of the impasse depended primarily on the attitude of third-party payers. Consequently, neutrals often have made direct contacts with third-party payers, partly to seek additional information on hospital reimbursement rates, and partly to obtain their approval for factfinding recommendations or binding arbitration awards.[67]

The new role of third-party payers in the wage determination process was vividly demonstrated in the well-known 1976 award of Arbitrator Margery Gootnick in the *League of Voluntary Hospitals of New York and District 1199* case. One of Gootnick's findings, on which she based her refusal to award a wage increase during the first six months of the contract, was that a major third-party payer, New York State, had "exhausted its capacity to raise additional revenues for service programs." This finding was based on the testimony of a state officer who was invited to testify. Arbitrator Gootnick entirely disagreed with the union's contention that "the hospital's financial woes should have no bearing on her decision."[68]

A recent political development is the growing body of health care cost-containment legislation. This legislation may have a profound impact both on the ability of health care institutions to pay and on the freedom of wage determination in the industry. According to a survey made by William Stodghill, as of spring 1978, the following 15 states had enacted voluntary or mandatory cost-containment programs: Arizona, California, Colorado, Connecticut, Maine, Maryland, Massachusetts, Minnesota, New Jersey, New York, Oregon, Rhode Island, Virginia, Washington, and Wisconsin. Cost-containment laws, wherever they exist, "are a factor in negotiations, since most of them try at least to review health care facilities within their jurisdictions."[69]

In Maryland, one of the earliest states to enact a health cost-containment law, the regulation of hospital charges by the Maryland Health Service Costs Review Commission has proved to be quite successful. "In a period of rapidly rising health costs, the State of Maryland had the lowest increase in charges of any state."[70]

The ability-to-pay criterion was further emphasized by the renewed efforts of the Carter Administration to contain increases in health care costs. An administration-supported bill (H.R. 2626), provided that hospital cost increases should not exceed the actual rate of inflation. Should this bill be reintroduced by the Reagan Administration, hospitals and other health care institutions would be under the double pressure of the federal government and private third-party payers to contain increases in labor costs. As a result, the ability-to-pay standard could become even more important in both wage bargaining and in the awards of interest arbitrators.

THE EFFECTS OF IMPASSE RESOLUTION PROCEDURES ON COLLECTIVE BARGAINING

What impact, if any, do impasse resolution procedures have on the collective bargaining process? This question is frequently asked by practitioners and students of industrial relations in the so-called public interest sector of the economy. Two schools of thought are clearly discernible. One school maintains that impasse resolution procedures (IRPs) exert no harmful effect on the bargaining process. The other group asserts that the interruption of the bargaining process by the use of various IRPs has a "chilling" or "narcotic" effect on collective bargaining inasmuch as the parties anticipate outside intervention and will not bargain as diligently as they would in the absence of such procedures.

James Scearce, a former director of FMCS, is among those who are not overly concerned with the effects of IRPs on bargaining in the health care industries. He remarked that "it did not appear that the parties were delaying bargaining in anticipation of a BOI appointment."[71] Irving Kurasch, President of Local 73 of SEIU—one of the two unions comprising HELP, which represents the majority of hospital service employees in Chicago—observed that so far IRPs had not had a negative effect on bargaining in the health care industry. In fact, they were beneficial to collective bargaining in that they exerted a pressure on the parties to reach an agreement without third-party intervention.[72]

Charles Morris is another expert who sees no conflict between collective bargaining and IRPs. On the contrary, "For an impasse resolution device to operate successfully and for an extended period, it must encourage and complement the bargaining process, not supplant it."[73] Robert Helsby, an expert on public sector industrial relations, concluded that on the basis of a survey of IRPs in various states, the availability of the process has not markedly chilled the bargaining process. In addition, almost no strikes occurred where interest arbitration was available.[74]

Members of the other school are equally convinced that IRPs have an adverse effect on the bargaining process. Kochan explained how IRPs retard bargaining:

> . . . The parties are expected to make significant compromise toward an agreement only when under pressure to do so. This explains why most intensive bargaining appears to occur in the final days or hours prior to the strike deadline. . . . To the extent that multiple steps are built into the impasse procedures (e.g., mediation followed by factfinding and/or arbitration) the final hour or moment of truth is even further removed from the initial bargaining process.[75]

Management representatives in the health care industry appear to agree with Kochan's evaluation. Norman Burns of Chicago's Northwestern Memorial Hospital believes that because the parties anticipate IRPs, they may leave the issues on the bargaining table. Burns goes on to say that the use of IRPs can create a lopsided settlement in favor of the union since it is the union that makes all the demands. Even if only some of these demands are granted by the factfinder or interest arbitrator, the union comes out the winner.[76] William Abelow, executive vice-president of the Voluntary League of Hospitals in New York, shares Burns's viewpoint: "It has been our experience that if we know in advance that outside IRPs are available or that factfinding or a BOI will occur, there is no real bargaining until such procedures run their course."[77]

These negative assessments are supported by the findings of an FMCS research study on the intensity of negotiations in the first two years following the passage of the 1974 Amendments.

> Both the mediators and factfinders thought that in approximately 42 percent of the situations, no effective bargaining had taken place prior to factfinding board appointments. This situation, however, seems to have improved somewhat since the first four months after the amendments became operative. . . . The mediators indicated that this absence of bargaining prior to factfinding was more prevalent with nursing homes than with hospitals, in initial vs. renewal contract negotiations, and in BOI's compared with factfinding boards resulting from stipulation agreement.[78]

Kochan also reports the following: "More recently, studies of actual movement or compromising behavior have reported evidence of a chilling effect on negotiations."[79]

What are the implications of these findings? In the public sector where collective bargaining is controlled by legislation to a varying degree, parties have little or no choice in electing to use IRPs, unless their negotiations proceed without reaching an impasse.

Parties in the private sector enjoy greater freedom and more discretion in designing their bargaining strategy. Although the 1974 Amendments make mediation mandatory (at least in principle) and factfinding a distinct possibility, in practice FMCS shows a considerable willingness to accommodate the parties. Therefore, parties in the private sector may have more time and opportunity to bargain without the intervention of a third party. Chicago is a case in point. During the past ten years, only two BOIs, two advisory arbitrations, and one interest arbitration have occurred in Chicago's health care industry. Although these figures show only one region of the country, they do indicate that IRPs do not interfere with the collective bargaining process in the great majority of these cases. In those exceptional cases where the parties do reach an impasse and are forced by law to accept factfinding or interest arbitration—or decide to submit themselves voluntarily to such procedures—the choice is clear: a strike that may threaten public interest, or the use of IRPs. The latter appears to be the lesser evil. In those situations where the use of IRPs cannot be avoided, the parties may prefer their own contractual arrangements to the IRPs prescribed by law. In that case, they should prepare for such eventuality and specify in their agreement voluntary IRPs that are compatible with the regulations of FMCS or the states.

NOTES

1. Theodore W. Kheel and Lewis B. Kaden, "Collective Bargaining in Hospitals: A Plan to Resolve Impasses," in the *Proceedings of the 22nd Annual Meeting* (Madison, Wis.: Industrial Relations Research Assn., 1970), p. 215.

2. Information obtained from Joel D'Alba, Attorney, Asher, Greenfield, Goodstein, Pavalon & Segall, Ltd. (July 1979).

3. Information obtained from Irving Kurasch, President of General Service Employees, SEIU, Local 73 (June 1979).

4. Information obtained from William J. Abelow, Executive Vice-President, League of Voluntary Hospitals of New York (August 1979).

5. Public Law 93-360, 1974.

6. *Impact of the 1974 Health Care Amendments to NLRB on Collective Bargaining in the Health Care Industry* (Washington, D.C.: Federal Mediation and Conciliation Service, 1979), p. 119.

7. *Ibid.*, p. 127.

8. *Ibid.*, p. 126.

9. Kurasch, *op. cit.*

10. Information obtained from Nancy C. Fibish, National Representative, Federal Mediation and Conciliation Service (August 1979).

11. *Impact, op. cit.*, p. 138.

12. *Ibid.*, pp. 147-48.

13. James Scearce and Lucretia Dewey Tanner, "Health Care Bargaining: The FMCS Experience," *Labor Law Journal* 27 (July 1976): 398.

14. *Ibid.*, p. 391.

15. Kurasch, *op. cit.*

16. Thomas A. Kochan, "Dynamics of Dispute Resolution in the Public Sector," in *Public Sector Bargaining*, Benjamin Aaron et al., eds., IRRA Research Series (Washington, D.C.: Bureau of National Affairs, Inc., 1979), p. 179.

17. *Ibid.*, p. 182.

18. Presentation of Anthony Sinicropi at the AAA/FMCS Interest Arbitration Seminar, Cedar Rapids, Iowa, April 28, 1979.

19. Jean McKelvey, "Fact-Finding in Public Employment Disputes: Promise or Illusions?" *Industrial & Labor Relations Review* 22 (July 1969): 535.

20. *Impact, op. cit.*, p. 181.

21. 418 F. Supp. 711 (N.D. 1976).

22. Keith A. Reed, "The National Labor Relations Act and Health Care Institutions: The Persistent Paradox," *Employee Relations Law Journal* 4 (Winter 1978-79): 374-75.

23. Jerome T. Barrett, "A Discussion," *Labor Jaw Journal* 28 (August 1977): 526.

24. *Impact, op. cit.*, p. 187.

25. *Ibid.*, p. 236.

26. Fibish, *op. cit.*

27. *Impact, op. cit.*, p. 243.

28. *Ibid.*, p. 253.

29. Norman Metzger, "NLRA Boards of Inquiry Have Been Used Sparingly," *Hospitals, JAHA*, July 1, 1976, p. 56.

30. *Impact, op. cit.*, p. 268.

31. *Ibid.*, p. 228.

32. *Ibid.*, p. 230.

33. *Ibid.*, pp. 255-57.

34. *Ibid.*, p. 275.

35. Hervey A. Juris, "Labor Agreements in the Hospital Industry: A Study of Collective Bargaining Outputs," *Labor Law Journal* 28 (August 1977): p. 506.

36. Public Law 95-454, 1979.

37. Anthony F. Ingrassia, "Reflections on the New Labor Law," *Labor Law Journal* 30 (September 1979): 543.

38. B.V.H. Schneider, "Public-Sector Labor Legislation: An Evolutionary Analysis," in *Public Sector Bargaining*, Benjamin Aaron et al., eds., IRRA Research Series (Washington, D.C.: Bureau of National Affairs, Inc., 1979), pp. 192-93.

39. Joseph R. Grodin, "Judicial Response to Public Sector Arbitration," in *Public Sector Bargaining*, Benjamin Aaron et al., eds., IRRA Research Series (Washington, D.C.: Bureau of National Affairs, Inc., 1979), p. 241.

40. Charles J. Morris, "The Role of Interest Arbitration in a Collective Bargaining System," in *The Future of Labor Arbitration in America*, Benjamin Aaron et al., eds. (New York: American Arbitration Association, 1976), p. 206.

41. *NLRB v. Massachusetts Nurses Assn.*, CA-1, 95 L.R.R.M. 2852.

42. Abelow, *op. cit.*

43. Kurasch, *op. cit.*

44. Julius Rezler and Donald J. Petersen, "Strategies of Arbitrator Selection," in *Labor Arbitration Reports (LA)*, vol. 70 (Washington, D.C.: Bureau of National Affairs, Inc., 1979), pp. 1307-20.

45. Morris, *op cit.*, p. 236.

46. *Ibid.*, p. 232.

47. James L. Stern et al., *Final Offer Arbitration* (Lexington, Mass.: D.C. Heath and Co., 1975), p. 184.

48. William B. Werther, Jr. and Carol A. Lockhart, *Labor Relations in the Health Professions* (Boston: Little Brown & Co., 1976), p. 151.

49. Harry Pollard, "Mediation-Arbitration: A Trade Union View," *Monthly Labor Review* 96 (September 1973): 63-64.

50. *Ibid.*, p. 64.

51. George W. Taylor, "Effectuating the Labor Contract Through Arbitration," in *The Profession of Labor Arbitration* (Washington, D.C.: Bureau of National Affairs, Inc., 1957), pp. 20, 35.

52. Sam Kagel, "Combining Mediation and Arbitration," *Monthly Labor Review* 96 (September 1973): 62-63.

53. Pollard, *op. cit.*, p. 63.

54. Karen Dunlap, "Mediation-Arbitration: Reactions from Rank and File," *Monthly Labor Review* 96 (September 1973): 65.

55. Frank Elkouri and Edna A. Elkouri, *How Arbitration Works*, 3rd ed. (Washington, D.C.: Bureau of National Affairs, Inc., 1973), pp. 79-80.

56. Remarks of Robert D. Helsby at the AAA/FMCS Interest Arbitration Seminar, Cedar Rapids, Iowa (April 28, 1979).

57. *Ibid.*

58. Morris, *op. cit.*, p. 244.

59. Gordon F. Bloom and Herbert R. Northrup, *Economics of Labor Relations*, 7th ed. (Homewood, Ill.: Richard D. Irwin, 1973), p. 330.

60. *NLRB v. Truit Mfg. Co.*, 351 U.S. 149 (1956).

61. Morris, *op. cit.*, p. 243.

62. *Ibid.*, pp. 243-44.

63. *Impact, op. cit.*, p. 366.

64. *Ibid.*, p. 367.

65. *Ibid.*, pp. 352, 354.

66. *Ibid.*, p. 359.

67. *Ibid.*, p. 362.

68. 67 LA 293, 294 (1976).

69. William Stodghill, "A Discussion on Health Care Issues," *Labor Law Journal* 30 (August 1979): 512.

70. Paul A. Weinstein, "Impact of Hospital Cost Review on Industrial Relations," *Labor Law Journal* 30 (August 1979): 599.

71. Scearce and Tanner, *op. cit.*, p. 398.

72. Kurasch, *op. cit.*

73. Morris, *op. cit.*, p. 200.

74. Helsby, *op. cit.*

75. Kochan, *op. cit.*, p. 176.

76. Information obtained from Norman Burns, Vice-President of Employee Relations, Northwestern Memorial Hospital, Chicago (June 1979).

77. Abelow, *op. cit.*

78. *Impact, op. cit.*, p. 245.

79. Kochan, *op. cit.*, p. 176.

Part III

Grievance Issues Facing Hospitals Today

The third section of this book is devoted to an analysis of the major grievance/ arbitration issues facing hospitals today: discipline and discharge, seniority, employee benefits, and others. The issues are illustrated by citing both published and unpublished hospital and nursing home arbitration awards. Of course, industry-based examples have maximum application for our readers. This approach is not without its limitations, however.

Typically, only a small fraction of the total number of private and public sector cases are published. Hospital cases represent an even smaller subset within this limited sample of published cases. Thus published cases may or may not be representative of the universe of cases. We have cited public as well as private sector hospital cases. Not only did this tactic increase the total number of cases for study, but more importantly, it gave broader coverage to the full spectrum of hospital proprietorship.

It has been claimed that the reporting services that publish the cases like to publish those that address unique issues or feature novel treatments or profound discussions, and therefore may not be "typical" of most arbitration cases. We acknowledge this possibility. We hope, however, that by citing both unpublished and published cases, this contingency might be reduced.

An informal comparison between published and unpublished cases has revealed no discernible differences in issues, treatment, or handling of disputes. Nor do we wish to minimize the importance of published cases. They are read carefully by practitioners, not only for educational purposes, but also as a means to assess the quality of the arbitrator-writers. And while published cases are not precedent-setting in the same way that court cases are, similar settlements on a given issue seem to develop over time into a kind of "common law" that may serve as a general guide to decision making.

In the hospital industry union representation seems to be concentrated around three cities: New York, Chicago, and San Francisco. It is no wonder, then, that a majority of cases cited in this book come from these areas—specifically, from the League of Voluntary Hospitals in New York City, the Bay Area hospitals, and Chicago Hospital Council members.

Our sources for cases were varied. Most were easily accessible, but others required a bit of digging. The majority of cases cited in the following chapters have awards dating back only 12 to 15 years at most, and thus reflect current arbitral thinking on the issues surveyed.

A brief description of our sources for both published and unpublished cases is given below. The reader may want to become familiar with these before reading on, as they provide a guide to the abbreviations used throughout the remainder of the book, as well as other pertinent information.

SOURCES FOR PUBLISHED CASES

1. *Labor Arbitration Reports*. Published by the Bureau of National Affairs (BNA), 1231 25th Street, N.W., Washington, D.C. 20037. The entire text of each arbitration award is reproduced in each volume. Volumes run from number one to the current number (Volume 72 at the time of this writing). Cases are indexed by employer and union. No special designation is made for hospital cases, so you must read every listing to find them. Case citations are given as: volume number, LA (for Labor Arbitration Reports), and the page number on which the case appears. For example, 70 LA 391 would mean the 70th volume of the Labor Arbitration Reports at page 391. There may be overlap between dates of awards from volume to volume.

2. *Commerce Clearing House* (CCH), 4025 W. Peterson Avenue, Chicago, Illinois 60646, publishes two volumes of arbitration awards for each calendar year. The CCH, like the BNA, publishes the full text of each arbitration award. There is some overlap between cases reported by the BNA and the CCH, but very little. A sample CCH case citation might read: 71-2 ARB ¶ 8414. This would be read: 1971 CCH Arbitration Awards, the second volume for the year 1971, at paragraph 8414.

3. *Government Employee Relations Reports* (GERR), published by the Bureau of National Affairs (address above). The cases reported, of course, deal strictly with local, state, or federal government employers, and accordingly one finds cases dealing with government-run hospitals. The entire text of the arbitration case usually is not published in the GERR, but there is a paragraph or two summarizing the case. Copies of the full text of the case may be obtained for 30 cents a page from the BNA. A sample citation in the GERR would read as follows: 773 GERR:30, which translates: the 773rd volume of the Government Employee Relations Reports on page 30.

4. *Labor Arbitration in Government* (LAIG), published by the American Arbitration Association, 140 W. 51st Street, New York, New York 10020. These

cases, like those in the GERR, are reported in excerpt form. Also like the GERR, the LAIG reports only government-run institutions, including hospitals. Full text of the cases may be obtained at 30 cents per page from the American Arbitration Association. Cases are listed in the index by employer only, and one must look at each listing to find hospital awards. A sample citation might read: LAIG 1735, meaning Labor Arbitration in Government at Section 1735.

5. *White Collar Reports* (WCR), published by the Bureau of National Affairs (address above). Some hospital cases are reported in this source. The WCR indexes cases by industry, making it relatively simple to locate hospital awards. A typical citation might be 1089 WCR A-6, meaning the 1089th volume of the White Collar Reports on page A-6.

6. *Other sources of published arbitration cases.* These include:

a. Florida Public Employee Reporter (FPER)
b. Indiana Public Employee Reporter (IPER)
c. New Jersey Public Employee Reporter (NJPER)
d. Pennsylvania Public Employee Reporter (PPER)
e. Public Sector Arbitration Awards (PSAA)
f. Unpublished awards (LAI).

These sources were not used for this research. All of the above are published by the Labor Relations Press, 550 Highland Avenue, Fort Washington, Pennsylvania 19034. All arbitration awards listed in the above sources can be obtained at 30 cents per page.

7. *Labor Arbitration Index* (LAI), published by the Labor Relations Press (address above), is a useful listing of arbitration cases of all agencies listed above. However, hospital cases are not grouped together, so one must search each entry to find them.

SOURCES FOR UNPUBLISHED CASES

1. *League of Voluntary Hospitals and Homes* (LVH) of New York, 60 E. 42nd Street, New York, New York 10017. The League has extensive numbers of arbitration cases that are listed by issue. Synopses of cases are available, and arrangements can be made to have cases reproduced.

2. *Kaiser Permanente Medical Care Program.* Information and cases may be obtained by special arrangement from Ken Dale, Regional Labor Relations Manager, P.O. Box 12916, Oakland, California 94604. Cases under this program are both listed and summarized.

3. *Chicago Hospital Council* (CHC). Cases may be obtained from John Comer, Director Employee/Labor Relations Services, 840 N. Lake Shore Drive, Chicago, Illinois 60611.

4. *Health Manpower Management* (HMMM). Cases may be obtained from Michael J. Phillips, Health Manpower Management, 2329 University Avenue Southeast, Minneapolis, Minnesota 55414.

5. *East Bay, San Francisco,* and *Peninsula Associations.* Cases from these West Coast associations are cited as BAHA.

Chapter 9

Management Rights and Union Security Issues

Few issues elicit so much emotional response from the parties as those involving management rights and union security. Both unions and management ultimately see their survival as institutions resting on these issues. Management tries to preserve its ability to run the organization with a minimum of union interference, while unions attempt to protect themselves from possible management attempts to oust them or erode union benefits. A survey conducted some years ago by the U.S. Department of Labor showed that of the 1,773 major agreements studied (that is, those involving more than 1,000 workers), slightly less than half (48.5 percent) contained a formal statement of management rights.[1] However, almost 60 percent of manufacturing firms and slightly over 35 percent of service industries had such a clause in their agreements.[2]

RESERVED RIGHTS THEORY

The reserved rights theory, also referred to as the residual rights theory, holds, in its most basic form, that management retains all rights that are not expressly conceded in the collective bargaining agreement or limited by law. Adherents to this theory believe that when the contract is silent regarding a particular issue, it should be assumed that the issue is a management prerogative and thus not arbitrable.

On the other side some unions hold to a point of view as extreme as this one. They claim that management has no rights (reserved or otherwise) beyond those stated in the collective agreement. Proponents argue that where the contract is silent, management must bargain or at the very least, consult with the union before taking any action.

While the reserved rights doctrine is a valid and necessary frame of reference for contract interpretation, the notion that it admits no qualifications stems from a failure to grasp the true nature of the collective agreement.[3] Those familiar with collective bargaining know that there are times when purposefully vague clauses are negotiated into agreements because it is known that the parties will never be able to agree on more precise terms. Examples are legion: "overtime shall be distributed *as equally as possible*," "*just cause*," "union stewards shall be granted a *reasonable* amount of time to adjust grievances," and so on.

The Supreme Court recognized the difficulty of negotiating precise language into collective agreements in the 1960 "Steelworkers Trilogy,"[4] one of its landmark decisions.

> . . . [I]t is not unqualifiedly true that a collective bargaining agreement is simply a document by which the union and employees have imposed upon management limited, express restrictions of its otherwise absolute right to manage the enterprise, so that an employee's claim must fail unless he can point to a specific contract provision upon which the claim is founded. There are too many people, too many problems, too many unforeseeable contingencies to make the words of the contract the exclusive source of rights and duties. One cannot reduce all the rules governing a community like an industrial plant to fifteen or even fifty pages. Within the sphere of collective bargaining, the institutional characteristic and the governmental nature of the collective bargaining process demand a common law of the shop which implements and furnishes the context of the grievance. We must assume that intelligent negotiators acknowledged so plain a need unless they stated a contrary rule in plain words.

The Supreme Court thus points out that only the most forceful (plain) language in the agreement will prevent an issue from being substantively arbitrable. This is because the administration of the contract develops a common law that recognizes practices the parties have used and precedents they have set in living with the agreement they have negotiated. Also, the arbitration of numerous cases has developed a body of common law that has interpreted vague contract clauses such as "just cause."

Moreover, unions have given up their right to strike in many collective bargaining agreements, and the application of the strict residual rights theory would cause them to seek to remove the no-strike, no-lockout clause to balance management's application of the principle. Basically, when a contract is silent with respect to an established benefit, that benefit cannot be withdrawn until the contract is open for changes or the employer provides the union with the opportunity to negotiate over that withdrawal. Failure to do so means that the benefit must be continued into the new contract.[5]

TYPES OF MANAGEMENT RIGHTS CLAUSES

Two types of management rights clauses appear in collective agreements. One type is called a "general" or "broad" management rights clause and consists of a very general statement or definition of rights. An example of a general management rights clause is:

> The management of the plant and the direction of the working forces,
> . . . are the exclusive function of the company.[6]

The second type is referred to as an "enumerated" rights clause because the reserved rights of management are spelled out in some detail. Though some enumerated rights clauses are relatively simple and short, others are lengthy, with particular rights illustrated in detail:

> The management of each employer and its operations, the direction of the work force, including the right to hire, retire, assign, suspend, transfer, promote, discharge, or discipline for just cause, and to maintain discipline and efficiency of its employees and the right to relieve employees from duty because of lack of work or for other legitimate reasons; the right to determine the extent to which the plant shall be operated; the right to introduce new or improved production methods, processes or equipment; the right to decide the number and location of plants, the nature of equipment or machinery, the products to be manufactured, the scheduling of production, the method of training employees, the designing and engineering of products, and the control of raw materials; the right to assign work to outside contractors and to eliminate, change, or consolidate jobs and operations (subject to giving the union notice of such change); and the right to enact company policies, plant rules, and regulations which are not in conflict with this agreement, are vested exclusively in the employer.[7]

Each approach has its advocates. Those who prefer the general statement say that in any enumeration of rights, important functions may be overlooked inadvertently.[8] If an issue involving an overlooked right reaches arbitration, the arbitrator could argue that the absence of this right was intentional and therefore the function can no longer be exercised by management unilaterally. On the other hand, proponents of enumerated rights clauses point to the Supreme Court's decision in the *Warrior and Gulf Navigation* case, when the high court noted that only specific language would preclude a grievance's arbitrability. Moreover, supporters feel that the enumeration of rights offers better protection against their erosion.

In terms of frequency of use, enumerated clauses were found in 83 percent of sample collective bargaining agreements studied by the U.S. Department of Labor; only 17 percent of the agreements studied featured general clauses.[9]

HOW MANAGEMENT LOSES ITS RIGHTS

Management loses its rights in two ways: voluntarily or involuntarily. Rights are surrendered voluntarily through collective negotiations and grievance settlements. Every management concession during contract negotiations represents the potential erosion of a management right. Of course, some concessions to union demands may have to be made in order to avoid an unfair labor practice charge for failing to bargain in good faith. Still, the cumulative effect of bargaining away management rights can be profound.

Management may also lose its rights when it accedes to a grievance. Although allowing a grievance, especially where the organization has made a mistake, frequently has a salutary effect on industrial relations, it may also set a precedent for the future.

Management may also lose its rights involuntarily: because of NLRB (or court) interpretation and/or application of the Taft-Hartley Act; because of new labor laws or amendments to the old ones; and through decisions of arbitrators. There is little that an employer can do, beyond political pressure and lobbying, to change the labor laws; the NLRB decisions are also beyond the reach of most employers. Arbitration, however, represents one area where management has considerable control.

Beyond careful preparation for arbitration and thoughtful selection of an arbitrator (see Chapters 3 and 4), management can have some impact on the arbitrator's decision. In *Warrior and Gulf Navigation,* the Supreme Court said that only the plainest (specific) language would exclude an issue from being arbitrable. This suggests that the proper place to limit an arbitrator's decision-making power is in the arbitration clause itself. Such action may be more important than whether the management rights clause is broad or enumerated, because by specifically excluding the arbitrator's authority to make decisions on certain issues (such as insurance, wages, etc.), management is in essence preserving its rights. Arbitrator authority should also be limited to the application and interpretation of the contract; the contract should specify that the arbitrator has no power to alter or amend the contract terms.

UNION SECURITY

According to a recent survey by the Bureau of National Affairs, nearly 84 percent of labor agreements provide for one of the following forms of union security: closed shop, union shop, modified union shop, maintenance-of-membership shop, agency shop, simple recognition shop, and dues checkoff.[10] However, the most common forms of union security are the union shop and the checkoff.[11] The inclusion of this kind of provision guarantees that the union will retain effective control over bargaining unit members and that its flow of dues will be sure and stable. Many management observers agree that a secure union is more reasonable in negotiations than one that feels constant tension with management and even feels that its institutional existence is threatened.

UNION-MANAGEMENT COOPERATION

In recent years, union-management relations have experienced a modest trend toward greater accommodation and cooperation. Many employers have realized the futility of attempting to destroy unions, while unions and their membership are increasingly aware that an organization must remain competitive (or at least, efficient, in the case of hospitals) if the jobs it provides are to continue. However, there has been relatively little union-management cooperation as specified and formalized in the collective agreement. This may reflect management's fear that such collaboration may lead to a diminution of its prerogatives. For example, in a government study of 1,773 major collective bargaining agreements, it was found that only about five percent of all agreements called for joint committees to deal with issues that are normally solely management's prerogative.[12] However, about 25 percent of the sample agreements did contain provisions for union-management cooperation on production problems, technological change, sales promotion, legislation, and similar managerial problems.[13] Most of these provisions took the form of pledges that the union would cooperate in achieving these goals or helping to facilitate them. Often the union's pledge was coupled with one from management—usually to cooperate on labor-management matters or to guarantee that workers would not be hurt by their participation in joint efforts. The other forms of cooperation involved joint committees and/or funds.

A growing form of union-management cooperation in Europe has been the formalization of worker participation—for example, workers serving on an organization's board of directors. More and more, these arrangements are being mandated by law. Such formalized worker participation is being studied for possible adaptation in the United States. However, at present it remains a very controversial issue.

A form of worker participation that is less controversial, but still not widespread, has involved attempts by employers to "enrich" workers' jobs or increase their job involvement by increasing the scope of their responsibility and decision-making power. These arrangements have been viewed suspiciously by unions; the on-going experiments have, for the most part, been the work of nonunion firms.

SELECTED ARBITRATION ISSUES INVOLVING MANAGEMENT RIGHTS

In the following pages we will examine a number of arbitration issues that center around management rights. Although management prerogatives may be raised in virtually any type of case, in these issues they are central to the resolution of the dispute. Arbitrations involving union security issues are at the end of the chapter.

Subcontracting

Subcontracting is one issue that seems to have more than its proportional share of cases dealing with management rights and union recognition clauses. The U.S. Supreme Court has held that management must not assume the authority to make a decision that will cause the loss of jobs in a bargaining unit without first negotiating with the union. The Court reasoned that such action involves the "terms and conditions of employment," and the Taft-Hartley Act expressly requires bargaining with respect to that issue.[14]

Arbitrator David Dolnick explains why subcontracting issues present difficulties:[15]

> Subcontracting is one of the most troublesome and perplexing problems in labor-management relations. It affects the concern of the recognized collective bargaining agent and the preservation of the bargaining unit. It triggers the fear of job loss and unemployment. Although arbitrators have extensively dealt with this subject, and although many excellent, scholarly treatises have been written, there is no fixed guideline which may be applied in every subcontracting dispute. Each case must be examined in the light of the applicable agreement, from the fixed, indisputed practices of the parties, from the implications that stem from either or both the contract and practice where they do not conflict, and from the circumstances and the evidence in each dispute.

One such subcontracting dispute involved a nursing home that attempted to place its dietary, laundry, and housekeeping services under the direct supervision of a management agency.[16] The subcontractor hired the old employees but refused to accept the nursing home-employee labor contract in its entirety.

In finding for the union, the arbitrator observed:

> The general position of arbitrators is that the right to subcontract depends upon reasonableness; and when a substantial portion of the regular work of employees is subcontracted, substantial business justi-

fication must be shown. To rule otherwise would place in the hands of the Employer the power to destroy the very essence of the bargain.[17]

The arbitrator found no evidence of substantial business justification in this case. He reasoned that even though a broad management rights clause existed in the agreement, the clause was limited by the requirement that the employer act reasonably. Because no substantial business justification was shown, the arbitrator ruled that the employer had acted unreasonably.

In another case the collective agreement provided that ". . . If the Employer intends to subcontract any work within the listed classifications, he shall give thirty (30) days prior notification to the Union."[18] At issue was the subcontracting of medical transcriptionists' work. A medical transcriptionist must have a high degree of knowledge of medical terminology and be able to type medical reports dictated by doctors. Because such work was backlogged on approximately five occasions—during the months of September, October, November, and December 1972, and January 1973—the hospital subcontracted some of the work to a transcription service. The hospital did not give the union 30 days' notice, but there was no objection by the union. In fact, there was no evidence that the union was even aware that the transcription work had been subcontracted.

The arbitrator excused the hospital's technical violation (failure to notify the union on one of the subcontracting occasions), because it appeared that the employer used its available and qualified bargaining unit employees to the fullest possible extent. However, he ruled that the employer was obligated to pay employees damages equivalent to the actual sum the hospital paid on two earlier occasions when it subcontracted work and failed to make full use of its existing bargaining unit employees or offer them a reasonable amount of overtime work.

In another case, a family practice center (FPC) was opened by a hospital for the purpose of training selected medical residents for so-called "family doctor" service.[19] The FPC was contained in a separate building on the hospital's grounds. It generated its own income and paid many of its own expenses. At issue was the retention of an outside cleaning firm that provided two cleaning women two hours per evening, six days per week, for a total of 24 hours of weekly service. For more than two years prior to the introduction of the outside service, the FPC had been using individual cleaning women hired on the basis of the recommendations of FPC staff members' wives. No layoffs resulted from the contracted service, nor were any housekeeping personnel on layoff status during the period of contracted service.

The union claimed the FPC had violated its recognition clause and demanded the job be posted. Although the arbitrator found that the type of cleaning work contracted for fell within the scope of bargaining unit work, he noted that the FPC had been subcontracting for a two-year period without a grievance being filed. Thus a past practice was created, which would permit the FPC to continue to subcontract so long as no more than 40 hours of work was involved and no qualified hospital personnel were on layoff.

When a Minnesota hospital substituted a vending machine operation, stocked by an outside supplier, for a small cafeteria line, the union claimed this new arrangement changed the working hours and duties of a cafeteria counter worker who worked as a cashier on the cafeteria line.[20] The parties' contract contained no clause prohibiting or permitting subcontracting or automation. The arbitrator brushed aside a "conventional" union argument that where no specific subcontracting language exists in the agreement, the wage clause, the union security clause, the seniority clause, the recognition clause, and the general intent of the entire agreement as a whole requires that subcontracting be prohibited on the grounds that it basically defeats the union's lawful right to represent the bargaining unit. The arbitrator found that the fact situation warranted a different analysis. First of all, he pointed out that the cashier duties, performed at least 50 percent of the time, were specifically excluded from bargaining unit jurisdiction. Second, the employee's job was incidental to the employer's main function. Third, other employees' wage rates and the union contract wage rates were not affected by the change. Fourth, although the employee's hours were changed, she did not receive a demotion, nor were her pay rate and working conditions affected. Finally, the hospital did not act capriciously or arbitrarily.

The collective agreement of another hospital provided that "Nothing herein contained shall be deemed to prevent supervisors and volunteer workers from performing those tasks which they have performed in the past."[21] A chemistry technician was promoted out of the bargaining unit to the supervisory position of chief laboratory technician. Management had this employee continue to perform most of the advanced aspects of testing he carried out while a member of the unit. The less advanced tasks were made part of a new job, that of assistant chemistry technician. In the meantime, the position of chemistry technician was abolished.

Arbitrator LeWinter found that the clause stated above was ambiguous, particularly the use of the word "they." In resolving the ambiguity he noted:

> The answer comes, therefore, from the concept of bargaining unit. It is this general concept and its ramifications which gives to labor-management relations an astigmatic approach to law. It is the need of the collective bargaining process to preserve the rights of both sides in that delicate balance of collective bargaining which created and developed the arbitral process along lines so often misunderstood by our brethren at the bench and the bar.[22]

After reviewing other arbitral opinions, the arbitrator found that while supervisors were permitted to perform some bargaining unit work, the work the supervisors carried out could not be used to destroy bargaining unit positions.

According to the arbitrator, the new supervisor's performance of the most advanced aspects of testing resulted in the elimination of a unit position, that of chemistry technician. He therefore directed the hospital to reinstate that position.

The Hospital for Joint Diseases and Medical Center had maintained laundry facilities since its inception. However, in 1977 it closed down most of its laundry facilities.[23] While some laundry services were still performed at the hospital, others were now done by a commercial laundry. When conferences between the union and hospital over the subcontracting issue proved unproductive, the hospital proceeded to lay off workers in the laundry area, rather than spend the $500,000 it estimated it would need under the New York State health code at the old laundry facility. This expenditure seemed particularly absurd to the hospital board when a new hospital was currently being built.

The arbitrator, in finding for the union, pointed out that the parties had negotiated a stringent no-subcontracting clause. While the arbitrator agreed that it was absurd for the hospital to spend $500,000 to reopen the old facility when the new one was so close to being completed, he reasoned that this was known to the hospital at the time the collective bargaining agreement was being negotiated. He observed:

> The Hospital elected at that time to agree to a non-subcontracting clause and in making that agreement effectively made the election in the expenditure of funds that they now ask be eliminated. Such a change would be an effective alteration of the essence of the contract. The parties have specifically agreed that no hospital signatory to the Collective Bargaining Agreement would subcontract to any profit or non-profit organization, any service, maintenance, clerical or office work, including kitchen *laundry* services, dietary housekeeping or day-to-day services. The parties, in creating the agreement, provided that all modifications be subject to approval of both sides in writing. That has not been done in this case.[24]

The arbitrator concluded that he could reach no other decision but that the hospital had violated the collective agreement by subcontracting the laundry facilities—an award that cost the hospital $500,000.

Performance of Bargaining Unit Work by Supervisors

One highly sensitive area involves situations where a supervisor allegedly performs bargaining unit work. Unions view such action as a threat to their security and to the security of bargaining unit members. While some contracts are silent regarding this issue, others specify that management representatives may perform bargaining unit work only in specified circumstances, such as in emergencies or when training new employees.

In one case, prior to the inclusion of the pharmacy in the bargaining unit, the hospital had assigned pharmacy personnel in any manner it desired.[25] After the pharmacy employees became members of the bargaining unit, the hospital's authority was curtailed by the collective bargaining agreement. The hospital attempted to justify the performance of bargaining unit work by supervisory personnel on the grounds of necessity and efficiency. However, the arbitrator found the hospital to be in violation of the agreement, because efficiency was not one of the conditions that allowed nonunit personnel to perform unit work. He did find, however, that the contract did permit interns to work in the pharmacy and perform bargaining unit work as part of their internship; the contract also permitted volunteers to work in the pharmacy and perform the same duties they had performed over the past several years.

In another case, a hospital was found not to be in violation of the contract when two security guards, who were not members of the bargaining unit, were observed making a key in the maintenance shop, a task reserved to bargaining unit members.[26] The hospital claimed the guards were acting without permission in making the key for a private vehicle. The union contended the hospital's defense was based on hearsay evidence consisting of the written statements of the two guards. The arbitrator held that it was the burden of the union to disprove the statements, and the union failed in this regard.

Arbitrability

A fulcrum point for many management rights disputes involves the question of a grievance's arbitrability. Such a defense may be very effective, because if an arbitrator finds that a grievance is not arbitrable, the merits of the dispute no longer matter and management's final answer becomes controlling.

There are two types of arbitrability claims: (1) procedural arbitrability, and (2) substantive arbitrability. Procedural arbitrability involves situations where the union violates the collective agreement, which bars further processing of the grievance. Frequently, the question of procedural arbitrability is raised when a union allegedly fails to present a grievance within the time limits indicated in the agreement. When an employer contends a grievance is not substantively arbitrable, the claim is often based on the allegation that a strict management prerogative is involved. Arbitration cases that raise the issue of arbitrability are of course not confined to any particular type of issue. The cases treated here involve substantive arbitrability.

In one case, the discharge of an ophthalmic photographer was upheld by an arbitrator because his job was not covered by the collective bargaining agreement, and hence the dispute was not arbitrable.[27] The union claimed that the employee was a technician who should be attached to the hospital's technician unit. However, the arbitrator noted the contract was completely silent regarding the existence of such a technical unit, and the union did not produce any evidence that a technician's unit existed. Moreover, the employee testified he had "nothing to do" with the technicians and therefore did not share a community of interest with them.

In a similar case, Arbitrator Lauritzen found that a hospital's failure to post a vacancy for the job of p.m. supervisor was not arbitrable because the job was not part of the bargaining unit.[28] The recognition clause of the agreement specified the union was the exclusive bargaining agent for employees "whose classifications are listed" in the agreement; "supervisors" were excluded as were "such other classifications as may have been historically excluded from the unit." In sustaining the hospital's claim that the grievance was not arbitrable, the arbitrator noted that: (1) the p.m. supervisor was not listed or mentioned in the agreement; (2) the responsibilities and functions of the position were supervisory in nature; and (3) testimony of past p.m. supervisor incumbents showed they never paid union dues or had to join the union and therefore could be considered "historically excluded from the unit."

In a Detroit case, the arbitrator ruled that four employees, sent home after less than four hours of work at a health clinic, were entitled to a full day's pay because the decision to release the employees from duty was not for "legitimate reasons," as required by the management rights provision.[29] When a broken boiler at the clinic caused temperatures to drop as low as 49°, the grievants were told they could go home. However, though the malfunction continued, the clinic remained open and all employees were required to work the remaining days of the week. The city paid the grievants for four hours, though they had worked only three and one-half hours. They were told they would not be paid for the remainder of the day.

The arbitrator held the grievance was arbitrable despite the fact that the union failed to specify the contract provisions allegedly violated. The contract did not call for dismissal of a grievance for such a reason, and the union processed the grievance through four steps in the grievance procedure without the city's objection. Thus, the arbitrator concluded the city had waived its right to later object to the union's omission.

Working Scheduling

While some contracts are silent on the subject, others regulate shifts, or fix the work week, or make scheduling the exclusive function of management. Many arbitrators have recognized that if there is no contract language expressly restricting management's right to schedule work, it remains a management prerogative.

In one case, a hospital unilaterally changed the shift starting times from 6:30 a.m. to 7:30 p.m. on certain days of the week.[30] The hospital justified this change on the basis that emergency surgery and the birth of babies often occurred outside the 6:30 a.m. to 3:00 p.m. time period, and no employee was available to clean up the emergency and operating rooms until the next morning. However, the hospital failed to provide a lunch period or premium pay for the late work shifts.

The arbitrator permitted the change of work shift starting times on these grounds:

> . . . [A]bsent a specific prohibition in the contract the arbitrator feels it
> is inherent in the collective bargaining agreement that the Company has
> the right to set the starting times for employees as long as such starting
> times are reasonable under the circumstances and not oppressive or
> burdensome to the employees.[31]

Even though one section of the contract established normal starting times, the arbitrator said it was "obvious" this section did not prohibit the hospital from setting up other starting times. However, he did find the hospital had erred in not giving late shift workers premium pay or permitting a paid lunch as required by the collective agreement.

In a similar case, an arbitrator ruled that a hospital had the right to schedule an employee to work a six-day week, including two four-hour days.[32] There was nothing to indicate that the collective bargaining agreement's broad management rights clause did not apply to all types of scheduling. Though there was evidence that the x-ray aide would be inconvenienced by the new schedule, the arbitrator found that the arrangement was necessary to the hospital from a business and operational standpoint.

Another arbitrator did not permit a hospital to unilaterally change the method of scheduling weekends off in the nursing services department.[33] Even though the contract stated that "the Hospital will attempt to distribute the weekend time off evenly in each job classification," other language in the agreement cited the authority of past practice for working conditions not "specifically mentioned" in the contract, unless adjusted by mutual agreement. Brushing aside the hospital's argument that the language of the agreement was specific enough to discontinue the past practice, the arbitrator ruled that the previous method of scheduling weekend time off met the criteria of an established practice and consequently could not be altered unilaterally by the employer. In addition, there was no evidence to indicate that the employer had attempted to revise the applicable language during the negotiations that had culminated in the current contract.

In other cases, management has been permitted to rotate shifts under the management rights clause;[34] unilaterally transfer an employee from the night shift to the day shift;[35] and change shift hours.[36]

Job Assignments

Job assignments, like work scheduling, represent another area where management has considerable discretion. In general, arbitrators have accorded management wide latitude in making work assignments, in the absence of contract restrictions to the contrary. The following cases illustrate this.

In one arbitration, the union objected to a hospital order mandating that a registered nurse (nonunit employee) and a surgical technician (unit employee) would make up the standby operating room team, instead of two surgical technicians as had been the practice for the past five years.[37] The hospital contended that HEW requirements for Medicare participation required that registered professional nurses be in charge of operating rooms. It had delayed in such staffing due to a scarcity of registered nurses.

The arbitrator felt the actual threat of loss of accreditation was not needed to justify the hospital's action—it was sufficient that the change was "necessary and reasonable to provide better patient care and greater efficiency," and also to comply with HEW and the American Osteopathic Association's staffing requirements.[38]

In a closely related case, the arbitrator ruled that a hospital association did not violate its contract when employees classified as gardener-helpers were assigned the task of picking up and delivering mail prior to the arrival of the truck driver-messenger on days when the chief gardener was unable to perform this work.[39] The union contended that the job of picking up and delivering mail was a duty of the truck driver-messenger, and thus the grievants should be paid a higher rate when they performed such work. However, the arbitrator ruled that the chief gardener routinely picked up and delivered mail before the messenger started his work day, and the grievants had been advised before placement that they would be required to perform this task occasionally.

However, when a ward clerk at a mental hospital was assigned to a work station where she was subjected to embarrassment (her station faced toilets and showers where there were no curtains)—not to mention increased fear of bodily harm, diminished efficiency, and mental anxiety by being behind locked doors—the arbitrator ruled that she be provided an alternate work area. While he recognized management's right to make the assignment and that the assignment was prompted by a need for efficiency, he nevertheless ordered that the worker in question be provided a work area where she would have less exposure to some of these stressful situations.[40]

When a vocational nurse was alleged to have caused "unbearable tension" in her former duty station because of a "personality conflict" and "impaired communications" with her colleagues, her reassignment back to the ward was justified, despite the union's charge that the action violated the due notice requirement in the work week article of the contract.[41] The arbitrator noted that the contract itself waives the due notice requirement in cases of emergency. A breakdown in communications, teamwork, and morale constituted an emergency situation because it represented a "clear and present threat" to "the level of patient care."

In yet another case, a contract violation was found when a hospital transferred the duties and responsibilities of a higher paid clerk-typist to the distribution worker's classification, but did not negotiate a revision of the job description or an appropriate wage rate.[42] The issue was remanded to the parties for negotiation and revision.

Looking at another grievance in the same case, the arbitrator ruled that contract language gave the hospital broad discretionary power to determine "when and whether certain employment is required only on a part-time basis."[43] No full-time employees had been replaced by the use of a part-timer, so violation of the contract had occurred. The hospital was accorded the right to avoid the necessity of paying full-time workers overtime, by using part-time workers.

In a Collyerized case, the arbitrator held that the management rights clause of the hospital contract gave management the right to remove five LPNs from the intensive care unit (ICU).[44] The hospital made a "good faith" effort to find alternate employment for the five employees. The arbitrator observed, "It may not seem fair, but there is nothing in the contract that prohibits it."[45]

A very interesting case involved a hospital that, according to the union, had violated the recognition clause of the agreement by laying off certain ward clerks and "giving their work" to employees (RNs) outside the bargaining unit.[46] The arbitrator found that the layoff was for "sound business and economic reasons and was free from any Union or non-Union employee relationship considerations." In finding for the hospital, the arbitrator ruled that the recognition clause required that the hospital recognize the union "for employees whose classifications" are listed in the contract; there was no reference to "work" or "work functions." Therefore, the arbitrator reasoned that the "work" of ward clerks is not performed solely by ward clerks. As he saw it, ". . . the Union was recognized for Ward Clerks employed at the Hospital—not for work that was being performed or could be performed by such Ward Clerks."

Overtime Assignments

Overtime assignments frequently are coveted by hospital workers because they can be so lucrative. On the other hand, there are occasions when an employee may see working overtime as an inconvenience, possibly because of a prior commitment or because he or she is fatigued from working an already heavy schedule. Management may wish to exercise its right to require overtime in order to maintain efficiency in the hospital. Conflicts arise when employees wish to decline overtime. Normally, management's right is recognized unless there is a contractual limitation to the contrary.

While many hospital cases have involved the issue of overtime, very few have involved overtime assignment. In one such case, Arbitrator Yarowsky ruled that a collective agreement did not prohibit an employer practice of occasionally assigning employees to work two consecutive tours of duty.[47] Management argued that the union, in submitting the grievance, intended to eliminate compulsory overtime, which was disliked by many employees. The hospital contended that satisfaction of the union's wish would improperly impinge on the rights of management. The arbitrator added that, even if he wanted to, he was without authority to order the elimination of the work shift assignments.

SELECTED ARBITRATION ISSUES INVOLVING UNION SECURITY

The remainder of this chapter deals with issues that involve either union security alone, or union security in collision with management rights.

An issue that sometimes becomes the subject of arbitration involves the status of the union when one hospital becomes a successor to another, is merged, or is purchased. In one such case, a hospital that acquired another only six-tenths of a mile away—where the employer administered both facilities as a single unit in terms of hiring and firing, payroll, and interfacility transfers—was required to recognize the employees of the other hospital as part of the existing bargaining unit.[48] It was reasoned the recognition clause did not limit the union to acting as bargaining agent for the employer's first facility, while the employer was making interfacility transfers to achieve economy and efficiency in operation. Such actions to achieve economy were not held to be an "emergency" under the contract provision that permitted the employer to assign unit work to nonunit employees, and the hospital was forced to recognize the employees of other hospitals as part of the bargaining unit.

In a different type of union security case, an employer's right was upheld to establish a ruling that specified a maximum of six union officials could attend a union training seminar because of heavy workload and budget limitations.[49] This ruling came despite a contract clause that provided:

> Authorized absence to attend seminars, workshops and official functions of mutual interest will be granted Union representatives ordinarily not to exceed 8 hours in a 12 month period. Additional time may be granted providing the agendas submitted show matters of mutual interest.

The arbitrator observed that the contract made no provision regarding the number of representatives who had to be given authorized absences.

In a different case, an arbitrator ruled that a union chairperson and steward were entitled to be paid wages for appearing as witnesses in an arbitration hearing involving an employee's grievance.[50] The contract provision in question gave the chairperson, chief steward, and stewards the right to process grievances during working time, and the processing of grievances includes testifying at arbitration hearings. The grievance procedure includes arbitration as its terminal step, the arbitrator observed.

In yet another case, the visitation rights of a union business agent were suspended by an arbitrator because the agent had entered the hospital and visited work areas without notifying "designated management officials" as required by the contract. Furthermore, the agent had talked to employees during work time, in violation of contract language that required visiting business representatives to confer with employees "only upon their own free time" and in "public areas." The business agent also had distributed literature to employees in their work areas during work time, in violation of a contractual mandate that stated that business representatives "shall not distribute any material on hospital premises." The arbitrator reasoned the employer clearly was not obligated to honor such unreasonable conduct.[51]

Another aspect of union security was involved when a hospital reassigned the local president and vice-president from the day to the evening shift.[52] The contract provided that such assignments could be made only if the employees volunteered or if "staffing needs of an emergency nature so require." The arbitrator held this language was designed to give the union officers protection in their shift assignments.

In another discrimination case, an arbitrator set aside a union steward's reprimand and consequent docking (for an hour and fifteen minutes) for allegedly leaving her work station without authority.[53] The arbitrator found that management procedures for authorizing and taking such leave were lax, and the supervisor had failed to clearly indicate whether the union steward would be allowed to leave her work station on union business during the period in question.

In another case a nurse was found to have been discriminated against by management when the hospital removed some of her duties, denied her additional assignments, and improperly evaluated her job performance.[54] The evidence showed that the hospital had taken these actions only after she protested the fact that nurses in the bargaining unit were being given compensatory time off instead of being paid overtime pay, as the contract required. In view of its discriminatory treatment, the hospital was ordered to restore her workload and pay her for overtime work when so assigned. It was also ordered to refrain from further discrimination against her.

Thus, arbitration cases involving management rights and union security issues are often highly charged, emotional issues as the institutional security of either or both may be perceived as being threatened. Practitioners may find that arbitration cases involving these issues are among the hardest fought they may encounter.

NOTES

1. U.S. Department of Labor, Bureau of Labor Statistics, *Management Rights and Union-Management Cooperation* (Washington D.C.: U.S. Government Printing Office, 1966, Bulletin No. 1425-5), p. 5.

2. *Ibid.*, pp. 4, 5.

3. Paul Prasow and Edward Peters, "New Perspectives on Management's Reserved Rights," *Labor Law Journal* 18 (January 1967): p. 6.

4. United Steelworkers of America v. Warrior and Gulf Navigation Company, 363 U.S. 574 (1960). See Chapter 1.

5. Prasow and Peters, *op. cit.*, p. 11.

6. U.S. Department of Labor, *op. cit.*, p. 5.

7. *Ibid.*, pp. 6, 7.

8. *Ibid.*, p. 6.

9. *Ibid.*, p. 7.

10. *Collective Bargaining: Negotiations and Contracts*, vol. 2. (Washington, D.C.: The Bureau of National Affairs, Inc., 1978), p. 65:1.

11. There are, at present, 20 states that have banned the union shop agreement. The closed shop is outlawed by the Taft-Hartley Act except in certain industries, such as contract construction.

12. U.S. Department of Labor, *op. cit.*, p. 25.

13. *Ibid.*, p. 26.

14. Fibreboard Paper Products Corp. v. NLRB, 85 S.Ct. 398, 57 L.R.R.M. 2609 (1964).

15. American Air Filter and the United Auto Workers, Local 1346, July 1, 1970. 54 LA 1251.

16. Greater Pennsylvania Avenue Nursing Center and National Union of Hospital and Health Care Employees, District 1199E, June 6, 1977. 77-2 ARB 8343.

17. *Ibid.*, p. 4472.

18. Kaiser Foundation Hospitals and Hospital and Institutional Workers' Union, Local 250, November 9, 1973. 61 LA 1008.

19. Akron City Hospital and American Federation of State, County and Municipal Employees, District Council No. 11, Local 684, March 27, 1977. 74-1 ARB 8098.

20. Rochester Methodist Hospital and Hotel, Hospital, Restaurant and Tavern Employees Union (Rochester, Minn.), Local 21, November 22, 1976. 67 LA 927.

21. Monongahela Valley Hospital, Inc. and United Steelworkers of America, Local 8041, May 11, 1976. 76-2 ARB 8368.

22. *Ibid.*, p. 6137.

23. Hospital for Joint Diseases and Medical Center and District 1199, National Union of Hospital and Health Care Employees, RWDSU, November 3, 1978. LVH.

24. *Ibid.*, p. 13.

25. Akron (Ohio) City Hospital and American Federation of State, County and Municipal Employees, Local 684, August 11, 1978. LAIG 2191.

26. Akron (Ohio) City Hospital and American Federation of State, County and Municipal Employees, Local 684, November 13, 1978. LAIG 2215.

27. Brookdale Hospital and Medical Center and District 1199, National Union of Hospital and Health Care Employees, RWDSU, May 24, 1977. 68 LA 908.

28. Peralta Hospital and Hospital and Institutional Workers Union, Local 250, June 5, 1969. BAHA-10.

29. City of Detroit (Mich.) and Registered Nurses Organization, Unit I, October 25, 1977. LAIG 2012.

30. Miami Inspiration Hospital, Inc. and United Steelworkers of America, April 26, 1977. 68 LA 898.

31. Ibid., p. 900.

32. Quincy (Mass.) City Hospital and Massachusetts Hospital Workers, Service Employees International Union, Local 880, March 8, 1977. LAIG 1804. Same case reported at 4 PSAA 77480.

33. Marinette General Hospital and Marinette General Hospital Employees Union, Local 1752, AFSCME, February 19, 1974. 73-2 ARB 8616. Same case reported at LAIG 1023.

34. Herrick Memorial Hospital and Hospital and Institutional Workers Union, Local 250, September 19, 1970. BAHA-14; also Associated Hospitals of the East Bay, Inc. (Merritt Hospital) and Hospital and Institutional Workers Union, Local 250, June 8, 1965. BAHA-6.

35. Marshall Hale Memorial Hospital and International Union of Operating Engineers, Stationary Local No. 39, June 7, 1978. 78-2 ARB 8281.

36. Grant Hospital of Chicago and International Brotherhood of Teamsters, Local 743, Local 73, SEIU, August 11, 1977. CHC-12.

37. Saginaw (Mich.) Osteopathic Hospital and Service Employees International Union, Local 79, April 29, 1977. LAIG 1865.

38. Ibid.

39. Youngstown (Ohio) Hospital Association and Service Employees International Union, Local 627, September 17, 1975. LAIG 1431.

40. Veterans Administration Hospital (Murfreesboro, Tenn.) and American Federation of Government Employees, Local 1844, August 7, 1972. 479 GERR: 279.

41. Veterans Administration Hospital (Palo Alto, Calif.) and American Federation of Government Employees, Local 2110, undated. 588 GERR: A-1.

42. Akron (Ohio) City Hospital and American Federation of State, County and Municipal Employees, Local 684, September 30, 1978. LAIG 2175.

43. Ibid.

44. Metropolitan Medical Center and the Minnesota Licensed Practical Nurses Association, October 9, 1978. HMMM-5.

45. Ibid., p. 3.

46. Peralta Hospital and Hospital and Institutional Workers' Union, Local 250, January 19, 1971. BAHA-15.

47. Veterans Administration Hospital (Lincoln, Nebr.) and American Federation of Government Employees, Local 2219, February 24, 1978. 754 GERR: 40.

48. W.A. Foote Memorial Hospital, Inc. and Operating Engineers, Local 547, January 19, 1976. 66 LA 24.

49. Veterans Administration Hospital (Salt Lake City, Utah) and American Federation of Government Employees, Local 2199, September 15, 1977. 69 LA 364. Same case reported at 77-2 ARB 8455.

50. Board of Mental Retardation, Lucas County and American Federation of State, County and Municipal Employees, Council 46, Local 544, November 10, 1977. 69 LA 862.

51. Franklin Medical Center and Hospital and Institutional Workers Union, Local 250, August 16, 1976. 67 LA 323. Same case reported at 76-2 ARB 8495.

52. Veterans Administration Hospital (Fayetteville, N.C.) and American Federation of Government Employees, Local 2080, June 21, 1976. 682 GERR: C-11.

53. William Beaumont Army Medical Center (El Paso, Texas) and American Federation of Government Employees, Local 2516, January 30, 1978. 750 GERR: 27.

54. Hurley Hospital and Hurley Hospital Head Nurses Staff Council, September 6, 1972. 72-1 ARB 8366.

Chapter 10

Discipline and Discharge of Professional and Nonprofessional Staff

Discipline and discharge cases are far and away the most frequently arbitrated issues, both in industry and in hospitals. For this reason alone, they are of vital concern to hospital administrators and union officials. Some unions, in fact, have a policy of automatically taking any discharge to arbitration, regardless of the merit of the case.

Obviously, the loss of one's job is the worst work-related fate that can befall a hospital employee. Consequently, unions tend to be vigilant protectors of rank and file rights. On the other hand, a hospital decision to arbitrate a discipline or discharge can have serious implications for management as well. Reinstated employees can become hospital "heroes" as they proudly explain to their enraptured audience how they "beat the system" or "how the hospital couldn't keep them fired." Such episodes encourage other employees to take liberties with hospital rules. If such attempts become widespread, they can lead to a general breakdown in the disciplinary climate.

JUST CAUSE

It is widely held in arbitration that the right to discharge, in the absence of contract language to the contrary, is dependent on proving that the discharge (or discipline) is supported by just cause.[1] According to Juris et al., hospital contract clauses calling for either "just cause," "cause," or a mix of "cause" with particular offenses specified, are found in almost 75 percent of all such agreements.[2] Contracts containing no such provision accounted for only 18.5 percent of the total.[3] Even if the contract is silent regarding "just cause" or "cause," many arbitrators will read this obligation into the agreement, absent contract language to the contrary.[4]

Hospital management, because it initiates discharge action, also has the burden of establishing just cause. To meet the just cause standard, a hospital must be cognizant of the following criteria:

- Rules covering the offense must be known to employees and should be enforced consistently.

- Rules should be reasonable.

- Rules and disciplinary actions should be nondiscriminatory.[5]

- Due process should be given to each grievant. For example, there should be a full and fair hearing of the facts before administering discipline.[6]

Unless these criteria are met, the hospital will not prevail in sustaining its disciplinary action.

WEINGARTEN OBLIGATIONS

In addition to management's "just cause" obligation, the hospital may also have a due process duty. This means the hospital must permit an employee to have union representation where the employee has good reason to fear that the interview with his or her supervisor might result in disciplinary action.[7] This so-called *Weingarten right* has been extended, on the basis of another case,[8] to include an employee's right to prior consultation with the union steward, even before the interview. However, the NLRB has held that an employer is not required to postpone an investigatory interview with an employee simply because the *particular* union representative desired by the employee is unavailable for reasons beyond the employer's control.[9] The employee could request that another union representative who is available be present.

Arbitrators, though not usually obligated to observe these NLRB (court) decisions, may nevertheless add such responsibilities to a hospital's obligation to provide "due process."[10] Some arbitration cases are "Collyerized"[11] and consequently, with the NLRB scrutinizing the decision, an arbitrator will undoubtedly take cognizance of the *Weingarten* doctrine, if relevant.

PROBATIONARY EMPLOYEES

Under many hospital collective agreements, an employee does not have seniority rights until the end of a probationary period. Thus an employer does not have to meet "just cause" standards when terminating a probationary employee.[12] However, some arbitrators would subject this general rule to the test that the discharge was made in "good faith"[13] and that there was no evidence that a hospital discriminated against an employee on grounds set forth in the nondiscrimination clause in the collective agreement,[14] or that the discharge was "arbitrary or capricious."[15] However, the burden of proof may be placed on the probationer to show that a hospital's actions were arbitrary or capricious.[16]

DISCHARGE VERSUS RESIGNATION

A fundamental but important distinction may be made between discharge and resignation. In the case of resignation, an employer does not have a just cause obligation, provided the employee quits *voluntarily*. If a hospital accepts the resignation, it has no further duty to reinstate an employee should that employee change his or her mind. There are times, however, when an employee is coerced to resign. In such situations, the alleged resignation will be treated as a discharge and subjected to just cause standards. To many arbitrators the deciding factor is the *intent* of the employee. If the employee intended to quit, then it is a voluntary resignation. If not, it is a construct discharge. The affirmation of intent to quit was a key factor in the *Mount Sinai* case.[17] When a woman walked off her job because she refused to accept a transfer, the arbitrator argued it could not be considered a quit because the hospital would not rehire her to her former position. The arbitrator found, however, that though the woman was constructively discharged, she was nevertheless discharged for just cause.

In another case an arbitrator concluded that the grievant had resigned because she had assumed she would have to work extended weekend shifts in the future, but had not checked with supervision to determine whether her fears were founded.[18] Moreover, she did not use the grievance procedure to protest what she thought would be long hours of work. Arbitrator J. Fred Holly concluded:

> As previously indicated, the resignation must be viewed as a voluntary act on the part of the Grievant, and there is no basis for concluding that the Employer withheld essential information from her. After all, the Grievant did not elicit information concerning her assumed future hours of work. She made the assumption and acted on it without attempting to obtain verification.[19]

DISCIPLINE AND DISCHARGE ISSUES AT THE WORK PLACE

Disciplinary issues fall into two broad categories: (1) employee conduct while on the job or at the work place, and (2) off-duty conduct. Hospitals normally promulgate rules regarding acceptable employee behavior, and these may become part of the just cause requirement.

This chapter will consider on-the-job violations first, in the following order:

Work Performance
  • negligence
  • incompetence
Misconduct
  • absenteeism
  • leaves of absence
Troublemaking
  • fighting
  • disrespect to fellow employees
Insubordination
  • refusing orders
  • leaving the work station
Dishonesty
  • improper personal conduct
  • theft
  • punching another's time card
  • falsification of application blank
Sex Discrimination
Personal Appearance

The final sections of this chapter deal with off-duty conduct, including alcoholism. The chapter ends with a discussion of the factors arbitrators use to evaluate disciplinary penalties.

Discipline and Discharge for Poor Work Performance

Negligence

Employee negligence describes a situation where an employee is qualified to do a job, but due to carelessness, inattention, or failure to follow established procedures, does not perform the work properly. One case involved two registered nurses who were faced with a heavy patient load. The nurses therefore decided to prepare medication in advance. They stored the medication in an unused refrigerator in an open area and covered the medication with a towel labeled "Do not touch." Storing the medication in this uncontrolled area made it accessible to almost anyone. Both the advance preparation of the medicine and its subsequent storage in the refrigerator were violations of hospital policy. Arbitrator Florey, in sustaining the nurses' three-day disciplinary suspensions, observed:

> Whatever the grievants' motivation was, and however harmless their
> action may have been in their eyes, their failure to follow standard

procedure, without proper authority, opened the door for the possibility of interference by whatever agent, with the correct administration of medication, and created a potentially dangerous situation.[20]

In a closely related case, an arbitrator sustained the discharge of a hospital pharmacist who made three errors in filling prescriptions over the course of one year. The arbitrator brushed aside union's defense that the work load was so great that mistakes were inevitable. Indeed, the arbitrator found that the potential seriousness of the errors was great.[21]

Carelessness was the issue involved in a case where a surgical orderly who was responsible for preparing male patients for surgery, was given a one-day suspension for leaving on the nightstand hair removed from a patient and the razor used for removing the hair. Arbitrator Lauritzen sustained the penalty after deciding that this carelessness was becoming a habit with the grievant. Nevertheless, he observed:

> From all the evidence adduced, there is no question in the mind of the Arbitrator that M_____ has been and will no doubt continue to be a good Orderly, and that he will be a better Orderly in the housekeeping aspects of his job by reason of the discipline imposed.[22]

In the absence of a written policy governing the handling of a procedure, an employee must consult with a supervisor to clarify a nonstandard situation.[23] A registered nurse had stayed beyond her shift to attend a patient in distress. Although the hospital had no written policy regarding continuity of notewriting past normal shift hours, the nursing personnel had been advised of the importance of chart entries, both as legal documents and as a guide for proper patient care. Arbitrator Hy Fish sustained the nurse's ten-day suspension for failing to consult with her supervisor on how to handle the situation, asking an aide to write on the chart, and signing the names of other nurses without adding her initials to show they were not actual signatures.

Incompetence

A distinction may be made between negligence and incompetence, although at times the line may be a thin one. As previously noted, negligence occurs when an employee has the ability to do a job, but does not perform it well through inattention, carelessness, or noncompliance with established procedures. On the other hand, an incompetent employee is one who has never mastered the job due to lack of ability, poor health, and so on. However, an employer must not permit an incompetent employee to pass the probationary period and then later discharge that employee when that person subsequently performs at the same level as during the evaluation period.[24] A nurse's discharge for incompetence was reversed despite the nurse's decline in performance earlier in the year. Subsequently, her performance improved to an extent that she was promoted (temporarily) to head nurse. The arbitrator saw an inconsistency between the temporary promotion and the hospital's claim that the grievant was incompetent.[25]

It is also widely held that an employer must give adequate training to an employee in order to later sustain discipline for unsatisfactory performance.[26]

One arbitrator has held that while an incident of incompetence leading to a discharge was insufficient in itself to sustain that discharge, the employee's entire past record combined with the incident to establish just cause.[27] In one case an 18-year employee lost her job after a medical leave of absence forced her to accept a different job. She was unable to perform the new job adequately during the probationary period and was thus terminated. But there was no evidence of discrimination nor arbitrary or capricious action by the hospital.[28]

In another case a registered nurse was found to have been properly discharged after she had agreed to take a review course in medication administration, but refused or repeatedly failed to take it. The hospital action followed discipline for failing to check a patient's chart before giving the patient insulin and administering a contraindicated drug. The arbitrator observed in part that "the real danger is not so much the possession of a malpractice claim, but the threat to the patient's health."[29]

Discipline and Discharge for Misconduct

Absenteeism

Absenteeism is an issue that has plagued hospitals. Hospital cases analyzed in this study indicate disciplinary action fell into four main categories: (1) discipline or discharge for "excessive" absenteeism; (2) discipline or discharge for failing to call in to work when absent; (3) falsification of the reasons given for absences; and (4) absence from work several days without reporting in.

There is no doubt that arbitrators take excessive absenteeism very seriously, particularly in hospitals. One arbitrator observed in this regard:

> It would constitute a very unfair decision and would place a tremendous burden upon the hospital if the hospital was forced to retain employees who could not attend work regularly—continual legitimate absences due to sickness beyond the allowable paid sick leave cannot and should not mitigate the hospital's right in this respect.[30]

No competent arbitrator will go on record to state unequivocally how many days off constitute excessive absenteeism. This depends in part on the reasons for the absences, the contract, and the rules and practices of the parties. Frequently the parties themselves fail to specify the number of days that will result in termination. In one case an arbitrator did not find six days in five months to be excessive.[31] The arbitrator stated: "When discharge has been upheld a much stronger and conclusive pattern of absences is ordinarily present."[32]

Another arbitrator upheld a discharge for 56½ days of absence over more than a three-year period, even though the grievant was ill part of that time. He observed:

> A review of the grievant's record sets forth a pattern of excessive absenteeism which supports the Hospital's position in this matter. While it is true that the grievant was suffering from various illnesses and had certain family problems, the general principle is that an employer is not required to retain in employment an individual upon whom it cannot rely in terms of constant work attendance. While this rule may be harsh, it is a fact of industrial life that an employee who is
> · absent on a repeated basis for longer than average reasonable periods of time, becomes a liability which the employer cannot be required to maintain.[33]

The discharge of a food service employee was upheld when the record showed that from January 1, 1972 through August 24, 1977, the grievant had been absent over 297 days, approximately 60 days per year.[34] However, in another case an aide's discharge was reduced to a long suspension despite an absence record of 74 days in a three-year period. The reason for such reduction was that the employee's last absence, the one leading directly to her discharge, was due to a back injury. The hospital assumed such absence represented another attempt on her part to extend a vacation. The arbitrator nevertheless noted:

> An unreasonable absence record, regardless of how valid the reasons for non-attendance may be, relieves an employer of the obligation to retain the person as an employee because the person has, by his or her record of non-attendance converted a full-time or regular employment relationship into a part-time or casual employment relationship. Grievant's absence record cannot be said to have reached this point but it may very well be on the way unless Grievant corrects her attitude toward regular attendance.[35]

As with other forms of discipline, the parties will often offer evidence of an employee's past work and disciplinary record. This evidence may have either a mitigating effect or add to the severity of the penalty imposed.[36]

Many hospitals have a policy requiring employees to call in when absent. Such policies should be clearly communicated to employees in writing. A hospital was instructed to remove a warning notice given to a housekeeping aide for being

AWOL, when it was learned the employee had called in but the supervisor had been unavailable. The employer did not have a policy instructing employees what to do in such an instance.[37]

When an employee fails to call in to report his or her absence for a specified time, frequently three consecutive working days, hospital rules will consider the employee a quit. This could possibly escalate into a dispute if the employee claims he or she called in or had a valid reason for not calling in, and the employer alleges otherwise. A building service employee was ordered reinstated when the arbitrator found that the grievant had a medical statement from a clinic which the hospital would have accepted had it been presented; the clinic (affiliated with the hospital) had neglected to transmit the statement. It therefore had to bear some responsibility for the grievant's plight.[38] In a closely related case, Arbitrator Pearce Davis found that when a grievant's supervisor told him that he would not be permitted to return until released by his physician, "it was not unreasonable for the grievant to conclude that he did not have to call in every day thereafter."[39]

Hospitals often require that beyond calling in, they have the right to check on the veracity of excuses offered by employees. Even where a hospital does not have a rule requiring "truth in absence reporting," one arbitrator equated this requirement to "common knowledge" or "common sense," and thus it "negates the need for a warning as a condition precedent to a summary discharge."[40]

However, in one case an arbitrator ordered reinstatement with partial back pay when an employee who called in sick at 9 a.m. on a Friday morning was seen at a football game at 7 p.m. the same day. The discharge had been based on the conclusion that if the employee was not at home, she could not have been ill. But the hospital had failed to even discuss the incident with the employee or determine if she had received medical treatment on that day (which she had).[41] It can be seen then that thorough investigation of an employee's excuse is of paramount importance.

Leaves of Absence

Typically, discipline or discharge for a leave of absence comes about when hospital employees allegedly fail to return from such a leave on an appointed date. Also at issue is whether or not permission was granted for the leave.

A discharge was set aside where there was confusion regarding an employee's return date, because the hospital and employee both were at fault.[42] Hospitals should give an employee sufficient notice when a leave is granted or denied and should not arbitrarily withhold permission for a leave of absence.[43] Moreover, rules regarding leaves of absence should be clearly communicated, preferably in writing.[44] However, discipline will be upheld when an employee is AWOL in cases where the supervisor has withheld permission for the leave after determining that staffing needs cannot be met otherwise.[45] In fact, supervisors are obligated to determine the propriety of leave requests in light of hospital staffing needs.

Discipline and Discharge for Troublemaking

Fighting

The pressure of the hospital work environment may indeed tend to foster fights and other acts of aggression, but virtually all hospitals ban fighting on the premises. As one arbitrator put it:

> Obviously, a Hospital cannot be operated in a manner conducive to the safety and well-being of its patients if the employees of same are allowed to engage in conduct which is not only injurious to themselves but is also potentially injurious to fellow employees, patients and even visitors to the Hospital. Fighting on the job, and irrespective of whether the antagonists are of the male or female species, is a serious offense in an industrial plant. In the judgment of this Arbitrator it is even more serious in a Hospital.[46]

Arbitrators, in attempting to resolve cases involving fighting, frequently will attempt to discover who the aggressor was. If an attack is unprovoked, of course, the individual defending himself or herself cannot be said to be engaging in fighting. One arbitrator held that while he found the grievant equally responsible for the argument that preceded the actual fight, the discharge was not based on the argument, but only on the fight itself. He explained: "The evidence failed to establish that Grievant provoked the fight or was the ultimate cause of said fight. In other words, after the original argument, for which Grievant was equally responsible, had ended, Mrs. B_____ resumed the affair."[47] For that reason the arbitrator reinstated the grievant, but without back pay.

In another case, a nursing assistant was discharged for an unprovoked assault on the charge nurse. Though there was conflicting testimony, other witnesses corroborated the charge nurse's version. The arbitrator observed:

> Striking a supervisor in charge of a Hospital nursing area in a reaction to being reported for a *de facto* refusal to perform a vital task in the fullest sense of the term—is an offense against administrative discipline which warranted severe punishment, up to and including the discharge option open to and chosen by the Employer. A hospital is no ordinary work place. The timely completion of an assignment which is a crucial link in the process of providing needed medication to patients is a responsibility which has few counterparts in manufacturing or other service industries.[48]

In another case, following a discussion between a technician and her supervisor, the supervisor started to turn away. The technician grabbed her arm and the two then began to fight. Arbitrator Yaffe concluded: "Because the grievant clearly provoked the incident, the undersigned agrees that serious discipline was warranted."[49] However, the arbitrator found that neither woman instigated the fight, but rather that "both women simultaneously began striking each other, partially out of anger and partially in self-defense."[50] Nevertheless, in light of the grievant's length of service and satisfactory work record, he modified the discharge to suspension without pay.

An x-ray technician's discharge was also converted to a suspension without pay in a case where the technician contributed to the incident by his antagonistic behavior. The arbitrator noted:

> On the other hand, his supervisor's militant and taunting response was hardly the quintessence of managerial dignity or tact, no matter how justifiably resentful he was. Surely the behavior of both employees that morning was not in keeping with the professional or para-professional decorum one should expect in a respected institution, as here, for the care, treatment and healing of the sick and wounded.[51]

According to one arbitrator, an employee must not use excessive force, even in the performance of duty, and even when provoked by physical or verbal abuse.[52] At issue was a hospital parking lot security officer who, when assaulted by another employee, struck him three times causing profuse bleeding from the head. The arbitrator converted the security officer's discharge to reinstatement without back pay, particularly in light of the fact that the other employee who instigated the incident was given only a two-day suspension.

There is no doubt that arbitrators place great importance on the quality of the investigation that follows the fighting incident. In one case a licensed practical nurse (LPN) disobeyed the head nurse by refusing to follow instructions concerning a patient's call. She slapped the head nurse, but only after the nurse had grabbed her by the nose and told her to go immediately to the patient.[53] The arbitrator observed that the entire incident might have been "easily resolved" had the nursing supervisor conducted an investigation to determine fault and mitigation. The supervisor was "duty bound" to check the truth or falseness of the head nurse's story before making any decision. Accordingly, the grievant was reinstated with partial back pay.

Disrespect to Fellow Employees

Disrespect to fellow employees involves abuse (other than physical) or harassment of one employee by another. Normally an employer has a contractual, if not legal, obligation[54] to keep its work place free from such abuse and harassment. In one such case, where the contract provided that "proper respect must be shown to medical staff, patients, visitors, or fellow workers," an arbitrator upheld a three-day suspension for an employee who complained about being "worked like a nigger.''[55] A black sitting at the table where the remarks were made complained to hospital management. The arbitrator observed:

> Thus the Arbitrator is of the view that no reasonable person living in contemporary America can offer as a defense that the use of such a phrase is not socially desirable and racially derogatory. It is even more pointed in this particular work environment where a sizeable minority constitutes the work force and where the testimony in the record shows there is no use of the word "nigger" in that work environment. Consequently the word has a racial bias which indeed is a form of discrimination.
>
> In effect words alone can be discriminatory in that they can create an aura which affects the entire work place. Words may be intimidating and are often the basis upon which more overt discrimination occurs. It cannot be concluded that the words as used here can not be construed to be anything other than a violation of both the contract and the law.[56]

A hospital may also take disciplinary action against an employee who is belligerent and profane to others. However, the hospital must take pains to make sure that it has sufficient evidence to support such a charge. For example, the Akron City Hospital was ordered to reinstate a discharged grievant because it had failed to produce witnesses. The hospital had relied solely on signed statements of employees accusing the grievant of misconduct. Arbitrator Geissinger thus observed:

> Although the grievant was loud-mouthed, profane and belligerent, I am not convinced that his fellow-employees actually were in immediate danger of physical harm. There is a difference between a verbal threat of violence and conduct which can be construed as threatening immediately physical violence. In the absence of testimony by the person or persons allegedly threatened it is virtually impossible to evaluate the conduct complained of. Under the circumstances I am not giving weight to the signed statements in reaching my decision.[57]

Discipline and Discharge for Insubordination

Refusing Orders

The record is replete with hospital cases revolving around the issue of insubordination. It appears to be a very sensitive issue in the health care field, particularly because failure to follow orders not only leads to inefficiency but also to possible harm to the hospital (including financial liability) and its patients. Insubordination may take many dimensions. Perhaps the best known is where an employee is given a direct order and refuses to carry it out. However, insubordination may also take the form of refusing overtime where the hospital has the right to require it; or directing abuse and threatening language toward a supervisor. The latter may have the impact of diminishing authority within the hospital environment.

In labor relations the usual principle is that employees are to follow orders and complain later if they feel they have been mistreated. This point was underlined by one arbitrator's comment: "The importance of not following orders in this area is even more detrimental to the grievant than such an act in the private sector. Patient care is the fundamental and prime existence for a hospital facility."[58]

While no one denies the importance of following orders, an employee is accorded the right to refuse an order that "outwardly appears to be hazardous to his and/or her health and safety, and the same may be taken into consideration in mitigating the degree of penalty imposed by an employer where discipline is imposed."[59] However, a "mere assumption" that a dangerous and/or extra-ordinary hazardous condition exists in the work place cannot act as a bar to a finding of insubordination.[60]

In order to sustain a claim of insubordination, there must be evidence that a direct order was given. A grievant's three-day suspension for insubordination to a nutrition aide was reversed when the evidence showed that at no time was the grievant given a specific directive to do a cleaning job usually performed by a part-time employee, nor was the grievant advised that a supervisor would take care of her regular duties while she cleaned the cabinet.[61]

Employees must work, even on scheduled days off, if the contract so provides.[62] The fact that an order to report is given close to quitting time the day preceding an overtime assignment does not destroy the validity of the order.[63] Only if the hospital request is unreasonable or in bad faith, or if compelling reasons prevent the employee from coming to work, is it permissible for employees to refuse overtime, absent contract language to the contrary.[64] In one case, the suspensions of two pharmacy aides were upheld. They had refused overtime where the contract required it. Arbitrator Matthew Kelly noted:

> . . . the controlling fact is that the contract clearly alerts all employees that they are subject to being required to work overtime when needed and that the contract does not require Management to give prior notice of overtime assignment. Management, of course, need be reasonable in its assignment of overtime.[65]

Where the contract gives employees the right to refuse overtime, the exercise of that right does not constitute insubordination.[66]

Abusive language directed at a supervisor may also be considered an act of insubordination. An LPN's discharge was upheld where after receiving a reprimand from her supervisor, she continued her loud and abusive language. The arbitrator noted that the grievant's behavior was not in keeping with the hospital's need for peace and quiet, required for patients' welfare. The grievant had been defiant of authority, had tampered with official hospital records, and had written an insubordinate note to her supervisor. Subsequently, her "persistently loud and disrespectful language" became the "last straw."[67]

In another case, a grievant threatened his supervisor in the presence of patients, and later threatened a guard. Arbitrator Rutledge noted that the arbitration process is "implacably at odds with self-help threats."[68]

A medical attendant's five-day suspension was upheld even when there was no evidence to substantiate a direct order, in a case where the grievant's answer to the supervisor was "flippant and disrespectful," and her attitude indicated that she did not accept the properly established authority.[69] In this case the contract stated that an employee could be disciplined for "reasons detrimental to the interests of the patients." The arbitrator found the grievant's action (failing to remove a bedpan from a patient's tray) was detrimental to the patient's interest.[70]

A somewhat different twist is shown in two cases where employees performed tasks outside their classifications, under orders, and were later discharged for insubordination. In the first case, an orderly working under the general supervision of the charge nurse had been told to take orders from the nurses and not the doctors. An emergency room doctor asked if the orderly wanted to suture a patient. He was observed doing the suturing and was discharged. The arbitrator reduced the discharge to a one-week suspension after finding that the failure to carry out "long-range instructions without any defiance" is not considered insubordination. In addition, the arbitrator noted, "The seriousness of the offense is mitigated by the doctor's encouragement of his act and approval of his conduct."[71]

In a similar case, an admitting clerk was discharged for participating in a surgical procedure after his shift was over. A staff physician had asked the grievant to get some materials and also to hold a retractor. In ordering the clerk's reinstatement with full back pay, the arbitrator observed:

> In an Emergency Room, if a Staff Physician orders something to be done, the Grievant has the right to expect that the Staff Physician knows what he is doing and would not order an Admitting Clerk to do something except based upon the Physician's professional judgment. If that judgment is lacking, it is not the Admitting Clerk who should suffer thereby.[72]

Leaving the Work Station

Leaving one's work station without permission is related to insubordination, discussed above. The abandonment of the work station can be an especially serious problem in a hospital, because emergencies arise with little or no warning. A written warning to a nurse's aide was upheld even though she left her post to obtain wash cloths that were needed on her floor. The arbitrator ruled she should have obtained permission from her supervisor before leaving.[73] Other cases reveal that discharges for abandoning the work station are sustained after several warnings for such action.[74]

Dishonesty

Improper Personal Conduct

Violations of personal conduct run the gamut from abuse of hospital property to the carrying of weapons. In one case, a hospital employee's discharge for making unauthorized telephone calls was reduced to a one-week disciplinary suspension. The arbitrator noted that while the hospital had a policy forbidding certain uses of the telephone by employees, there was a procedure for collecting personal telephone charges. Moreover, the grievant's use of the telephone was researched by the hospital, but there was no evidence of similar research conducted for other unauthorized calls the hospital knew were being made by other employees.[75]

In a similar case, Arbitrator Koven ordered reinstatement and back pay for an employee who used the hospital's Xerox machine to make copies of a personal letter. While the employee first denied using the machine, she later admitted making the copies and was subsequently discharged. Koven felt the incident did not warrant discharge.[76]

An arbitrator reduced a discharge to a suspension without pay in a case where a hospital food service worker pulled a knife at the stockman who had attacked and struck him. The arbitrator found that the knife was on the grievant's person through carelessness. While hospital policy stated that the possession of a lethal weapon was cause for discharge or suspension without pay, the policy did not indicate one penalty was more appropriate than the other. Based on the employee's good prior work record and that fact that he did not threaten the other employee with the knife, the arbitrator imposed the lesser penalty.[77]

A hospital worker was correctly terminated after he was identified as the man who had exposed himself in an indecent manner in front of female hospital employees on two separate occasions. Though the grievant's past work record was spotless, the arbitrator believed the female employees' stories, particularly because they both noted the peculiar hat always worn by the exhibitionist. This lent credence to their identification.[78]

Theft

Because stealing usually results in discharge and leaves a lasting stigma on the employment record, arbitrators will require the hospital to produce a high degree of proof. Theft can, of course, also be grounds for a civil action, although failure to file criminal charges usually has no effect on the outcome of the arbitration case.[79] Of course occasionally a hospital will prosecute an employee in addition to terminating that employee.[80] However, even though the arbitrator gives weight to an employee's conviction in court for the same offense, dismissal of criminal charges will not automatically render the hospital's case moot. "The dismissal (of charges) does not independently act to negate the effect of the evidence presented at the arbitration hearing."[81]

In one arbitration case, a hospital relied heavily on the grievant's confession of guilt to a member of the sheriff's department who had been investigating the thefts in which the grievant was allegedly involved. The court later found the confession to be of dubious value because it had been obtained under duress. Without the confession there was "no independent evidence" of the alleged thefts and consequently management could not meet the "clear and compelling standard" of evidence needed to support the LPN's discharge.[82]

Hospitals will be reversed by arbitrators in cases where they cannot show the material allegedly stolen was hospital property,[83] or where the "hospital had no proprietary interest in retaining [the] articles for further use" and had never told employees they could not keep for their own personal use items slated to be tossed out.[84] However, the value of the object(s) stolen does not always determine whether or not the discharge will be sustained.[85]

In one case, a worker in the receiving department was discharged following the inspection of a large shopping bag he was carrying. Two pieces of frozen meat were found, one weighing about 11 pounds and the other about 3½ pounds. The arbitrator upheld the discharge.[86]

A hospital projectionist was properly suspended for ten days when he refused to permit a security guard to inspect the package he was carrying. The employee knew that hospital policy stated that when an employee takes out material that has been or still is hospital property, a package pass must be obtained and signed by an authorized supervisor. The employee was stopped because he did not have such a pass and consequently refused to let the guard inspect the package. Moreover, the grievant had been warned on several previous occasions for the same offense.[87]

In another theft case, an undercover operative was hired by a hospital after management became aware of substantial losses in food inventories. A housekeeping worker was subsequently discharged after he was observed independently, both by the undercover man and a hospital patient, as the person who was taking material out of the hospital and depositing it outside. In sustaining the discharge, the arbitrator noted:

The strength of separate identifications, when the two observers were not even together, both coming not long after the observations, leaves little question about their accuracy. It would be entirely too coincidental otherwise. It offers no realistic basis for predicating a decision on the vague possibility of double error by unrelated witnesses. The separate identifications of the Grievant by two witnesses, unknown to one another, in the presence of a Security officer, thus is deemed conclusive, absent reason to doubt the *bona fide* nature of the observations. The offense involved is universally considered a reason for discharge.[88]

Punching Another's Time Card

Punching another employee's time card normally is considered by hospitals to be a first-offense dischargeable violation. Arbitrator Kelliher sustained a nurse's discharge where she was clearly seen punching a second employee's time card, and it was her second offense. The arbitrator observed that she worked in an area requiring "an intense level of medical care" and thus "a failure to be on the job could seriously affect the proper care of the patients."[89]

An arbitrator may look to the purpose of the time card rule to establish just cause. In a case where a nurse punched out another employee's card because she feared the other employee would get unwarranted overtime, and there was no intent to defraud the employer, the arbitrator reinstated the nurse without back pay. The arbitrator did point out, however, that the rule was reasonable and was known to the grievants. Moreover, the nurse had admitted punching the card.[90]

Falsification of Application Blank

It is generally held that management has the right to discharge an employee for falsifying work records, including an employment application blank. Employers argue that had the application not contained misleading, erroneous, or even missing information, the employee would not have been hired in the first place. Arbitrator Bernard J. Fieger observed that to sustain a discharge based on falsification of an employment application, the case must show:

1. that the falsification was intentional,
2. that the falsification related to material information relative to the job being sought,
3. that the employer acted with dispatch in ascertaining facts, after becoming aware of the falsification,

4. the performance and disciplinary record of the employee, and
5. injury to the employer.[91]

In addition, Arbitrator Fieger found that arbitrators have followed a "one-year rule" in such cases and have refused to sanction an employee's discharge if the employer had not discovered the falsification within a year and the employee had performed his or her duties adequately. The one-year rule acts as a statute of limitations, especially where an employee has had a good record. Thus an employer cannot show injury to support the drastic action of discharge.[92]

A somewhat different position was taken by Arbitrator Louis Yagoda, in a case involving a worker who deliberately falsified his application by omitting his record of arrests. His work record was good, however. Yagoda's discussion is summarized below:

> I am convinced from the evidence put before me that inquiry into the arrest record of a prospective employee is of material importance to this institution in determining whether or not it shall hire an employee. I am further convinced that the Employer is justified in reserving to itself the right to dismiss an applicant who misrepresents his application form it put before this employee for his signature and to which the applicant consented by his signature.
>
> I do not believe that I may look behind these critical determinants into the wider moral questions of alleged societal injustices so eloquently described by Union counsel which, in his view, transcend these conventional norms of an Employer's right to know, to evaluate and to act on this aspect of an employee's record. I have neither the evidentiary resources nor the authority to re-try or re-order the society, the circumstances and the behavior which made this arrest a fact when the applicant stated that it was not.
>
> There may be some merit in the contention of Union counsel that the favorable record of the grievant for the nine months during which he was employed speaks more forcefully for him than the arrest record which he concealed. But I do conclude that this was an entitled judgment for the Employer to make and I do not find evidence that the making of it was an impermissible exercise of management discretion, bearing in mind that the decision took into consideration (a) the protection of management's need to secure pertinent information of this kind, (b) querying the grievant concerning the nature of the record itself after it had been discovered, (c) consideration of the kinds of arrests and convictions involved and their potential pertinence to the expectations put on employees' performance and responsibilities as members of the maintenance staff of the hospital.[93]

Sex Discrimination

The charge of sex discrimination is, of course, one for which arbitration represents only one of several possible forums for complaint. Obviously, a grievant can also seek redress under the provisions of the 1964 Civil Rights Act or Equal Pay Act. Moreover, arbitration of a sex discrimination (or other discrimination) case does not prevent the grievant from seeking further consideration of the complaint under the Equal Employment Opportunity Commission (EEOC) or state Fair Employment Practices (FEP) agency.[94]

Obviously these considerations raise the issue of whether an arbitrator, in attempting to resolve a discrimination complaint, should apply contract terms or relevant EEO law, if these are in dispute. Though this seems to be a matter of individual arbitrator's preference, resolution of the dilemma may not be so difficult when the discrimination is also prohibited by the collective agreement.

Despite these considerations, a hospital was permitted to discriminate against male employees by refusing to promote them to the position of LVN (licensed vocational nurse) wherever in the hospital system that classification would routinely be responsible for intimate care of female patients.[95]

Personal Appearance

The major issue involved in disputes concerning personal appearances may be summed up this way:

> An employer is entitled to prescribe reasonable rules governing the conduct of its employees. Similarly, the employees are entitled to freedom of expression in their adornment and personal appearance. The problem is, how are these equally important rights to be reconciled when they come into conflict?[96]

In attempting to resolve such conflicts, arbitrators will ask themselves whether the appearance and dress standards in question were reasonably related to the necessities of the organization and the duties that the employee was expected to perform.[97]

In one case, a psychiatric aide was discharged for wearing a neatly trimmed beard. The arbitrator, in sustaining the discharge, observed that it was debatable whether or not the standards of medical care were adversely affected by the aide's beard, but there were numerous complaints by patients. Where there are health, sanitation, or safety reasons for regulation of dress, appearance, or adornment, these regulations are scrupulously enforced by arbitrators.[98] Complaints by patients regarding dress or adornment may also serve as tangible evidence of their inappropriateness.[99]

DISCIPLINE AND DISCHARGE FOR OFF-DUTY ACTIVITIES

Arbitrators have generally held that an employer has no control over an employee's outside activities unless the effects of those activities influence on-the-job performance. Such a situation may occur where an employee is moonlighting and reports to work in an unfit condition, or where an employee uses drugs or alcohol off the job and arrives at the job unfit for work.

What about a situation where an employee gets into difficulty with the law and is consequently arrested and convicted for a crime? Such a situation occurred at the Fairmont General Hospital.[100] A housemaid employed at the hospital for about six years was apprehended by a department store security guard and charged with shoplifting. The housemaid admitted the shoplifting. Subsequently she was discharged. In upholding the hospital's action, the arbitrator stressed the sensitive nature of the grievant's job:

> Here the employer is a community hospital whose "product" is that of serving the sick people of a relatively small community. It is established in evidence that aside from drugs and other property of the Hospital and of employees, easy access exists as a matter of course to the personal property of the patients who, despite the best efforts of the Hospital, inevitably leave valuables in and around their rooms often at times when they are unable to prevent such property from being stolen. In addition, the evidence establishes that in recent years there has existed a serious theft problem at the Hospital.[101]

In another case, a hospital employee belonged to a worker organization.[102] He spent some of his off-duty (hospital) time handbilling the public for various worker causes. One of the handbills decried certain conditions at the hospital where he was employed. Though the hospital warned him about the consequences of his actions, the employee persisted. In upholding the discharge, the arbitrator noted:

> And while it is true that the employer does not (by virtue of the employment relationship) become the guardian of the employee's personal action and does not exercise parental control, it is equally true that in those areas having to do with the employer's business, the employer has the right to terminate the relationship if the employee's wrongful actions might injuriously affect the business.[103]

Occasionally employees are disciplined for excessive wage assignments. Federal law prohibits discharge of an employee for only one wage assignment, but state laws may be even more restrictive.[104] Thus, in setting discipline and discharge policies regarding wage assignments, relevant federal and state laws should be considered. In one hospital case, a medical supply clerk's discharge was reduced to a 60-day suspension even though the employee had ten wage attachments since 1970. The mitigating factors were: (1) the attachments were in all probability partially the result of underpayments on her husband's income; (2) the hospital failed to establish and enforce clear rules on wage attachments; (3) a previous two-week suspension and the discharge resulted from attachments covering the same year in which the grievant had managed to reduce the principal sum owed; (4) the grievant took steps to correct the malperformance and agreed to the obligations; (5) all garnishments were for tax delinquencies and not "promiscuous purchases of luxuries;" and (6) the grievant had a record of sixteen years of "good and faithful service."[105]

Alcoholism

We have chosen to treat alcoholism as an off-duty issue even though some discipline is meted out for "drinking on the job." The justification for this is that most employees acquire the habit of drinking while off the job, and the problem carries over to on-the-job drinking when addiction is well advanced. Thus, alcoholism as an outside activity can manifest itself on the job through either lowered job performance and/or actual drinking on the job.

An example of the latter situation occurred at Maimonides Medical Center, where the hospital was sustained in terminating one employee in the Escort Service but not another.[106] The first employee was found with a cup of blackberry brandy in front of him while playing cards. The second employee was not seen drinking and did not have a cup in front of him. The arbitrator indicated:

> Drinking on a hospital's premises is a serious offense and, indeed, it should be stamped out with offenders seriously disciplined. But at no time were efforts taken to correct laxities in this regard. Seemingly, the sole objective was to catch employees in the act and to make an example of them. In L_____'s case, specifically, there was never a caution and never an admonition to remind him of the seriousness of having even an occasional beer or blackberry brandy with milk on the premises.[107]

In a similar case, an employee was reinstated with back pay where a supervisor saw the employee with a cup of liquid in his hand and a bottle of liquor nearby.[108] The supervisor confiscated the bottle but not the cup. The arbitrator felt that the whole case depended on whether the grievant was pouring liquor from the bottle into the cup. Because the supervisor did not have the cup, she couldn't tell whether it contained liquor. Arbitrator Sandler enumerated nine factors that would convince an arbitrator to sustain a discharge for drinking on the job (if one or more of them are present):

1. frequent absenteeism as a result of drinking;
2. other serious improper behavior;
3. inability to perform the work;
4. overt evidence of intoxication;
5. a destructive effect on the morale of other employees;
6. chronic alcoholism with no effort at rehabilitation;
7. where the employee is in personal contact with the public;
8. where the job is such that drinking will endanger the safety of others (*e.g.*, driving a truck); or
9. past warnings about drinking on the job.[109]

A hospital is not required to administer a medical test to determine intoxication for any employee who reports to work with an odor of alcohol on his or her breath, staggers, lacks coordination, has a fixed and glassy stare, or whose speech is thick and slurred.[110]

The mere possession of alcohol is not the same as drinking on the job, and if possession of alcohol is a punishable offense, there must be a clearly established and published rule.[111] If the hospital deals out inconsistent punishment for the same offense, this also can mitigate a discharge for alcoholism (or any other violation).[112]

FACTORS IN EVALUATING PENALTIES

In many of the decisions cited in this chapter where discipline or discharge penalties were reversed or modified, arbitrators took into account many different factors when evaluating the appropriateness of the penalty assessed. Some of the most significant factors are discussed below:[113]

1. *Nature of the offense*. If the nature of the offense does not warrant immediate discharge, arbitrators will require that corrective action or progressive discipline be followed by management.

2. *Due process and procedural requirements*. Basically, due process involves the notion of fairness. Did the hospital permit a disciplined employee a hearing?[114] Did it give the employee an opportunity to question his or her accuser? Was there undue delay in notifying the employee of the discipline/discharge? Had the hospital abided by the grievance procedure? These are a few of the key questions one may ask to determine due process.

3. *Postdischarge conduct or charges*. Most arbitrators agree that employees should be given all reasons for the discharge action at the time of discharge. The hospital cannot add reasons when the case reaches arbitration. It should also be noted that sometimes the discovery of new information regarding the grievant's postdischarge actions may be given favorable consideration.

4. *Double jeopardy.* Once discipline has been imposed and accepted, it cannot thereafter be increased.[115] Double jeopardy will also be held applicable where the hospital unduly delays the assessment or enforcement of discipline.

The concept is not relevant, however, where the hospital, say, puts an employee on indefinite suspension pending the outcome of an investigation, and later determines the suspension should be converted to a discharge. Neither does double jeopardy apply where a hospital considers an employee's (poor) past record in fixing a penalty.

5. *Grievant's past record.* An offense may be mitigated by a good past record and aggravated by a poor one. Often the employee's past record is the major factor in determining an appropriate penalty.[116]

6. *Length of service with the hospital.* Long service with the hospital, particularly if the employee's past record is a good one, weighs in the employee's favor when an arbitrator reviews the discharge.

7. *Knowledge of rules: Warnings.* Basic to virtually all arbitration of discipline and discharge cases is that there must be reasonable rules or standards, widely known, and consistently applied and enforced.

8. *Lax enforcement of rules.* Arbitrators do not hesitate to modify penalties in cases where the hospital has in the past and over a period of time condoned violations of the rule. The lax enforcement of rules leads employees to believe that their conduct is sanctioned by management. However, an employer can strictly enforce a rule, even after being lax, when it gives clear notice of intent to do so.

9. *Unequal or discriminatory treatment.* Arbitrators usually agree that enforcement of rules and assessment of discipline must be done in a consistent manner.[117] Discipline should be meted out to the same degree for all employees guilty of the same infraction, unless some reasonable basis exists for variation (such as degrees of fault or mitigating or aggravating circumstances).

10. *Anti-union discrimination.* Unions occasionally will argue that discipline/ discharge was based on anti-union animus alone, and not on the alleged offense. Such charges must be supported by clear evidence.

11. *Management also at fault.* Where an employee is guilty of wrongdoing, but management (usually the supervisor) contributes to the situation by issuing unclear or incorrect instructions, to take but one example, an arbitrator may be persuaded to reduce or set aside the penalty imposed by management.[118]

NOTES

1. See, for example, Grace Hospital Northwest Unit (Detroit, Mich.) and Service Employees International Union, Local 79, November 10, 1971, 71-2 ARB 8676, p. 5573.
2. H. Juris et al., "Employee Discipline No Longer Management Prerogative Only, *Hospitals, JAHA* 51 (May 1977): 68.

3. *Ibid.* Also, a BNA Survey of 400 contracts showed that 80 percent of the sample agreements had provision for discharge for "cause" or "just cause" and 65 percent contained specific grounds for discharge. Basic Patterns in Union Contracts, as reported in the (BNA) *Daily Labor Report,* January 16, 1979, p. 2.

4. See Grace Hospital, *op. cit.,* and Dameron Hospital and Hospital and Institutional Workers, Local 250, March 12, 1976, BAHA 23. In the latter case, Arbitrator Dykstra equates just cause and cause (see pages 5 and 6).

5. See, for example, Chicago Osteopathic Hospital and Chicago Osteopathic Nurses Association, March 17, 1976. LAIG 1610.

6. An excellent discussion of this subject is found in Harry T. Edwards, "Due Process Considerations in Labor Arbitration," *Arbitration Journal* 25 (1970): 141-169.

7. NLRB v. Weingarten, Inc. 76 Labor Cases 10,662 (February 19, 1975).

8. Climax Molybdenum Company (1977) 1976-77 CCH NLRB 17,792.

9. Coca-Cola Bottling Company of Los Angeles (1977) 1976-77 CCH NLRB 17,787.

10. In a post-Weingarten decision, Arbitrator Eaton declined to extend a union representation clause that provided for union representation during certain formal discussions and during the grievance procedure to occasions whenever an "employee feels threatened" or whenever an employee "wanted" representation. Arbitrator Eaton felt that this change in the agreement would be beyond his scope of authority. Veterans Administration Hospital (Palo Alto, Calif.) and American Federation of Government Employees, Local 2110, December 15, 1978. LAIG 2265.

11. See Chapter 1 for a discussion of the Collyer Doctrine.

12. Veterans Administration Hospital (Perry Point, Maryland) and American Federation of Government Employees, Local 331, February 7, 1977. 750 WCR 27.

13. Jackson County (Mich.) Medical Care Facility and American Federation of State, County and Municipal Employees, Local 139, December 19, 1973. LAIG 1014.

14. Bernalillo County (N. Mex.) Medical Center and Bernalillo County Medical Center Employees Association, December 18, 1976. LAIG 2234.

15. New York City (N.Y.) Health and Hospitals Corp. and Individual Grievant, September 11, 1978. LAIG 2186.

16. *Ibid.*

17. Cedars-Sinai Medical Center and Mt. Sinai Division and Building Service Employees, Local 399, May 30, 1967. 67-1 ARB 8315.

18. Oak Ridge Hospital of United Methodist Church and Service Employees International Union, Local 150-T, April 25, 1978. 78-1 ARB 8207.

19. *Ibid.,* p. 3997.

20. Harrisburg (Pennsylvania) Polyclinic Hospital and Pennsylvania Nurses Association, November 23, 1976. LAIG 1748.

21. Booth Memorial Medical Center and Drug and Hospital Union, Local 1199, March 17, 1972. LVH.

22. Samuel Merritt Hospital and Hospital and Institutional Workers Union, Local 250, September 17, 1963, BAHA-2. See also City of Detroit (Mich.) Emergency Medical Service and Emergency Mobile Medical Technicians Association, April 2, 1979. LAIG 2325.

23. Cook County (Ill.) Health and Hospitals Governing Commission and Illinois Nurses Association, February 2, 1977. LAIG 1819.

24. Kaiser-Permanente Medical Care Program and Office and Professional Employees Union, Local 29, April 24, 1978. 70 LA 799 and 70 LA 804.

25. Youngstown Hospital Association and Ohio Nurses Association, March 31, 1972. 72-1 ARB 8129.

26. Cabell Huntington Hospital and National Union of Hospital and Health Care Employees, West Virginia Local 1199, April 6, 1978. 70 LA 979.

27. Puget Sound Hospital and Washington State Nurses Association, November 9, 1977. 77-2 ARB 8540, p. 5361.

28. Barberton Citizens Hospital, Inc. and American Federation of State, County and Municipal Employees, Local 684, March 9, 1973. 72-2 ARB 8694.

29. Schuylkill County (Pennsylvania) Commissioners and American Federation of State, County and Municipal Employees, April 18, 1979. LAIG 2328.

30. St. Joseph Hospital and Pennsylvania Nurses Association, December 21, 1976. 77-1 ARB 8016, p. 3076.

31. Franklin Hospital and Hospital and Institutional Workers Union, Local 250, February 14, 1968. BAHA-9.

32. *Ibid.*, p. 4.

33. Michael Reese Hospital and Medical Center and Health Employees Labor Program of Metropolitan Chicago (HELP), July 15, 1975, CHC-3, pp. 6, 7. See also St. Joseph Hospital, *op. cit.*

34. Brooklyn Methodist Hospital and Drug and Hospital Union, District 1199, December 6, 1977, p. 6. LVH.

35. New York University Institute of Rehabilitation Medicine and Drug and Hospital Union, Local 1199, p. 6. LVH.

36. See, for example, Samuel Merritt Hospital and Institutional Workers' Union, Local 250, July 12, 1977. BAHA-33.

37. Veterans Administration Hospital (Ill.) and American Federation of Government Employees, Local 2107, March 27, 1978. 758 GERR:37. See also Barberton (Ohio) Citizens Hospital, Inc., and American Federation of State, County and Municipal Employees, District 11, October 24, 1975. LAIG 1487.

38. Michael Reese Hospital and Medical Center and Hospital Employees Labor Program (HELP) of Metropolitan Chicago, February 21, 1976. CHC-7.

39. Rush-Presbyterian-St. Luke's Medical Center, Chicago, Illinois and Hospital Employees Labor Program (HELP) of Metropolitan Chicago, August 10, 1976, p. 6. CHC-10.

40. Dameron Hospital and California Nurses Association, December 30, 1975. 76-1 ARB 8102, p. 4942.

41. Appalachian Regional Hospitals, Inc. and International Union of District 50, United Mine Workers of America, Local 14585, April 21, 1970, 70-2 ARB 8515, pp. 4685, 4686.

42. Grace Hospital (Detroit, Mich.) and Service Employees International Union, Local 79, February 20, 1976. LAIG 1583.

43. Carney Hospital (Dorchester, Mass.) and Massachusetts Nurses Association, undated. LAIG 1632. In one case, a suspension of a part-time LPN was reversed even though she was ten hours past the deadline to file her request for a three-day leave, but took the leave anyway for important reasons. She nevertheless requested her leave one month prior to the time she requested off.

44. Michael Reese Hospital and General Service Employees Union, Local 73, March 25, 1976. CHC-8.

45. Veterans Administration Hospital (Asheville, N.C.) and American Federation of Government Employees, Local 446, March 28, 1977. LAIG 1817. See also Veterans Administration Hospital (Baltimore, Md.) and American Federation of Government Employees, July 3, 1972. 475 GERR:247.

46. Saint Francis Memorial Hospital (San Francisco, Calif.) and Service Employees International Union, Local 250, January 18, 1975. 64 LA 31 and 32.

47. *Ibid.,* 64 LA 33.

48. Methodist Hospital of Brooklyn and Hospital and Health Care Employees, Local 1199, June 9, 1977, pp. 10-11. LVH.

49. Michael Reese Hospital and Medical Center and Health Employees Labor Program (HELP) of Metropolitan Chicago, May 13, 1977, 1057 WCR A-8.

50. *Ibid.*

51. Flower Fifth Avenue Hospital and Drug and Hospital Union, Local 1199, May 17, 1973, p. 3. LVH.

52. New York City (N.Y.) Health and Hospitals Corp. and Individual Grievant, September 30, 1977. LAIG 1950.

53. Women's General Hospital (Cleveland, Ohio) and Service, Hospital, Nursing Home and Public Employees Union, Local 47, November 30, 1973. LAIG 1028.

54. There have been several court and EEOC decisions under the 1964 Civil Rights Act that have held an employer must maintain a work environment free from sexual, racial, or other forms of harassment.

55. Memorial Hospital and International Brotherhood of Teamsters, Chauffeurs, Warehousemen and Helpers, December 18, 1978. 71 LA 1252.

56. *Ibid.,* 71 LA 1255. See also Alta Bates Hospital and Service Employees International Union, Local 250, September 28, 1977, BAHA-35, which also involved harassment of employees.

57. Akron (Ohio) City Hospital and the American Federation of State, County and Municipal Employees, Local 684, February 15, 1974. LAIG 1049. A closely related case occurred at the same hospital. See Akron (Ohio) City Hospital and American Federation of State, County and Municipal Employees, Local 684, July 1, 1975. LAIG 1399.

58. Memphis and Shelby County (Tenn.) Hospital Authority and American Federation of State, County and Municipal Employees, Local 1733, March 11, 1976. LAIG 1645.

59. Barberton Citizens Hospital Co. and American Federation of State, County, and Municipal Employees, District Council, Local 684, August 18, 1972. 59 LA 280.

60. *Ibid.,* 59 LA 282.

61. Metropolitan Hospital and Health Centers (Detroit, Mich.) and Office and Professional Employees International Union, Local 42, April 29, 1975. LAIG 1376.

62. Akron (Ohio) City Hospital and American Federation of State, County and Municipal Employees, Local 684, September 15, 1976. LAIG 1719.

63. *Ibid.*

64. *Ibid.* Also see Michael Reese Hospital and Medical Center and Health Employees Labor Program (HELP) of Metropolitan Chicago, February 13, 1976. CHC-6; and Roosevelt Memorial Hospital (Chicago, Ill.) and Health Employees Labor Program (HELP) of Metropolitan Chicago, June 30, 1976. LAIG 1657.

65. New York University Medical Center and National Union of Hospital and Health Care Employees, District 1199, March 29, 1978, p. 5. LVH.

66. Barberton (Ohio) Citizens Hospital and American Federation of State, County and Municipal Employees, District Council 11, March 30, 1972. 72-1 ARB 8089, p. 3306.

67. Memphis and Shelby County (Tenn.) Hospital Authority, *op. cit.* September 27, 1977. LAIG 1965.

68. University Hospitals of Cleveland (Ohio) and Individual Grievant, September 29, 1977. LAIG 1992.

69. Metropolitan Hospital (Detroit, Mich.) and Office and Professional Employees International Union, Local 42, September 3, 1975. LAIG 1466.

70. *Ibid.*

71. Akron (Ohio) City Hospital and American Federation of State, County and Municipal Employees Union, Local 684, December 30, 1976. LAIG 1763.

72. Dameron Hospital Association and Hospital and Institutional Workers Union, Local 250, September 27, 1976. BAHA-29.

73. Veterans Administration Hospital (Canadaigua, N.Y.) and Service Employee International Union, Local 200, May 19. 1978. 767 WCR:25.

74. Merritt Hospital and Hospital and Institutional Workers Union, Local 250, October 26, 1960. BAHA-1. Pacific Medical Center and Hospital and Institutional Workers Union, Local 250, December 17, 1976. BAHA-31. French Hospital and California Nurses Association, December 18, 1978. BAHA-42.

75. Kaiser Hospital (Redwood City, Calif.) and Hospital and Institutional Workers, Local 250, September 8, 1975. LAIG 1514.

76. Kaiser Foundation Hospitals and Hospital and Institutional Workers Union, Local 250, February 22, 1971. 733 WCR:A-5.

77. University Hospitals of Cleveland and Individual Grievant, January 7, 1977. 77-1 ARB 8053. The same case in an abbreviated form is found at 700 GERR:15.

78. Youngstown Hospital Association and Service Employees International Union, Local 627, June 4, 1976. 76-2 ARB 8409.

79. Michael Reese Hospital and Medical Center and Hospital Employees Labor Program (HELP) of Metropolitan Chicago, November 11, 1974. CHC-2.

80. Pacific Medical Center and International Union of Operating Engineers, Local 39, September 6, 1974. BAHA-19.

81. *Ibid.*, p. 11.

82. Bixby Hospital (Adrian, Michigan) and Michigan Licensed Practical Nurses Association, June 3, 1976. LAIG 1633.

83. Michael Reese Hospital, *op. cit.,* p. 11.

84. Northwest General Hospital (Wis.) and Service and Hospital Employees International Union, Local 150, March 3, 1975. LAIG 1288.

85. Alta Bates Hospital and Hospital and Institutional Workers Union, Local 250, February 16, 1978. BAHA-38. In this case, the arbitrator sustained a discharge of the grievant for taking an empty bottle of wine from the hospital's kitchen. The bottle was going to be used for a home decoration. The employee's past work record was not a good one, however.

86. Morris J. Bernstein Institute of Beth Israel Medical Center and Hotel, Hospital, Nursing Home and Allied Health Services Union, Local 144, January 2, 1975. LVH.

87. Roosevelt Hospital and Hospital and Health Care Employees, District 1199, March 24, 1978. LVH.

88. Bronx-Lebanon Hospital and Hospital and Health Care Employees, District 1199, February 15, 1979. LVH.

89. Rush-Presbyterian-St. Luke's Medical Center and Hospital Employees Labor Program (HELP) of Metropolitan Chicago, July 29, 1975, p. 5. CHC-4.

90. Palm Harbor General Hospital and United Nurses' Associations of California (Palm Harbor Registered Nurses' Association), July 30, 1976. 76-2 ARB 8479.

91. Southwest Detroit Hospital Association and Service Employees International Union, Local 79, July 29, 1976. 1018 WCR:A-8 and A-9.

92. *Ibid.*, p. A-9.

93. Long Island Jewish Medical Center and Drug and Hospital Union, Local 1199, October 2, 1972, pp. 6, 7. LVH.

94. See Chapter 1.

95. Kaiser Foundation Hospitals and Building Service Employees International Union, Local 399, June 26, 1967. 67-2 ARB 8471.

96. St. Mary's Hospital and Medical Center (San Francisco, Calif.) and Hospital and Institutional Workers Union, Local 25, June 28, 1973. 60 LA 1144.

97. *Ibid.*, 60 LA 1145.

98. Veterans Administration Hospital (Marion, Ind.) and American Federation of Government Employees, Local 1020, May 23, 1977. 716 GERR:31.

99. St. Mary's Hospital, *op. cit.* 60 LA 1144.

100. Fairmont General Hospital and Retail, Wholesale and Department Store Union, June 20, 1972. 58 LA 1293.

101. *Ibid.* 58 LA 1295.

102. Abbott-Northwestern Hospital (Minneapolis, Minn.) and Hospital and Nursing Home Employees Union, Local 113, April 29, 1974. HMMM-1.

103. *Ibid.*, p. 5.

104. For example, in Illinois, state law forbids the discharge of an employee regardless of how many wage assignments he or she accumulates.

105. Clearfield (Pa.) Hospital and American Federation of State, County and Municipal Employees, Council 85, undated. LAIG 1758.

106. Maimonides Medical Center and Drug and Hospital Union, Local 1199, July 15, 1975. LVH.

107. *Ibid.*, pp. 5, 6.

108. Home and Hospital of the Daughters of Jacob and Drug and Hospital Union, Local 1199, May 6, 1974. LVH.

109. *Ibid.*, p. 4.

110. Dearborn Medical Center Hospital, Inc., and Service Employees International Union, Local 79, January 3, 1973. 493 GERR:B-7-B-9.

111. Children's Hospital of the East Bay and Hospital and Institutional Workers' Union, Local 250, August 28, 1971.

112. Evansville State Hospital and American Federation of State, County and Municipal Employees, April 14, 1969. 69-2 ARB 8585.

113. This section borrows heavily from Frank Elkouri and Edna Elkouri, *How Arbitration Works* (Washington, D.C.: Bureau of National Affairs, Inc., 1973), pp. 630-647.

114. Chicago (Ill.) Osteopathic Hospital and Chicago Osteopathic Nurses Association, March 17, 1976. LAIG 1610. See also Metropolitan Hospital (Detroit, Mich.) and Michigan Nurses Association, December 4, 1970. 71-1 ARB 8197. Audie Murphy Memorial Veterans Administration Hospital and American Federation of Government Employees, Local 3511, May 3, 1978. 763 GERR:32.

115. Veterans Administration Hospital (San Antonio, Texas) and American Federation of Government Employees, May 3, 1978. 772 GERR:27.

116. Elkouri and Elkouri, *op. cit.*, p. 638.

117. New York City Health and Hospital Corporation and Individual Grievant, March 22, 1976. LAIG 1611.

118. Grace Hospital, Northwest Unit (Detroit, Mich.) and Service Employees International Union, Local 79, November 10, 1971. 71-2 ARB 8676, pp. 5573, 5574.

Chapter 11

Seniority Issues in Arbitration

There is no doubt that seniority is important to health care workers, and it may be even more greatly prized in a time of economic downturn. Workers place so much importance on seniority because it is the only viable and equitable method known for resolving employee competition.[1] Some of the reasons are:

1. Length of service does reflect experience, and experience is an asset both to workers seeking advancement and to those who must manage or direct the work process.
2. Seniority systems provide employees with reasonable opportunities to plan their careers based on some judgment of personal preference and projected potentials. Thus, an employee can plan to achieve jobs or types of work that seem appropriate and possible, taking into account the relative seniority of others who are potential competitors.
3. A proper seniority system should also permit persons who are victims of job, process, or operation abandonment to choose a new career with consideration given for past service and past general work experience.
4. As workers grow older, there is a tendency for their immediate economic needs to increase; seniority tends to dovetail with this general condition. As workers grow still older, their needs tend to peak, but in many establishments their last years of employment determine the amount of their pension. A higher base during preretirement years often generates higher pensions and even determines the level of benefits to the surviving spouse.
5. As a worker advances, because his or her standard of living tends to increase, the impact of pay reduction or layoff creates economic hardship. The alternative for the older worker—planning one's life around the plant's minimum rate—would be unrealistic indeed.
6. An older worker tends to lose mobility. Many factors discourage older workers from moving. They cannot learn new ways so easily. Work and

193

social habits become fixed. Often changing jobs means changing residence, and departing from a well-established place in a community or neighborhood becomes more difficult as a worker (and the worker's family) ages. Thus, an employee's dependence on the place of employment tends to grow.

7. In balance, management does better with a stable work force. Retraining entails significant cost for management. Usually training is not accomplished by some formal process, but more often comprises exposure to the job, to the nearby jobs, to the specific work process, to the safety hazards—all this plus countless work practices. Seniority systems that are well conceived tend to give reasonable weight to stability factors.[2]

While some management representatives especially appreciate the last point, they tend to be suspicious when seniority is used to determine promotions. But management does not seem to question seriously the use of seniority as a basis for layoffs and recalls.

The benefits of seniority are a matter of contractual privilege, and not law. If seniority provisions do not exist in the collective agreement, arbitrators will not assume that the parties meant for them to be there.

SUPERSENIORITY

Superseniority frequently is negotiated into labor contracts as a reward, as well as a protection, for union stewards. Because it places the steward at the top of the seniority list within the seniority unit, it prevents management from laying off a group of workers in order to eliminate a steward who is thought to be causing labor difficulties. The steward's superseniority would necessitate a layoff of everyone in the seniority unit before the steward would be affected—clearly a suicidal policy. Since the job of union steward is usually not highly paid, superseniority may represent one of the key benefits of the position.

Limitations have been placed on the union's ability to negotiate superseniority clauses. The National Labor Relations Board (NLRB) has held that such clauses must be limited to granting job preferences for union stewards in layoff and recall situations.[3] In the *Dairylea* case, it was held that superseniority protections must be limited to those union officers who play an on-the-job role in the processing of employees' grievances and the administration of the contract.[4] However, the NLRB approved a superseniority clause that permitted a steward to bump a more senior employee in the same job classification rather than a less senior employee in a lower job classification.[5] In a similar case, the Board countenanced a superseniority clause that permitted a steward to bump the least senior employee in his job classification *on another shift* after the *steward's shift* had been eliminated.[6]

Superseniority has been found to violate the Taft-Hartley Act when it is given to strike replacements or strikers abandoning a strike, because it necessarily discourages organizing activities; no proof of the employer's intent to discriminate is required.[7]

LOSS OF SENIORITY

According to a survey of 1501 agreements that referred to seniority, 1,329, or almost nine out of ten, established one or more conditions for its loss.[8] The survey looked at those situations under which seniority was completely lost. These fell into three major groupings. Most prevalent was loss of seniority due to voluntary quit, discharge, or failure to be recalled (from a layoff), or, if recalled, failure to report following a layoff.[9]

Less prevalent, but still common, were provisions that called for loss of seniority related to leaves of absence or shorter unreported or inexcused absences from work. Some agreements defined a violation of the terms of a leave of absence as a voluntary quit.

A third category of seniority loss, occurring less often, consisted of miscellaneous conditions ranging from transfer out of the bargaining unit (see next section) to medical discharge.

Status of Seniority When an Employee Leaves the Bargaining Unit

As previously noted, seniority is not a right guaranteed by law; it exists only when granted by the collective agreement. Therefore, it follows that when an employee leaves the bargaining unit—to either another bargaining unit or to a nonbargaining unit position—that employee may also leave behind any accumulated seniority. A number of hospital contracts provide that an employee loses his or her entire accrued seniority (but not length of service, of course) upon leaving the bargaining unit. Some hospital agreements specify that an employee's seniority vests at the date he or she leaves the bargaining unit, but does not continue to accumulate while outside the unit. A few contracts actually permit seniority to grow while an employee is employed beyond the limits of the bargaining unit.

SENIORITY AND THE CIVIL RIGHTS ACT

No discussion of seniority would be complete without considering the impact of Civil Rights legislation on negotiated seniority clauses. Decisions by the EEOC (Equal Employment Opportunity Commission) and the courts have won notable gains for women and minorities. In addition, affirmative action programs, as mandated under Executive Order 11246, have prompted employers to seek out minorities and women for hiring and promotion. One basic problem arises when the traditional seniority rule of "last hired—first fired" has an adverse impact on women and minorities new to the organization, and consequently, possessing the least seniority. Such layoffs can negate an employer's effort in implementing affirmative action plans. A corollary problem develops when minorities and women are denied promotional opportunities because of a requirement that seniority play a partial or complete role in determining who will be promoted.

The Civil Rights Act makes explicit reference to seniority only at Section 703(h). This is an exclusionary clause that reads as follows:

> Notwithstanding any other provisions . . . it shall not be an unlawful employment practice for an employer to apply different standards . . . pursuant to a bona fide seniority or merit system . . . provided that such differences are not the result of an intention to discriminate because of race, color, religion, sex or national origin . . .

A series of recent Supreme Court decisions have served to interpret and clarify the application of Section 703(h) to seniority clauses existing in collective agreements. In *United Airlines, Inc.* v. *Evans,* [10] the high court held that the airline did not commit a present, continuing violation of Title VII by refusing to credit a female flight attendant with seniority accrued before she was rehired in 1972 in the absence of any contention that the airline's seniority system, neutral in its operation, discriminated against former female employees or other victims of past discrimination. The court also barred her claim under Section 703(h), because it interpreted that section to permit different terms of employment, pursuant to a bona fide seniority system, if any disparity is not the result of intentional discrimination.

Upon remand from the U.S. Supreme Court, the U.S. Court of Appeals for the Fifth Circuit ruled in *East Texas Motor Freight* v. *Rodriguez, et al.* [11] that the federal government has no power under Executive Order 11246 to seek seniority relief for the victims of discrimination in employment beyond that authorized under Title VII of the 1964 Civil Rights Act. If a seniority system is "bona fide" within the meaning of Section 703(h) of Title VII, it is also immune from challenge under E.O. 11246. The respondents, Mexican-Americans, brought suit against petitioners and their union, claiming that they had been rejected for line drivers under the contract. East Texas Motor Freight employed both city and over-the-road or "line" drivers. Respondents claimed that their rejection came about as a result of the company's "no transfer policy" based on separate seniority systems for line and city drivers. The Supreme Court found the respondents were not qualified to be line drivers, and the seniority system could not be attacked on the ground that these practices perpetuated past discrimination and forced minorities into the less desirable jobs to which they had been discriminatorily assigned.

The capstone case of the "seniority trilogy" was the Supreme Court's decision in *International Brotherhood of Teamsters* v. *United States, et al.* [12] The high court ruled seven to two that union seniority systems are immune from attack under Title VII, even though they may perpetuate the effects of past discrimination that predates the 1964 Civil Rights Act. Justice Stewart, writing for the majority, found that when it adopted Title VII, Congress intended to immunize seniority systems "even where the employer's pre-Act discrimination resulted in whites having greater existing seniority rights than Negroes."

The case, similar to *East Texas Motor Freight,* involved the trucking industry's widespread practice of establishing separate bargaining units for city and line driver jobs. Under this system city drivers who wished to transfer to more lucrative line driver jobs had to forfeit their accumulated seniority.

Justice Stewart wrote that although a seniority system tends to perpetuate the effect of prior discrimination, Congress's intent was not to "destroy or water down the vested rights of employees simply because their employer had engaged in discrimination prior to the passage of the Act." The Supreme Court rejected the contention of the Justice Department and the EEOC that any seniority system that locks in the effects of past discrimination is not "bona fide" within the meaning of Section 703(h).[13]

The total impact of these three Supreme Court cases is yet to be felt. However, it seems clear that the court is saying that a seniority system is "bona fide" even though it may apply different terms of employment, and even though it perpetuates the consequences of pre-1964 Civil Rights Act discrimination, so long as it operates in a neutral fashion and is not intentionally designed to discriminate on the basis of race, color, sex, religion, or national origin. Of course, seniority systems initiated after the effective date of Title VII must not operate in a discriminatory manner.

DEPARTMENTAL VERSUS PLANT-WIDE SENIORITY

Ever since the 1968 district court ruling in *Quarles* v. *Phillip Morris, Inc.,*[14] departmental seniority systems that perpetuate past racial discrimination were assumed to be prohibited under Title VII. In a later case, the Supreme Court ruled that a remedy to such discrimination was to provide retroactive seniority to all employees affected, back to their date of application for work.[15]

However, in a case following the *Teamsters* v. *U.S.* case, the U.S. Court of Appeals for the Fourth Circuit rejected the contention made by a group of black drivers that the seniority system contained in the company's contract with Teamsters Local 71 in Charlotte, North Carolina, violated the 1866 Civil Rights Act (42 U.S.C. Section 1981) because it perpetuated discrimination in effect when they were hired prior to Title VII's effective date. As the court stated, "Both black and white employees were subject to loss of their former departmental seniority and they had to start at the bottom of the seniority list for line drivers even though they may have had more employment seniority than line drivers higher on the ladder." The appellate court relied on the Supreme Court's opinion in *Teamsters* v. *U.S.* that employees cannot obtain seniority relief under the 1866 Act that is not available under Title VII.[16]

However, the U.S. Court of Appeals for the Fifth Circuit said it would adopt a case-by-case approach in determining whether departmental seniority systems are subject to attack under Title VII of the 1964 Civil Rights Act. The court found that a seniority system in effect at the Birmingham, Alabama plants of the Stockham Valves & Fittings Company presented black employees the option of "seniority suicide" if they desired to transfer to more desirable jobs. It maintained that the Supreme Court's ruling in *Teamsters* v. *U.S.*, which immunized "bona fide" seniority systems, must be viewed in the factual context of the trucking industry, where separate bargaining units for line drivers and city drivers are common practice. The Fifth Circuit concluded that the seniority system at the Stockham plants had its genesis in racial discrimination, which was standard operating procedure in factories throughout the South.[17]

These cases suggest that further clarification will be needed to determine the legal status of departmental seniority. However, just because an employer-hospital has a departmental seniority system, it should not be assumed the system is *ipso facto* illegal. But until legal clarification is forthcoming, it is suggested that unions and hospitals consult their attorneys when contemplating changes in their seniority clauses.

ARBITRATION, CIVIL RIGHTS, AND SENIORITY ISSUES

As noted in Chapter 1, the *Gardner-Denver* case established that arbitration cases are not necessarily dispositive of civil rights violations. There is no deferral policy in civil rights cases as exists with the NLRB. However, occasionally arbitrators will rule on civil rights issues that arise under collective bargaining agreements. Two such cases (though not hospital cases) dealing with seniority issues are summarized below.

The first of these occurred at the Diamond Power Specialty Corps. Mirror, Control and Nuclear-Fossil plants in Lancaster, Ohio.[18] The union—United Steelworkers of America, Local 4708—was one of three locals that represented employees at the plants. Each local had a separate contract with separate plant-wide seniority provisions. The employer was a federal contractor, and a prior onsite review of its operations had led Defense Department officials to conclude that female employees hired after the company centralized its hiring operations were concentrated in lower-paying jobs in the plant, and that these workers constituted "an affected class" entitled to use company-wide seniority in filling job vacancies. Arbitrator Theodore High rejected a union grievance protesting three job awards based on company-wide rather than plant-wide seniority as called for in the agreement. He concluded that a federal contractor's obligations under Executive Order 11246 superceded the seniority provisions of a union contract. Moreover, he observed that remedial actions ordered by Defense Department compliance officers must be "held paramount to the provisions of the labor agreement" even though they may "drastically alter" its terms.[19]

In a case similar to the *Weber v. Kaiser Aluminum* decision, an issue developed in 1973 where a black worker was selected for an apprenticeship vacancy over a white employee with more seniority.[20] While both candidates were equally qualified, the company—a federal contractor—acknowledged that the black worker was selected under an affirmative action program designed to increase the number of minorities at the mill. Arbitrator F. Jay Taylor upheld the assignment, contending that the employer, International Paper Company's Southern Kraft Division in Bastrop, Louisiana, had no choice but to comply with federally imposed equal opportunity laws and Executive Order 11246. The arbitrator ruled that E.O. 11246 supersedes the seniority requirements of the local contract. In his decision, he claimed it was his responsibility to "consider the obligations of the equal employment policies of this nation, and the many laws and executive orders which spell out that policy," even though his authority under the contract was narrowly defined. He concluded, therefore, that the company's effort to comply with federal requirements and remedy past discrimination "is exempt from contractual obligations."

It should be noted here that a substantial number of arbitrators believe their fidelity is to the collective bargaining agreement, the source of their authority, and thus will refuse to sustain laws and/or executive orders that are at variance with the precise terms of the contract.[21] In any case, parties to arbitration should be alerted to this difference in opinion before selecting an arbitrator.

PROMOTIONS

Though most hospitals do not take serious issue with the use of seniority to determine layoffs or recalls, they do question using the seniority principle by itself to determine promotions. Management would prefer that promotions be based on merit and ability rather than on seniority, except where the qualifications of the employees are relatively equal. Unions, on the other hand, seriously doubt management's ability to judge accurately the relative qualifications of employees, and thus claim seniority is more equitable and objective.

The contractual provisions that attempt to reconcile these positions fall into four separate categories, according to the weight placed on seniority. These are sum-marized below.

1. *Strict seniority clause*. In this one the employer must give preference to the employee with the longest service, without regard to any other considerations.

2. *Relative ability clause*. Such a clause provides that seniority is a considera-tion in determining who will get a promotion only if the senior employee's ability, physical fitness, competence, etc. is "relatively equal" or "substantially equal" or "equal" to that of junior employees. For example:

> When there is an opening to be filled by promotion, employees in that division should be considered on the basis of their seniority and job qualifications. When job qualifications are approximately equal, then the employee with the greatest seniority shall be given the opportunity. Only in the event an employee with less seniority has superior job qualifications shall he be entitled to the promotion.[22]

3. *Sufficient ability clause*. Under this clause it is necessary to show only that the senior employee can do the job. Preference is given automatically to the senior job bidder. Thus, even though a junior job candidate may be much more qualified for a job, if the senior bidder can perform the work, comparing their relative abilities is unnecessary and improper.

> When a vacancy exists in a job classification covered by the contract, and the senior applicant for the job can meet the standards and qualifica-tions required to perform that particular job competently, the senior applicant for the job, who meets the above requirements, shall be offered the promotion, even though the senior applicant cannot meet the requirements for the next higher job, and may not be the most competent applicant for the job.[23]

4. *Hybrid clause*. This clause takes into account both seniority and relative ability. Usually, however, the weight or relative importance of these two factors is left purposely ambiguous to give management greater flexibility in dealing with various promotional situations. For example, "In giving preference for promo-tions and advancement, the company shall consider among other things, depart-mental seniority of service, ability and competence."[24]

Job Posting

The most common way to advertise promotional opportunities to bargaining unit members is through the posting and bidding technique. Frequently contracts will call for posting a notice on the bulletin board for a specified period of time, often three to five working days. Normally the posting will specify the job title, rate of pay or labor grade, and a brief job description. Usually if no one answers the posting and bids for the job, management has the right to attempt to fill the vacancy from outside the organization.

Disputes will sometimes arise when the employer fails to post a position opening and the union objects. In one such case, a hospital was held to have violated the contractual obligation to post an announcement of a vacancy in its maintenance department.[25] The hospital argued that although the contract did require posting and giving notice to the union of the vacancy, management had not always followed this policy and the union had not complained of deviations. While sustaining the union, the arbitrator noted that a past practice of tolerating contract violations can be honored only if the contract language is unclear or ambiguous. He, therefore, directed the hospital to post all vacancies. However, absent language to the contrary, a union has no authority to decide when there is a vacancy to post, or tell a hospital that it must make a vacancy and fill it when an employee retires.[26]

When a hospital makes an error in posting job requirements, it has the obligation to repost the position with the correct requirements, so that all eligible employees have an opportunity to bid for the position.[27] In one case, although the grievant was the only bidder who met all the requirements in the erroneous posting, she was not entitled to any monetary reimbursement because no one should have been selected on the basis of the erroneous posting.[28]

In another case, the state department of health (which was also the agency that certified the employer) recommended that a medical facility establish a new position, that of restorative care nurse. The employer therefore had the right to unilaterally establish the new position. Instead of posting for the new position from members of the employees' association, it hired a trained person to fill the vacancy.[29] The arbitrator found that the educational level required for this new position was an LPN. The classification of LPN was under a different bargaining unit than the one represented by the union in the grievance. Therefore, the employer's failure to post a position not covered by the contract between the association and management could not violate their agreement.[30]

Qualifications

A hospital was held not to have violated the contract when it failed to choose either of the two most senior applications for the position of inservice director.[31] Under a "relative ability" clause in effect, the evidence indicated that the ability of these two applicants was not relatively equal to that of the junior employee chosen. The hospital *did* violate the collective bargaining agreement when it did not promote the third most senior applicant of the four total applicants. Arbitrator O'Brien held that prior evaluations of the candidates were more objective than the recommendations of the director of nursing, the hospital superintendent, and the retiring inservice director.[32]

Another hospital's selection was reversed by an arbitrator under a hybrid promotion clause that provided "when a permanent position is created or vacated, it shall be posted for bid for five days and the senior qualified applicant shall be appointed."[33] The hospital had selected a candidate who bid for the job but was not a member of the bargaining unit. The hospital had based its decision on an alleged past practice that had established that where applicants were unequally qualified, the job was given to the best qualified candidate, regardless of whether he or she was a bargaining unit member. The arbitrator observed that the contract stated that vacancies were to be filled by the senior qualified applicant, and since it did not explicitly state that seniority must be determined solely within the unit, the arbitrator had to look to how the provision had been interpreted in the past. Arbitrator Sinclitico found:

> The evidence clearly shows that the past practice has been to fill vacancies with qualified unit members and that only when there are no qualified unit members who bid on the job would the vacancy be filled by someone outside the unit. Because there were unit member applicants who met the qualifications for the position as set by the employer, the arbitrator finds the employer violated the agreement as it has been interpreted by past practice by hiring outside the unit. Under the circumstances, the fact that the (successful) candidate (outside the unit) was the best qualified is irrelevant as there were qualified applicants within the unit.[34]

Under a relative ability clause calling for preference to seniority only where qualifications (ability and fitness to perform) were equal, a grievant seeking the position of in-house account representative was properly turned down where the contract provided that supervisory judgment was the sole criterion of ability and fitness.[35] The medical center's authority included the right to "hire, layoff, promote and transfer employees." Absent arbitrariness, unreasonableness, capriciousness, or discrimination in its judgment, the arbitrator found that management had acted correctly in refusing to promote the grievant because she lacked the requisite ability to perform the job.

Management was also sustained when it filled a vacant position by hiring an outsider over a bargaining unit employee. The hospital had a contractual requirement calling for a "merit promotion policy."[36] In denying the union's grievance, the arbitrator noted that the policy, which directed management "to utilize to the maximum extent the skills and talents of its employees," gave the hospital a great deal of flexibility in making personnel decisions. He commented that its fundamental objective was to find the "best qualified person available for the position." Under the agreement, the merit promotion policy also stated that promotion was only one method that could be used to fill positions and management could also use outside hires (appointments). The hospital, therefore, was using two methods to try to fill the position—promotion and appointment. The appointment method triumphed as an outsider was hired, but the duality of methods did not violate the merit promotion policy.

In another promotion case, a hospital had four separate occupational groupings: (1) building service, (2) laundry, (3) dietary, and (4) patient care. These were considered by the hospital to be separate departments covering separate occupational groupings.[37] A permanent, full-time vacancy was created in the linen room (under building service occupations) when a linen room worker retired. A woman who had previously held the job was promoted to the position. Her promotion was contested by a laundry worker (under laundry occupations) who had greater seniority. The contract provided that "when a permanent full-time vacancy occurs in a *higher classification of work and within the department* for which a regular full time or regular part time employee in a *lower classification of work* is qualified, seniority, together with skill and ability, will be considered." Arbitrator Lauritzen reasoned that the linen room worker job held by the person originally promoted was a lower classification of work than the grievant's job, on the basis of pay differential. The grievant worked in the laundry department, a different department from that in which the vacancy occurred. Moreover, the promoted employee was shown to have the necessary skill and ability to do the job.

In another case, a clinic had a relative ability clause calling for vacancies to be filled by the most senior employee "provided said employee is qualified. . . ."[38] When management awarded the job of private duty nurse in a physician's office to one of four qualified applicants, but not the senior bidder, the arbitrator decided that management had erred. He stated that the evidence established that the physician indicated "all four would make excellent office nurses," and because all were qualified, the senior nurse should have been given the job.

However, a mental health center had the right to award the posted job of "nursing assistant—male" to a male applicant instead of to a more senior female applicant under a "balanced-staff" concept that provided for a male/female staffing ratio roughly equivalent to patient population.[39] Although the collective agreement was silent regarding the balanced-staff concept, the arbitrator nevertheless upheld the center because he noted that: (1) the contract indicated that seniority was not the sole consideration in filling vacancies—rather "job requirements and qualifications shall be part of the posting;" (2) there was no issue of discrimination involved; and (3) the fact that male and female nursing assistants had been cross-assigned temporarily to cover for short-term vacancies did not establish that there was no need to maintain historical male/female ratio of nursing assistant for the personal care of patients.

Nonseniority Factors in Promotion Decisions

According to a survey by the United States Department of Labor,[40] nine-tenths of the collective agreements having promotion provisions specified those factors which, in addition to seniority, would be considered in promotion decisions. These included (in order of frequency):

1. skill and ability,
2. physical fitness,
3. education or training,
4. tests or examinations,
5. qualifications (not further defined), and
6. other.

These six factors are discussed below.

1. *Skill and ability.* These are factors that presumably qualify an individual to perform the job in question. What is meant by skill and ability may or may not be spelled out in the contract. When definitions are given, they may turn on very vague concepts such as "efficiency," "knowledge," "experience," "capacity to perform," and so on. Management normally uses a variety of means to assess skill and ability. Some rely on supervisory opinion. However, opinion without factual support will be suspect. But where several levels of supervisors, each familiar with the performance of the bidders and with the requirements of the job, all reach a unanimous decision, this can be persuasive.

Sometimes supervisors use performance reviews or merit rating plans to document their opinions of workers' skills and abilities. Arbitrators will give little weight to performance evaluations that focus on personal traits; they prefer measures that evaluate such job-related traits as ability, skill, and efficiency.

Production records can provide objective evidence of output or accuracy. Attendance records likewise may serve as tangible and objective evidence for assessing ability and qualifications, especially where a job carries a high degree of responsibility.

An employee's disciplinary record may be given some consideration. The disciplinary record reflects an employee's ability to perform the job, as measured by maturity, reliability, and a sense of responsibility. For example, in one case, a hospital was held to have violated its contract when it refused to consider a senior employee's bid for an assistant food service supervisor position because of her attendance record, where: (1) the contract "mandated" that the employee "with present ability to perform the work—shall be chosen in seniority order," and (2) denial of promotion is not a proper form of discipline.[41] The arbitrator reasoned that although the hospital was justified in wanting to hire supervisors upon whose attendance it could rely, it could not include good attendance within the term "present ability" when filling job vacancies. "A tendency to infraction of Hospital rules may and should be penalized, but that tendency does not detract from the grievant's present ability to do the job."[42]

Finally, actual job experience is a tangible and objective factor in determining fitness and ability. Naturally, if experience is not important to the job, it will be given little or no weight.

2. *Physical fitness.* While many contracts specify fitness, either physical or mental, some arbitrators argue that the term "ability" includes these concepts by implication. Current health records may serve as objective evidence of fitness and ability. Usually, unless the contract prohibits it, management has also been accorded the right to order a physical exam to determine physical fitness. Although management cannot order a physical exam arbitrarily, capriciously, or unreasonably, it may be obligated to protect the health of all employees, even those who are willing to perform the physically exerting work.

3. *Education or training.* Technical training gained through a trade school, union, or company-sponsored training program is highly important in determining fitness and ability, if such training is related to the job requirements. Formal education, such as high school or college, may also be relevant. Where the contract does not specify a formal education requirement for a particular job, arbitrators have taken several approaches to determine whether the employer may consider this factor, among them:

1. Management may require a high school education where the job is complex and carries with it automatic progressions through several classifications involving additional responsibility.
2. The formal educational background of the employee may be considered along with other factors.
3. The employer may not automatically disqualify an employee for want of a formal education, but may consider formal education in evaluating the employee's training and experience.
4. The employer violates the contract by denying a promotion to senior employees solely on the basis that they lacked a high school education or its equivalent.[43]

4. *Tests or examinations.* Even though there may not be a specific contract provision covering it, management has been accorded the right to give reasonable and appropriate written, oral, performance, and aptitude tests, as an aid in determining the ability of competing employees.

Arbitrators generally hold that tests used to determine ability must be: (a) specifically related to the requirements of the job; (b) fair and reasonable; (c) administered in good faith and without discrimination; and (d) properly evaluated.[44]

5. *Other factors*. Factors such as the sex, age, or personal characteristics of an employee are considered suspicious by most arbitrators and may also be violations of the Civil Rights Act.

DOWNWARD JOB BIDDING

Normally employees seek positions that represent a promotion to them in terms of expanded job responsibility, pay, or both. However, there are times when employees find themselves on a career path that seems to represent a "dead end." Or perhaps simply wish to reduce work load responsibility. For these and other reasons, they seek a lower level position. These downward moves are occasionally contested by hospitals or even by the union as prohibited under the agreement.

In one such situation, a hospital posted a clerk typist job in the Medical Administration unit.[45] A number of employees, including the grievant, bid for the job. Some time after the close of the bidding period, Mrs. T_____ requested the job. She was presently classified as GS-5, but the job of clerk typist was rated as GS-4. Mrs. T_____ was awarded the position by the hospital.

The grievant and union sought a decision to force the hospital to make its selection from the bid list. However, the arbitrator brushed aside their request because he pointed out that it was a *demotion action* and not a *promotion*. Under the guidelines for the merit promotion program, the hospital was not under obligation to make demotions by the same method as promotions, i.e., by posting the job opening. Moreover, the guidelines give the employer the right to deviate from the posting procedure. In addition, the arbitrator observed that previous jobs had been filled by demotion, without complying with posting and bidding procedures.

RECALLS FROM LAYOFF

Seniority, either by itself or in combination with an employee's past performance or ability, is the usual standard for determining the sequence of employees recalled from a layoff. When straight seniority controls, the administration's problems are minimized. However, when seniority is combined with job performance (or a related measure of ability), there are more problems in the application of the recall provisions.

Such a situation developed in a California hospital, where seven employees (the grievants in the case) were laid off due to a drop in the hospital census.[46] Several were laid off out of seniority sequence. At a meeting between the hospital and union, it was agreed that the temporary reduction in force was proper, but it was further agreed that the grievants would be recalled as soon as work was available. Later the hospital hired some nurse aides. While the hospital argued this was a different job classification from that held by the grievants, the arbitrator observed that the aides were hired into a department where there was only one job classification, namely, "nurse attendants." Thus he held that no distinction was made between Nurse Aide 1 or Nurse Aide 2 or between those classified as LVN. Moreover, the wage scale for all three was the same.

In another case a clinic failed to recall an employee laid off from its x-ray department, and instead hired a new replacement when it learned that the laid-off employee was pregnant.[47] The contract provided that the "Employer recognized the principle of seniority in layoffs, recalls and promotions—provided that the employee has the qualifications and ability to efficiently perform the required work." Although the employer argued that it had refused to reinstate the grievant because the x-ray equipment could endanger her fetus, it had nevertheless, in the past, permitted other pregnant women to work in that department out of personal and financial consideration, and the arbitrator held there was no reason why the same standard should not be applied to the grievant. Moreover, the evidence failed to establish the employer's claim that it would have been impossible to work out a rearrangement of job duties that would have permitted the grievant to avoid performance of dangerous functions.[48]

Due to a physicians' "walkout" occasioned by significant increases in malpractice insurance rates, a hospital's patient load fell and other staff layoffs were ordered. A number of hospital attendants were laid off, including the grievant. Although the grievant eventually was recalled to work, three junior hospital attendants had been recalled several days prior to her return. While the hospital claimed it had tried to reach the grievant but that she was not home, the arbitrator pointed out that many other recalls had been made without regard to seniority. This indicated to Arbitrator Koven that management had not really tried to call employees back to work on the basis of their seniority. Accordingly, the grievant was awarded back pay for the time the junior employees had been working.[49]

LAYOFFS

One of the most important uses of seniority is to determine the order of layoffs. A survey by the Bureau of National Affairs indicated that layoff provisions are included in 88 percent of 400 sample contracts analyzed. Seniority is *a factor* in selecting employees for layoff in 83 percent of the contracts—90 percent in manufacturing industries, and 72 percent in nonmanufacturing industries. Seniority is the *sole* consideration in selecting employees for layoff in 46 percent of the sample contracts, a *determining* factor in 26 percent, and a *secondary* factor in 10 percent.[50] When seniority is not the sole determinant, contracts usually will call for seniority in combination with some measure of past performance, such as fitness and physical ability.

Such a situation existed at a clinic in southwest Virginia.[51] The employer operated health clinics at four separate locations in the state. The grievant was originally hired in 1972 as an x-ray technician—*unregistered,* at the Big Stone Gap clinic. He later accepted an assignment in which he worked in all four clinics on a fill-in basis, with travel-time pay and mileage, but no change in his title or wage level. Meanwhile, the employer hired another person to work at the Big Stone Gap clinic as an x-ray technician—*registered.* When patient volume dropped off suddenly in 1973, a number of clinic employees, including the grievant, were laid off. The grievant, exercising his bumping rights under the contract, continued his employment at the same wage level, but at the Hanging Rock clinic, a location much further from his home.

The contract provided that in the event a layoff is necessary at a particular clinic, the layoff should be made within the department at the particular clinic, based on seniority. It was clear the grievant had more seniority than the registered x-ray technician. The arbitrator found that a distinction between a registered or unregistered technician is not required by law or by the parties' contract, and the duties and responsibility of each position were not consistently separated in clinical practice. Nor did the arbitrator see much merit in the employer's contention that the grievant's exercise of his right to bump precluded his reinstatement at Big Stone Gap. Thus the arbitrator ordered the grievant reinstated at Big Stone Gap.

But in another case, a grievant was held to be properly laid off by the hospital. The grievant, prior to his layoff on February 10, 1977, was employed in the engineering department as a maintenance engineer, doing general and preventive maintenance on hospital equipment.[52] Contractual provisions covering employment cutbacks stated: "In the event of layoffs due to job elimination or lack of sufficient work, seniority rule within the job family must be adhered to. . . ." The grievant was the least senior employee in the job family of "maintenance and engineering."

The union argued that the grievant had been laid off because of bias on the part of the chief engineer. The union also contended that the work previously performed by the grievant had not been substantially reduced. As far as the latter argument, the arbitrator pointed out that one must look to reduction of work in the engineering department and not to reduction of work of any particular individual. Moreover, the arbitrator concluded that there was no evidence that the grievant had been discriminatorily laid off, particularly in light of the fact he was eligible for rehire.

One interesting layoff case involved deciding the appropriate seniority date of two affected nurses.[53] Because of reduced needs in the hospital's surgery department, two nurses, M____ and C____, were laid off. These two nurses had more seniority as *registered nurses* at the hospital than did two other registered nurses in that department (though the issue of departmental versus hospital-wide seniority was not an issue in this case). However, the other two nurses had more continuous service as employees than did M____ and C____. Thus the issue was whether a registered nurse's seniority under the contract dated from the first day of service within the hospital in any capacity, or from the first day of employment within the hospital as a registered nurse.

The contract provided in part that "Where competency and ability of nurses are equal in the judgment of the Hospital administration, accumulated length of service with a given Hospital shall be a controlling consideration in redirection of force or re-employment. . . ." Arbitrator Myers found that this provision could be interpreted to favor either the association or the employer.

However, in finding for the hospital, the arbitrator cited a past practice regarding the status of employees. Those who had prior continuing employment at the hospital in other capacities are not considered as probationary employees during their first 90 days of employment as nurses. The arbitrator found this established practice to be especially significant because the provision regarding probationary employees was found in the same article with the language cited previously.[54]

BUMPING

Bumping is normally defined as the process where, under the seniority provisions, a more senior employee displaces a less senior employee in the same or a lower-rated job classification, provided that employee can perform the job into which he or she moves. This process is usually triggered by a cutback of hospital staff.

In a twist on the usual situation, two employees who were laid off by a hospital sought to bump into a higher classification than the one they held at the time of layoff.[55] The contract provided, in part, that "in the event of a layoff, employees shall be laid off in the reverse order of their seniority provided the employees retained are qualified and willing to perform available work." The grievants contended that there were no employees with less seniority in equal or lower classifications, but there were junior employees in a higher classification. They argued that the contract did not restrict them from bumping upward, particularly in light of the fact that the seniority unit was bargaining unit-wide.

Although the hospital counsel submitted a large number of arbitration cases as precedent, Arbitrator Howard Brown noted that a difference of opinion existed among arbitrators. He noted:

> While these cases cannot be entirely reconciled, those which have permitted upward bumping on a lay-off have done so on the basis of specific wording of the collective agreement involved, or on the premise that where the collective agreement has not otherwise restricted such movement, it can be allowed. On the other hand, arbitrators have held

that unless the specific right is found within the collective agreement to permit upward bumping, the right does not exist and cannot be inferred. Other arbitrators have referred to the possibility of inferring the right to displace junior employees without restriction, but subject to the question of whether such right is restricted or inconsistent with the collective agreement as a whole.[56]

In denying the union's arguments, the arbitrator pointed out that the grievants were, in effect, seeking a promotion, and that under the agreement the requirements for promotion were different from those covering layoffs and bumping.

A hospital was reversed, however, when it refused to allow seven part-time nurses in the medical-surgical ward to bump junior employees either in the nursery section of obstetrics or in the outpatient department, during a decline in the number of hospital patients. The contract was silent regarding qualifications required to perform work in any hospital unit.[57] Evidence established that nurses were taken from their regularly assigned units and placed in other units at the discretion of the hospital. The arbitrator ruled that an employee must be given the appointment to work in areas where they have worked in place of junior employees.

INTEGRATING SENIORITY LISTS

Whenever two hospitals merge or consolidate, problems sometimes arise over how to put together the separate seniority lists in a way that is fair to all employees concerned. Labor arbitrators have identified and used five major criteria for accomplishing seniority mergers.[58] These are:

1. the surviving-group principle,
2. the length-of-service principle,
3. the follow-the-work principle,
4. the absolute-rank principle, and
5. the ratio-rank principle.[59]

Each criterion is explained briefly below.

1. *The surviving-group principle.* This principle states that the employees of the acquiring or purchasing hospital should receive seniority consideration over the employees of the purchased or acquired hospital. In applying this principle, the employees of the purchased or acquired hospital are placed at the bottom of the seniority list. For obvious reasons, this principle has not been generally supported

by arbitrators as a fair and equitable means of merging seniority lists. Arbitrators use it only when the contract forces the principle to be applied.

2. *The length-of-service principle.* This principle states that when two seniority lists are merged, the final list is arrived at by ranking each individual according to length-of-service (or hire date). Like the surviving-group principle, it is easy to apply and it is in general harmony with the definition of seniority found in most labor contracts. However, where there is a considerable difference in either the average length of service or the degree of employment between the merging groups, the use of this principle alone may give one group a windfall at the expense of the other.[60]

3. *The follow-the-work principle.* The follow-the-work principle states that employees are given the opportunity to perform the same work they did when their organization was merged (provided it can still be identified), with the seniority rights to such work protected by continuation of the separate seniority lists. If the work becomes merged, the seniority lists may be integrated into a single list on a ratio basis, representing the amount of work brought to the consolidation by each group of employees. The main difficulty with the technique is that it sometimes is difficult to judge the percentage of work that each group brings to the consolidation.

4. *The absolute-rank principle.* Implementing this principle calls for retention of the same seniority rank one held at the time of merger. For example, in a consolidation of two hospitals, two employees would be ranked one, two employees ranked two, and so on. This system prevents windfalls to some employees and losses to others—where the groups to be merged are equal in size. But where the groups to be merged are of a different size, application of the principle may result in serious inequities.

5. *The ratio-rank principle.* In this system the two seniority lists are integrated by establishing a ratio based on the number of employees in each group to be merged, and assigning places on the new seniority list according to this ratio. Thus, if seniority list A has 200 employees and seniority list B has only 100 employees, the ratio is two to one. Therefore, of the first three places on the new seniority list, two are allocated to the first two employees on the A list and one is allocated to the first employee on the B list. Places 3, 4, and 5 on the new list are allocated to the third and fourth people on the A list and to the second person on the B list. This scheme is followed until all the A and B employees are placed on the new list.[61]

This method has an advantage over the absolute-rank method insofar as it can be used with different-sized groups. There are two difficulties, however: (1) the merged seniority list is not ranked according to length of service, which contradicts the usual definition of seniority, and (2) several employees may have equal rights to the same place on the merged list. Arbitrators have tended to use this principle to modify the length-of-service method, rather than as a sole determinant.

In one case involving the merging of seniority lists, a clerk typist had worked at Oneida County Hospital since November 3, 1957.[62] When this hospital was ordered to phase out some of its facilities in 1968, the employee on December 22, 1969 negotiated an employment contract with Rome Hospital. Her seniority date was given as November 3, 1957, the same date she had at Oneida. When her seniority date was posted, several other employees at Rome Hospital complained that her seniority date violated Article XV of the contract that provided, in part, "Seniority means an employee's length of continuous service with the employer since his last date of hire." In denying the clerk typist her seniority date, the arbitration panel agreed that "service" can only be established through employment at the Rome Hospital, and that conferring the earlier seniority date violated the agreement and had an adverse impact on employee morale.

United Hospitals, Inc. was formed in 1972 as a result of the merger of Miller Hospital and St. Luke's Hospital.[63] United has operated these two hospitals, located in St. Paul, Minnesota, as two divisions providing general hospital services. Prior to the merger, the union had separate contracts with Miller and St. Luke's since 1972. But since 1973, the union and United have had a series of single contracts covering the nonprofessional staff of both divisions in certain classifications, including the central supply room. The Children's Hospital of St. Paul since 1974 has had a management affiliation between it and United, whereby United furnishes administrative, executive, and some staff functions and services to Children's. The union also has a contract with Children's which is virtually identical to that of United.

In June 1978, United placed L____ and W____, central supply room aides at Children's Memorial Hospital, and assigned them a number 2 and number 7 place on the central supply room's seniority list. Their seniority was dovetailed with that of United's existing seniority list on the basis of their length of service at Children's (length-of-service principle). The union claimed that L____ and W____ should be placed at the bottom of the seniority list (surviving-group principle).

The arbitrator held, however, that neither method was acceptable. He opted rather for the "ratio-rank principle" ". . . which gives the optimum weight to the factors of length of service and also to employee rank on the seniority list at a minimum depreciation in the value of seniority to both groups of employees . . . is the most appropriate method of merging the two seniority lists in this case."[64]

This chapter documents the central position of seniority in labor-management matters. Seniority may regulate layoffs, recalls from layoff, promotions, choice of shift, overtime assignments, and as we have just seen, even play an important role in the merger of two or more seniority units. Workers place seniority on the same level of importance as protection from arbitrary treatment or discharge. Small wonder then that so many grievances involving interpretation and/or application of a contract provision dealing with seniority reach arbitration.

NOTES

1. Ben Fisher, "Seniority Is Healthy," in *Proceedings of the 1976 Annual Spring Meeting of the Industrial Relations Research Association*, May 6-8, 1976, Denver, Colorado, p. 498.

2. *Ibid.*, pp. 498-499.

3. Dairylea Cooperative Inc., (1975) 1974-75 CCH NLRB ¶16,036.

4. In a recent decision, the NLRB has ruled that recall or retention of union officials under a superseniority clause may be permissible for those officials involved in the administration of a collective bargaining contract or grievance process, but not for those whose duties are not thus involved. At issue in the case was a sergeant-at-arms for the union hall and a trustee in charge of the hall. The majority of the NLRB found that neither's duties were directly related to the representation of unit employees through the administration of the existing bargaining contract or grievance process. American Can Company, 1979-80 CCH NLRB ¶16,277.

5. Hospital Service Plan of New Jersey, (1976) 1976-77 CCH NLRB ¶17,683.

6. McGregor-Werner, Inc. and IATSE, Local 780, (1976) 1976-77 CCH NLRB ¶17,682.

7. Resistor Corp., (U.S. 1963) 47 Labor Cases ¶18,249.

8. U.S. Department of Labor, Bureau of Labor Statistics, *Administration of Seniority* (Washington, D.C.: U.S. Government Printing Office, 1972, Bulletin 1425-14), p. 25.

9. *Ibid.*

10. United Airlines, Inc. v. Evans, (U.S. 1977) 14 EPD ¶7577.

11. East Texas Motor Freight Systems v. Rodriguez et al., (U.S. 1977) 14 EPD ¶7578.

12. Teamsters v. United States, (U.S. 1977) 14 EPD ¶7579.

13. In a recent decision, the U.S. District Court for the District of Columbia ruled on a question left open in *Teamsters v. United States*. The open question was whether the court can use E.O. 11246 to declare unlawful the very seniority system the Supreme Court found lawful under Title VII. "The government charged that the Teamsters and the employer engaged in a 'pattern and practice' of discrimination with respect to hiring, assignment, transfer and seniority rights. The failure to grant seniority carryover for city drivers who apply for over-the-road (line) positions effectively 'locked' minorities into the undesirable city driver jobs, the complaint alleged." The district court held that although E.O. 11246 has the force and effect of law, it is not a statute and must not therefore "run afoul of the statutory construction of Title VII or the will of Congress." Bureau of National Affairs, *Daily Labor Report*, July 24, 1979, pp. 1-2.

14. Quarles v. Phillip Morris, Inc., (D.C. Va. 1968) 1 EPD ¶9843.

15. Bowman Transportation, Inc. v. Franks, 7 EPD ¶9401 and 8 EPD ¶9580.

16. Ryder Truck Line, Inc. in the Bureau of National Affairs, *Daily Labor Report*, May 11, 1978, p. 1.

17. Bureau of National Affairs, *Daily Labor Report*, September 27, 1977, pp. 1-2.

18. Bureau of National Affairs, *Daily Labor Report*, May 21, 1976, p. 1.

19. *Ibid.*

20. Bureau of National Affairs, *Daily Labor Report*, December 13, 1977, p. 2.

21. For example, see Edgar A. Jones, Jr. "The Role of Arbitration in State and National Labor Policy" and "comments" by Charles Morris; David Feller in "Arbitration and the Public Interest," both in *Proceedings of the 24th Annual Meeting of the National Academy of Arbitrators* (Washington, D.C.: Bureau of National Affairs, Inc., 1971), pp. 42-83. See also Lawrence R. Jauch, "The Arbitration of Racial Discrimination Cases as a Result of Employment Practices," *Labor Law Journal*[24] (June 1973): 367-376; and Kenneth Jennings, "Arbitrators, Blacks and Discipline," *Personnel Journal* (January 1975): 32-37ff.

22. U.S. Department of Labor, Bureau of Labor Statistics, *Seniority in Promotion and Transfer Provisions* (Washington, D.C.: U.S. Government Printing Office, March 1, 1970, Bulletin 1425-11), p. 6.

23. *Ibid.*, p. 5.

24. *Ibid.*, p. 6.

25. Veterans Administration Hospital (Big Spring, Texas) and American Federation of Government Employees, Local 1934, March 15, 1978. 758 GERR: 36.

26. Children's Hospital Medical Center and Hospital and Institutional Workers Union, Local 250, May 1, 1978, p. 6. BAHA-39.

27. Health and Hospital Government Commission (Cook County, Ill.) and Illinois Nurses Association, November 10, 1975. LAIG 1499.

28. *Ibid.*

29. Benzie Medical Facility (Benzie County, Mich.) and Benzie Medical Employees Chapter American Federation of State, County and Municipal Employees, Local 1804, January 18, 1975. LAIG 1277.

30. *Ibid.*

31. Plymouth (Mass.) Hospital and Massachusetts Nurses Association, April 8, 1977. LAIG 1849.

32. *Ibid.* For a similar case, see Miners Clinics, Inc. and United Steelworkers of America, Local 14077, November 18, 1975. 986 WCR:A-1 and A-2.

33. Warm Springs (Mont.) State Hospital and Warm Springs State Hospital Independent Union, January 6, 1977. 699 GERR: 9. Same case reported at LAIG 1787.

34. *Ibid.*

35. Michael Reese Hospital and Medical Center and Hospital Employees Labor Program (HELP) of Metropolitan Chicago, April 24, 1979. CHC-15.

36. Veterans Administration Hospital (Roseburg, Ore.) and American Federation of Government Employees, Local 1042, January 16, 1978. 70 LA 491. Same case reported at 754 GERR: 38 and 39.

37. Herrick Memorial Hospital and Hospital and Institutional Workers Union, Local 250, September 5, 1969. BAHA-11.

38. Clinch Valley Clinic Hospital (Bluefield, W. Va.) and Hospital and Nursing Home Employees, Local 1199, February 26, 1975. 64 LA 542.

39. Brown County Mental Health Center and Brown County Employees Union, Local 1901, July 7, 1977. 68 LA 1363.

40. U.S. Department of Labor, Bureau of Labor Statistics, *Seniority in Promotion and Transfer Provisions, op. cit.*, p. 7.

41. Chippewa County (Mich.) War Memorial Hospital and American Federation of State, County and Municipal Employees, Local 301, August 8, 1974. LAIG 1171.

42. *Ibid.*

43. Frank Elkouri and Edna Elkouri, *How Arbitration Works* (Washington, D.C.: Bureau of National Affairs, Inc., 1973), pp. 594-595.

44. *Ibid.*, pp. 578-579.

45. Veterans Administration Hospital (Danville, Ill.) and American Federation of Government Employees, Local 1963, November 4, 1977. 69 LA 822.

46. Merritt Hospital and Hospital and Institutional Workers Union, Local 250, November 17, 1964. BAHA-3.

47. Centerville Clinics, Inc. and Office and Professional Employees International Union, Local 457, May 1, 1973. 60 LA 691.

48. *Ibid.*

49. Affiliated Hospitals of San Francisco (Mary's Help Hospital) and Hospital and Institutional Workers, Local 250, January 14, 1976. 76-1 ARB 8140.

50. Bureau of National Affairs, *Daily Labor Report,* January 29, 1979, p. 2.

51. Southwest Virginia Community Health Services, Inc. and United Steelworkers of America, Local 15220, February 3, 1978. 1089 WCR:A-4.

52. Dameron Hospital Association and Hospital and Institutional Workers Union, Local 250, September 16, 1977. BAHA-34.

53. Peralta Hospital and California Nurses Association, July 15, 1976, BAHA-28.

54. *Ibid.,* p. 17.

55. Toronto General Hospital and Canadian Union of Public Employees, Local 2001, July 31, 1978. 71 LA 295.

56. *Ibid.,* p. 298.

57. St. Joseph's Hospital (Hazleton, Pa.) and Pennsylvania Nurses Association, January 10, 1977. 68 LA 658.

58. Thomas Kennedy, "Merging Seniority Lists," in *Labor Arbitration and Industrial Change, Proceedings of the Sixteenth Annual Meeting of the National Academy of Arbitrators* (Washington, D.C.: Bureau of National Affairs, Inc., 1963), p. 5.

59. *Ibid.,* p. 5.

60. *Ibid.,* p. 16.

61. *Ibid.,* p. 26.

62. Rome Hospital and Murphey Memorial Hospital and American Federation of State, County and Municipal Employees, Local 1088, December 18, 1970. 386 GERR: B-12.

63. United Hospitals, Inc. and Hospital and Nursing Home Employees, Union No. 113, April 17, 1979. HMMM-7.

64. *Ibid.,* p. 14.

Chapter 12

Arbitration Issues Involving Employee Benefits

The total compensation of hospital employees can be divided into two basic components: (1) wages or salaries, and (2) fringe benefits or wage supplements. Since World War II, the number and types of wage supplements have increased at an exponential rate. Fifteen years ago, Heneman and Yoder counted more than 100 fringe benefits that had achieved wide acceptance. They stated further, "A complete list if one were available would probably include at least 200 types."[1]

The large number of fringe benefits currently available to employees fully warrants their categorization. The biennial survey conducted by the U.S. Chamber of Commerce distinguishes among five major categories of employee benefits: (1) legally required payment (e.g., social security, unemployment compensation), (2) employer's share in pension and other insurance plans, (3) paid rest periods, (4) payments for time not worked, and (5) miscellaneous items (e.g., payments for employees' educational expenses, to union stewards, etc.).

As the number of fringe benefits has increased steadily their cost to the employer has taken up a growing portion of the total wage bill. According to the latest biennial survey of the Chamber of Commerce, costs of employee benefits, including those required by law, were 36.7 percent of the payroll in 1977, or $2.264 per payroll hour. In the health care industry, the corresponding figures were 25.7 percent and $1.295, respectively.

In health care institutions where employees are represented by labor organizations, the collective bargaining agreement controls the type and extent of fringe benefits and the conditions under which they are available to the members of the bargaining unit. As with other provisions of the agreement, those governing the delivery of fringe benefits frequently give rise to grievances, some of which eventually result in arbitration. Because of the extensive range of fringe benefits, a considerable number of arbitration cases deal with disputes growing out of the interpretation of those contract clauses that cover employee benefits. The following benefit cases are presented with the proviso that, although arbitrators are not

217

bound by precedent, they do take into consideration decisions delivered by arbitrators in analogous cases.

Of the five categories previously listed, the category of payments for time not worked appears to create the largest number of grievances in the health care industry. Benefits in this category include paid vacations, paid holidays, paid sick leave, and payments for special leave time such as for funerals of relatives, one's birthday, and educational meetings. This chapter will deal primarily with arbitration issues involving payments for time not worked.

According to a 1979 survey of collective bargaining agreements in Chicago area hospitals, the major "pay for time not worked" type of benefits and their average extent per year are as follows: paid holidays (nine days), vacations (15 to 25 days depending on length of tenure), funeral leave (a maximum of three days per death), sick leave (12 days). Their importance to the total benefit package received by hospital employees is indicated by the fact that, of the total package value (estimated at $1.295 per pay roll hour in 1977), payments for time not worked constituted 44.1 cents or 34 percent of the total benefit costs in the health care industry.

VACATIONS

Paid vacations constitute one of the fringe benefits most treasured by employees. Because this benefit is provided at considerable cost to the employer, both its conditions and extent are carefully delineated in the collective agreements. Nonetheless, every year a large number of grievances emerge with respect to such issues as eligibility, effective dates, scheduling, and so on. A number of arbitral decisions have established guidelines in these issues.

Effective Date of Increased Vacation Benefits

There is usually a direct relationship between the length of paid vacation due to an employee and the length of his or her tenure with the employer. However, the significance of this relationship may be affected by the contract terms. In health care institutions with an established contractual relationship, there is generally little doubt as to an employee's vacation rights. However, disputes may develop in situations where health care employees become covered by a collective agreement whose vacation benefits are superior to those granted either by the previous contract or, in the absence of such, by the previous practice of the employer. In such situations, there may be questions with respect to the effective date of the new improved vacation benefits. Specifically, the choice is between the effective date of the contract or some other date (such as the employee's hiring date).

In a case decided by Arbitrator Michael H. Beck, the agreement, the first between the parties, became effective on April 17, 1977. Under this new agreement, employees with ten or more years of continuous full-time service were entitled to four weeks' paid vacation. An employee who had completed almost 15 years of service as of April 17, 1977 was granted only three week's vacation in May 1977 on the ground that she would not qualify for the four-week vacation until her first anniversary of employment under the new contract. The arbitrator sided with the employer's interpretation and ruled that

. . . the intent of the parties was to extend an additional benefit of a four week vacation to an employee who had ten years of continuous full-time employment with the hospital as of their next anniversary date and not as of the effective date of the agreement . . . the Grievant is not entitled to any additional vacation benefits until she reaches her first anniversary year under the Agreement.[2]

In a somewhat similar case, a new contract provided more favorable vacation benefits than the old contract. Two employees of a New York hospital reached the fifth anniversary of their employment in 1974. The contract in force at that time called for three weeks' paid vacation for employees with more than five but less than six years of service. The grievants believed that they were entitled to four weeks of vacation in 1975 because the contractual provision, which took effect January 1, 1975, specified four weeks of vacation for persons having five or more years seniority. The hospital contended that employees who had reached their fifth anniversary as of 1974 were entitled to three weeks' vacation, and only when they reached the anniversary of their employment in 1975 would they be entitled to four weeks' vacation. The arbitrator ruled in favor of the hospital, stating that if the parties "had intended to make the four-weeks-after-five-years-provision effective earlier than January 1, 1975, they could have and would have said so. . . ."[3]

In a third case, the issue involved the manner in which vacation benefits should be computed in a year when a new agreement providing for increased benefits went into effect. The dispute centered on whether the method used should have been an "accrual" (pro rata) method or an "absolute" method of vacation computation. The Nurses' Association contended that vacation eligibility should date from the anniversary of the individual employee's first employment with the member hospital, and that benefits should be paid on the basis of that anniversary date—even when the new agreement, with its increased eligibility, became effective. On the other hand, the hospital contended that increased eligibility should be computed from the effective date of the new contract, and the benefits should not be applied retroactively.

Arbitrator William Eaton agreed with the hospital's position, stating that

> The accrued or pro rata method had become a part of the accepted practice of the parties prior to the negotiations leading to the latest contract. This practice was incorporated into a letter of memorandum appended to the previous agreement. During the latest negotiations, either by inadvertence or due to an assumption that the accrual method was accepted, the letter of understanding was left out of the new agreement. However, the arbitrator decided that said letter was still in force because of past practice and because of the absence of any discussion during the latest negotiations to delete that letter from the new contract. Therefore, he ruled "that the computation of vacation eligibility shall continue to be made on the accrual or pro rata basis, and not on an absolute basis. . . ."[4]

The effective date was at issue in yet another case. The employer had refused to pay any vacation benefits to a number of employees on the ground that the seniority on which such benefits were based should be computed from the effective date of the contract. Arbitrator Melvin Lenard disagreed with this interpretation of the contract. He found that the agreement stated clearly that, for the purpose of the employees' personal benefits, seniority was to be determined by an employee's date of hire and not the effective date of the contract. Accordingly, in an *ex parte* proceeding, he ruled that vacation pay was to be computed from the date of employment. In addition, he directed the company to pay interest on the vacation pay awarded to the grievants since "its defense to the claims for vacation pay was known to it to be without merit."[5]

In an interest arbitration case involving the length of paid vacation, Arbitrator Morris P. Slushien awarded 22 days of annual vacation to social workers who had completed one year's service, although under the contract all members of the bargaining unit, even PhD's and physicians, were entitled to only 20 days of vacation. He found that a 22-day vacation period was standard for social workers in the New York metropolitan area, and the "Uniformity of working conditions within an industry is proper goal of every union . . . to withhold this benefit from the MSW's in St. Luke, while it is granted everywhere else is likely to be a bridgehead for friction and unrest throughout the unionized industry."[6]

Computing Vacation Pay for Quitting Employees

Another common problem in the area of vacation benefits involves the proration of such benefits upon termination of employment. In a typical case, decided by Arbitrator Thomas L. Yaeger, a nurse aide quit her job three months prior to her vacation year. The union contended that she was entitled to a pro rata share of her

1974 vacation. The employer argued that an employee is not "due" any sub-sequent year's vacation unless and until that employee has worked the full prior year. Although the contract did not provide for prorating vacation benefits, the arbitrator ruled that the most reasonable way to calculate the pro rata share of this employee's vacation was to multiply one-twelfth of the vacation benefits by the number of full months the employee worked after her anniversary date in the year in which she was terminated. Since the grievant's anniversary date fell on March 1 and she worked until December 3, she was entitled to seven-twelfths of her vacation pay.[7]

In a similar case, the contract specified that employees were eligible to take earned vacation time after completing 2,080 work hours. Each of the three grievants voluntarily quit between their first and second anniversary of employment. The employer contended that during the last negotiations the definition of a "year" was changed from a calendar year to a 2,080-hour period, and since the terminating employees did not complete their most recent 2,080-hour period, they were not entitled to any vacation pay earned between their last anniversary dates and their quitting dates. The arbitrator ruled that this contractual provision did not mean that vacation was not earned until employees worked 2,080 hours after their last anniversary date, and directed the employer to "pay each of the three grievants vacation pay for the vacation time they earned between their last anniversary dates and their dates of termination."[8]

Vacation Scheduling

While in the private industry many firms schedule vacations during the annual plant shutdown, this practice is not feasible in the health care industry where institutions must operate year round without any interruption. Since the majority of employees prefer to take their vacations during the choice seasons, scheduling vacations may create problems for both supervisors and employees. In order to avoid understaffing and scheduling conflicts, most contracts in the health care industry provide for an orderly allotment of vacation periods, established mainly on the basis of seniority. However, some scheduling problems still are created by ambiguous contract language.

In one case, the hospital allowed full-time registered nurses to select vacation dates before part-time nurses with greater seniority. The contract did make a distinction between full-time seniority and part-time seniority. A part-time nurse filed a grievance because her vacation preferences were "preempted" by full-time nurses with less seniority. Arbitrator Charles T. Douds decided that the above practice violated the agreement, since seniority should have been the basis for vacation scheduling regardless of the number of hours worked per week. He recommended a procedure according to which "each group of nurses, part-time and full-time, make their selections of dates for vacation separately. . . . Where there are conflicts the hospital can work out a procedure to resolve the conflict. One would toss a coin and the winner would have first choice."[9]

In an unusual case, conflict developed between the vacation preferences of the most senior bargaining unit employee and a supervisor outside the bargaining unit. Arbitrator Harry J. Dworkin decided in favor of the bargaining unit employee. He ruled that although the hospital retained the right to schedule vacations according to its needs, it did not have the right to give a nonunit employee vacation preference over a senior unit employee. The question of whether the nonunit employee had greater seniority than the grievant was not relevant. Said Dworkin, "To equate the seniority of a non-bargaining unit employee with that of a bargaining unit employee, as to vacation and scheduling, would operate to comingle the rights of bargaining unit employees with those of excluded employees."[10]

Vacation Rights of Part-Time Employees

Most contracts grant vacation benefits to all employees. However, on this issue some contracts make a distinction between full-time and part-time employees. In a case decided by Arbitrator Charles M. Rehmus, the grievant had a total of 15 years seniority and, on that basis, claimed four weeks vacation. Her request was denied by the hospital on the ground that during ten of those years she had worked part-time. The union contended that employees' vacations were to be computed on the basis of total number of years worked, regardless of the number of hours worked per year. The arbitrator ruled that since the agreement was ambiguous on this issue, past practice should guide his decision: "Here, the Hospital had a long and well established past practice of administering the Agreement in conformity with its interpretation of vacation rights." Therefore, it would be inappropriate "to grant a benefit in arbitration that a party sought but failed to achieve in collective bargaining." On this basis, he ruled in favor of the hospital.[11]

Failure to Return from Vacation

Contractual vacation benefits involve not only the employee's right to paid time off, but also the employee's obligation to return from scheduled vacation on the agreed time. Failure to return from vacation on schedule may result in severe discipline, as illustrated by the following case. A hospital employee missed the date on which she was supposed to return to duty and, as a result, she was discharged. The grievant claimed that she failed to return because of circumstances beyond her control. She claimed further that there was a mix-up in scheduling and coordinating the vacation trip. The arbitrator sustained the grievant's discharge because "her testimony in this matter could not be credited. Much of what grievant said was inherently improbable." Furthermore, she had made several requests for an extension of her vacation time, but these had been denied.[12]

PAID HOLIDAYS

Paid holidays constitute another important category of benefits. The majority of the contracts in the health care industry provide their employees with nine to ten paid holidays. The interpretation of contract clauses controlling paid holidays has given rise to a number of grievances centering primarily on such problems as eligibility for holiday pay, the method of payment for work performed on contractual holidays, and time off before major holidays. We will review some arbitral decisions on these issues.

Eligibility for Holiday Benefits

Most contracts require employees to fulfill certain conditions in order to be eligible for holiday benefits. Such conditions may include working immediately before and after the holiday in question. Other provisions may make part-time employees ineligible for holiday pay.

In one arbitration case, the union contended that under the new contract both full-time and part-time employees of a health care institution were eligible for a birthday holiday and a paid personal day. However, the contract specified full-time employees, and the employer contended that it was not the intent of the parties to extend the new holiday benefits to part-time personnel. The arbitrator agreed with the employer's interpretation. He found that "there was no attempt at all to negotiate the specific language needed to institute this important addition. . ." and in the absence of such language, he was "unwilling to impose upon the employer such a significant contract modification. . . ."[13]

Compensation for Holiday Work

In health care institutions, work cannot stop on holidays. Therefore, management must decide how to compensate employees who are required to work on a holiday. Most contracts call for double-time pay for any employee scheduled to work on days specified by the contract as paid holidays. However, some hospitals pay straight time to these employees, and compensate them for their holiday work by giving them an extra day off with pay. As a result, these employees receive straight pay for a 40-hour work week, although they work only 32 hours, including a holiday.

Arbitrators are divided in their rulings with respect to grievances involving compensatory time off in lieu of double-time pay for holiday work. In one case, Park Community Hospital introduced a new policy under which employees who were scheduled to work on a contractual holiday did not receive double-time pay but were required to take an extra day off during the pay period on which one of the holidays fell. The contract called for double-time pay to employees who worked on holidays. The arbitrator ruled that "There is no indication in the Agreement for compensatory time. . ." and, therefore, "The scheduling of employees for thirty-two hours of work week preceding or subsequent to a holiday week . . . is violative of contractual benefits pertaining to holiday pay."[14]

However, in a similar case, Arbitrator William Belshaw upheld the practice of compensatory time off for holiday work. He found that "since at least 1969, the employer had consistently maintained a policy of granting a later day off to those performers who served on holidays." He also referred to a booklet distributed to employees. The booklet spelled out that those employees assigned to work on holidays would receive a compensatory day off with pay. Furthermore, for more than one year "the employer applied its compensatory-day-off policy without objection."[15] While in the Park Community Hospital case, clear and unequivocal contract language called for double-time pay for holiday work, in this case, practice prevailed over ambiguous contract language.

Arbitrator Bernard H. Cantor decided a case involving the loss of two contractual holidays. In 1976, both Christmas and New Year's Day fell on Saturdays. Hospital management laid off the employees of the x-ray department on the day before the Christmas and New Year's Day holidays, thereby depriving them of an extra day's pay in each of the two weeks involved. The hospital contended that its action was economically justified because the doctors' clinic from which the x-ray department got most of its business was closed on the day preceding each holiday. The arbitrator denied the grievance on the ground "that Management has a full and plenary right to schedule the employees and to adjust their hours to suit Management's need . . . and in this case the scheduling in question was economically justified."[16]

Past practice was the determining factor in another case involving one-half day off with pay on either Christmas Eve or New Year's Eve. The arbitrator found that the contract was silent on this issue, and therefore he turned to past practice for guidance. Evidence showed that "employees of long standing of the x-ray department and of the hematology laboratory . . . had been dismissed for a half day at Christmas and New Year's Eve and had always received pay therefore." Furthermore, the contract contained a provision that listed past practices that were superseded by the agreement, and the practice in question was not among them. Therefore, the arbitrator ruled, "The past practice is to give employees not responsible for direct patient care and not providing essential care one-half day off with pay either Christmas Eve or New Year's Eve.[17]

Scheduling Holidays

Since most holidays are fixed by the calendar or by law, the scheduling of paid holidays usually should not cause problems. However, a contract between a hospital and its employees provided for a so-called "floating" holiday. It was the understanding of the union that this holiday could be scheduled by the employee on any day, provided that the employee gave two weeks' notice of the date desired. However, when a nursing assistant scheduled her floating holiday for a particular Sunday, the hospital refused to permit it. The hospital argued that, according to the contract, it must agree to the scheduled time. The arbitrator ruled that the hospital had not violated the contract by refusing the employee's request, because it had reasonable grounds for this action. "Sunday is normally a day on which it is difficult to provide adequate staffing" and therefore the hospital's decision was based on a "just and equitable basis consistent with its needs."[18]

SICK LEAVE

Health care institutions, perhaps because of their involvement in healing, appear to show more understanding toward the health problems of their employees than do other industries. However, even hospitals may exempt certain infirmities and disabilities from the coverage of sick leave benefits, and they may set up certain conditions under which the sick leave provisions of the contract may be exercised. Some of the guidelines established by recent awards are surveyed here.

Kaiser-Permanente Medical Care Program refused paid sick leave for an employee who had a pregnancy-related health problem. The employer argued that, on the basis of past practice, an employee was entitled only to a leave of absence without pay for periods of prenatal and postnatal care surrounding a cesarean operation. Arbitrator Daniel J. Dykstra ruled that the employee was entitled to contractual paid sick leave because the past practice reflected a unilateral action on the part of the employer and lacked the mutual acceptance needed to make the practice binding. Furthermore, the employer's action also violated a clause in the present agreement that prohibited discrimination on the basis of sex.[19]

In another case, eligibility for sick leave was conditioned on the requirement that the employee serve advance notice of absence before the start of his or her shift. Since the employee failed to notify the employer in due time, her entitlement to sick leave was denied. The arbitrator agreed with the hospital on the ground that the employee would have been exempt from the requirement of advance notice if she had been able to show that circumstances beyond her control prevented her from giving the advance notice. Since the employee was unable to prove that, her grievance was denied.[20]

The employer's right to limit the extent of unpaid sick leave was the issue in another arbitration case. The nurse who filed the grievance had used up all her paid sick and personal leave days. When she requested two additional sick days, this time without pay, the employer refused to comply with her request and, instead, charged the two days to her vacation time. Arbitrator Jonas Aaron denied the grievance on the ground that, although the contract stated that a leave without pay "may" be granted, the employer had the right to set forth reasonable rules as to how it would exercise its discretion.[21]

Abuse of sick leave may result in disciplinary action against the employee involved. In one case, a nurse was disciplined for abusing sick leave privileges. For this employee, each day of sick leave taken in her one year of employment had been either preceded or followed by a leave-of-absence day or a scheduled day off. The hospital took a rather unusual measure: it withheld the nurse's annual wage increase for six months. The grievant never had been told that she risked this form of discipline. The arbitrator ruled that the withholding of a contractual wage was not a permissible form of discipline.[22]

In quite a few contracts, sick leave days and personal days are interchangeable. Therefore, in connection with the discussion of sick leave issues, questions involving policy on personal days may also be addressed. One problem that emerges is the rate at which personal days, allotted to a contract year, may be used up. In one case, the union contended that an employee's total number of personal days per year may be taken by the employee at any time after the beginning of the contract year. The employer countered that benefits must be earned and that they accrue to each employee by virtue of service. Arbitrator Charles F. Ipavec supported the employer's position and ruled that "where the contract language merely states that registered nurses are entitled to three non-accumulative personal days per year, it was not improper for the Hospital to determine that one personal day would be earned after each four months of service. . ."[23]

FUNERAL LEAVE

The majority of contracts in the health care industry call for paid funeral leave. As with other leave provisions, differences in interpretation may give rise to grievances. Disputes in this area usually center on such questions as the meaning of "immediate family" (that is, the number and kind of relatives whose demise would entitle the employee to paid funeral leave), the extent of the funeral leave, proof of attendance, and the coincidence of funeral leave with other types of paid time off (vacation, holidays, weekends).

In one arbitration case, a hospital refused to grant funeral leave to one of its employees when her father's funeral took place during her paid vacation time. The hospital concluded that the purpose of funeral leave was to compensate an employee for any pay lost during the time he or she attended the funeral; however, in this case the employee did not suffer any loss of pay as she was on paid vacation. The union contended that the hospital's position was contrary not only to the express terms of the contract but also to the intent of the parties. Though the employee did not actually incur a financial loss, she did lose three days off with pay—days she would have gotten had the death and the funeral occurred during nonvacation time. The arbitrator upheld the grievance because the hospital had failed to advise the grievant of its position at the time when she notified the hospital of her father's death. Furthermore, during negotiations for the current contract, a proposal encompassing the hospital's position had been deleted.[24]

Arbitrator Jesse Simons came to an entirely different conclusion in a similar case where the death of a family member fell during an employee's paid vacation time. The hospital declined to grant the three days' funeral leave provided by the contract, on the basis that said leave was not a "guaranteed bonus;" secondly, "grievant was scheduled to be off duty with compensation when the three days leave for her mother's death would normally have been payable, and thus grievant did not suffer any loss of compensation. . . ; third, such payment is specifically prescribed solely for 'three days absence' and grievant was not absent from work. . . ." Arbitrator Simons accepted the hospital's position that grievant was not entitled to paid funeral leave because "she was not assigned to or absent from work" during the period of bereavement. He therefore denied the grievance.[25]

In another grievance submitted to arbitration, the dispute centered on the question of whether the employee was required to take the three-day funeral leave before and during the funeral, or whether some of it might be used after the day of the funeral. The hospital argued that it was the intent of the parties to provide "up to three days" depending on the circumstances of each case, and that this interpretation was supported by past practice and by an announcement in the employee newsletter. The arbitrator ruled in favor of the grievant on the ground that, in accordance with the contract, the hospital had full discretion to determine the number of leave days when the funeral is for an employee's spouse or child, but an employee is guaranteed three days' paid leave when the funeral is for some other member of the family. The hospital's past-practice argument was rejected because requests for bereavement leave were personal matters and "unless brought to the attention of the Union . . . the Union has no knowledge of the manner in which the provision is administered."[26]

PAID TIME FOR ATTENDING EDUCATIONAL MEETING

This type of benefit is important to those hospital employees who obtained professional training and are inclined to maintain professional skill and competence. Many health care institutions are willing to support the continuing education of their professional staff by granting them paid time to attend professional conventions and workshops.

In one case, two registered nurses were denied full pay for the week they attended a meeting sponsored by the Association of Operating Room Nurses. The hospital contended that it had the right to determine what is reasonable time off, and in this case two days off with pay was deemed to be reasonable. Arbitrator Daniel G. Mills ruled that the hospital improperly denied the full week with pay. Although the contract uses the term "reasonable time off," past practice must be considered. In the past the hospital had considered a week off with pay for one or two nurses to be reasonable. Furthermore, the grievants' absence did not interfere with the operating needs of the hospital.[27]

LEAVES OF ABSENCE WITHOUT PAY

Although there is no payment with this type of leave, such leave may affect the employee's claim to certain benefits the contract grants to full-time employees. Moreover, the hospital may change an employee's assignment upon return from a prolonged leave. These and other problems involving interpretation of relevant contract clauses may require arbitration.

In one case, an employee requested and was granted five weeks' leave of absence without pay. As a result, her paid-time package of 33 days for the year was reduced by one-twelfth. Management maintained that she was not entitled to the full 33 days since this benefit was reserved for full-time employees and she had worked less than full-time that year. The arbitrator found that the relevant contract language contained the terms "proportionate," "pro rata," and "prorated." On this basis he ruled that the grievant was not entitled to all 33 "package-deal" days when not working, since this benefit must be earned. She was entitled only to a proportionate share of these days.[28]

In another arbitration case, the hospital failed to reassign a registered nurse to her previous shift when she returned from an authorized leave of absence. The hospital argued that the day shift, on which the nurse worked prior to her leave, was overstaffed. Arbitrator Fred E. Kindig found that the hospital had violated its contract in the above action. He ruled that the hospital, having authorized the leave and knowing that the grievant would return on a certain date, should have reinstated her to her former position and shift in conformance with the contract; the hospital could have then laid off less senior nurses to eliminate overstaffing.[29]

In a third case, a nursing assistant was granted a one-day leave of absence to attend his sick brother. While on leave, the brother's condition worsened, and the employee asked to extend the leave by another day. The hospital refused to comply with the request and charged the employee with being AWOL when he did not report to work. The arbitrator ruled that the situation constituted an emergency since the brother's doctor would not administer a certain medication to the sick brother unless the employee were present. The arbitrator therefore decided that the employee's leave should have been extended and that he had been improperly charged with being AWOL.[30]

The preceding review of arbitration awards involving "time off" cases clearly indicates that arbitrators frequently disagree in their evaluations of similar situations. Therefore, awards should be carefully analyzed for clues that explain the apparent differences in arbitral decisions.

NOTES

1. Herbert G. Heneman, Jr. and Dale Yoder, *Labor Economics*, 2nd. ed. (Cincinnati: South-Western Publ. Co., 1965), pp. 506-507.

2. St. Patrick Hospital and St. Patrick Local Unit of Montana Nurses' Association, November 14, 1977. 77-2 ARB 8575.

3. John M. Malkin, Beth Israel Medical Center (New York City) and District 1199, National Union of Hospital and Health Care, RWDSU, March 23, 1976. LVH.

4. Association of Hospitals of Santa Clara County and the California Nurses' Association; March 8, 1974. 74-1 ARB 8035.

5. Sunshine Convalescent Hospital (Paramount, Calif.) and Service and Hospital Employees Union, Local 399, February 27, 1974. 62 LA 276.

6. St. Luke's Hospital Center (New York, N.Y.) and Drug and Hospital Union, Local 1199, November 16, 1973. 63 LA 71.

7. Morningside Nursing Home and Service and Hospital Employees International Union, Local 150, April 19, 1974. 74-1 ARB 8118.

8. Providence Medical Center (Seattle, Wash.) and International Operating Engineers, Local 286, March 31, 1977. 68 LA 663.

9. St. Joseph Hospital and Pennsylvania Nurses Association, October 12, 1976. 1031 WCR:A-8.

10. Akron (Ohio) General Medical Center and Akron General Medical Center Employees Union, December 6, 1974. LAIG 1220.

11. W. A. Foote Memorial Hospital and International Union of Operating Engineers, Local 547, March 26, 1974. 74 ARB 8076.

12. Joseph F. Gentile, Community Hospital of San Gabriel (Calif.) and SEIU, Local 399, January 19, 1978. 78-1 ARB 8061.

13. A. Dale Allen, Jr. Hillsdale Community Center and Local 36 of Retail Store Employees' Union, September 27, 1978. 1128 WCR:A-6.

14. E. J. Forsythe, Park Community Hospital and Service Employees International Union, Local 70, April 5, 1975. 75 ARB 8037.

15. Grant Hospital of Chicago and Hospital Employees Labor Program (HELP) of Metropolitan Chicago, May 4, 1978. CHC-14.

16. Appalachian Regional Hospitals and United Steelworkers of America, Local 14491, July 20, 1977. 77-2 ARB 8354.

17. Oscar Ornati, Metropolitan Hospital (New York, N.Y.) and National Union of Hospital and Health Care Employees, December 1976. LVH.

18. Bruce B. Laybourne. Akron (Ohio) General Medical Center and Akron Medical Center Employees Union, September 2, 1975. LAIG 1464.

19. Kaiser-Permanente Medical Care Program and Hospital and Institutional Workers Union, Local 250, January 16, 1975. 64 LA 245.

20. Samuel S. Kates, Sunny Acres Cuyahoga County Tuberculosis Hospital and AFSCME, Local 1746, June 7, 1972. 72-1 ARB 8305.
21. Westchester County (N.Y.) and New York State Nurses Association, May 7, 1976. LAIG 1707.
22. Edward C. Pinkus, Nantucket (Mass.) Cottage Hospital and Massachusetts Nurses Association, April 27, 1979. LAIG 3242.
23. Youngstown (Ohio) Osteopathic Hospital Association and Ohio Nurses Association, June 10, 1977. LAIG 1931.
24. Theodore Dyke, Mt. Sinai Hospital of Cleveland and Northeast Ohio Public Employees, AFSCME, Local 2679, March 12, 1976. 76-1 ARB 8249.
25. The Presbyterian Hospital and New York Nurses Association, May 19, 1976. LVH.
26. Dallas L. Jones, Gratiot Community Hospital (Alma, Mich.) and AFSCME, Local 1511, November 27, 1975. LAIG 1523.
27. Carney Hospital (Boston, Mass.) and Massachusetts Nurses Association, August 25, 1978. LAIG 2184.
28. Charles F. Ipavec, East Liverpool City Hospital (Ohio) and International Brotherhood of Pottery and Allied Workers, Local 333, August 25, 1975. 75 ARB 8295.
29. St. Ann's Hospital of Columbus (Ohio) and Ohio Nurses Association, September 25, 1976. 1021 WCR:A-17.
30. John W. Kennedy, Veterans Administration Hospital and American Federation of Government Employees, Local 2080, May 6, 1975. 75 ARB 8144.

Chapter 13

The Arbitration of Issues with Special Hospital Significance

This chapter focuses on arbitration issues of special interest to the hospital/ medical service industry. Perhaps only one issue—abuse of patients—is unique to hospitals. However, hospitals present conditions that often prompt or facilitate the development of certain types of issues. No other industry treats a group of ill people with varying abilities to care for themselves. Businesses have their customers who may not always be as astute as they should be, but rarely are completely dependent on the quality of care or service given—at least they seldom risk their very lives on it.

Because hospitals deal with life and death, issues frequently intensify in importance. For example, employees who sleep on the job present a problem for many industries. Yet in hospitals the problem is exacerbated because it is usually quiet during the evening hours (making it conducive for sleeping), and of course, hospitals run around the clock. Similarly drug use is not an issue unique to hospitals. But aside from drug stores and pharmaceutical labs, what other organizations have such quantities of drugs on hand? Furthermore, in hospitals drugs are not always well protected.

Or consider the grievances that arise over the payment for or care of uniforms. Hospitals are not the only businesses that require employees to wear uniforms. Yet, because such a high percentage of hospital workers wear a uniform of one type or another, the possibility for disputes over this issue is increased.

In hospitals it is not uncommon for staff members to question the adequacy of hospital staffing or the adequacy of equipment. This type of issue rarely is raised in a manufacturing concern, and if it does come up, it probably is voiced by management and not bargaining unit employees.

Hospitals also are sensitive to information flow about, and to, patients. Professionalism in hospitals demands ethical behavior. What happens when a union member appears to have breached the hospital's code of ethics?

ABUSE OF PATIENTS

The issue of patient abuse is unique to the health care industry. No other business is responsible for the safekeeping, and even the lives, of individuals who are totally dependent on the care the business provides. Some of the patients are old, some are extremely weak from debilitating illness, and some are mentally or even emotionally crippled. This vulnerability may make patients a target for various types of abuse, ranging from verbal assault to sexual attack.

At the same time, the fact that patients can be infirm, uncooperative, unresponsive, and even abusive themselves may be frustrating to hospital personnel. Hospital personnel are under pressure to complete their duties in an expeditious manner, and an uncooperative patient can spark a spontaneous reaction in the form of a slap, harsh language, or something similarly inappropriate.

The patient abuse cases we reviewed had three common denominators:

1. They were usually punished by discharge.
2. The cases frequently focused on resolving questions of credibility between the patient-accuser and the employee; often corroborating testimony helped resolve the credibility question.
3. It was important to establish whether the grievant was given due process.

Patient abuse cases fall into four categories: (a) verbal abuse, (b) poor attitude toward patients, (c) physical abuse, and (d) sexual abuse.

Verbal Abuse

In one case, a disciplinary suspension was justified when a hospital worker was found to have made threatening remarks to a patient.[1] The employee, a maid, recognized the patient as one of the policemen who had arrested and injured her son. According to witnesses, she told the patient to watch out because she might poison him. Brushing aside the union's argument that the threat was meant merely as a joke, the arbitrator noted:

> Whether or not she meant what she said could not be determined to a certainty. Hence, it is seen that the hospital, after notice of the Grievant's language toward this helpless patient, *came under an absolute duty to protect the patient from this* threatened harm. [emphasis added][2]

An LPN, working at a children's hospital, was properly discharged for screaming vulgarities at a child-patient after her clothing had been splattered by the child's grape juice.[3] Two co-workers testified they overheard the screaming coming from the room. Although the grievant denied that she screamed at the patient, the arbitrator believed the two witnesses because "nothing was offered to support a contention that the two co-workers conspired to fabricate the story about Miss H_____."[4]

However, in a majority of other verbal abuse cases, the discipline or discharge meted out by the hospital was reduced or even dismissed. A nurse aide's discharge for using abusive language to a patient was set aside because the employer had failed to discharge the employee for verbal abuse and roughness with patients several years earlier when discharge would have been warranted.[5] The arbitrator concluded that the medical center had been lax in handling the matter.

In a similar case, also involving a nurse aide, an employer was found not justified in discharging the employee after issuing her three oral warnings for unbecoming conduct, ranging from abusive language toward patients to refusal to meet their needs.[6] The arbitrator noted that the medical facility had failed to apply progressive discipline designed to correct the employee. Her record showed there were no written reprimands or suspensions putting the grievant on notice that her behavior was unacceptable. The arbitrator therefore reduced the discharge to a three-day suspension.

Another case involved a nurse aide discharged by a hospital for allegedly using obscene language to a patient. However, the hospital made no attempt to permit the grievant to reply to the patient's complaint. Moreover, because of conflicts in the patient's statements, the hospital was unable to prove that the aide had actually been abusive.[7]

In another case an attendant was reinstated with full back pay after a dismissal.[8] A patient had complained that the grievant had pushed him around and told him that if he did not take a shower he could "drop dead." In sustaining the attendant's grievance, the arbitrator found serious discrepancies in testimony between the patient, the supervisor, and the head nurse. While the patient placed himself outside of his room and in the hallway during part of the events in question, overwhelming testimony established he had never left his bed. Moreover, the "credibility of the patient's entire statement was undermined by serious errors in fundamental details."

Poor Attitude

There were a few hospital cases that involved claims that hospital personnel exhibited, or were alleged to show, disregard for patients in some way.

In one case, a hospital in a nonpunitive and friendly way tried to teach an uncooperative and unsympathetic nurse the proper attitude toward patients.[9] However, after two incidents in which the nurse's unsympathetic behavior caused great emotional distress to three patients, the hospital terminated her. The arbitrator dismissed the union's argument that the hospital had not given her progressive discipline. He said that it was immaterial whether prior corrective discipline had been imposed. He noted also that the decision had not been made in haste, but rather only after all facts were known and duly deliberated. Feeling that a suspension might make the nurse even more hostile, he concluded that the discharge was proper.

In another case, a nurse aide was discharged for alleged mistreatment of a patient.[10] Specifically, the grievant had: (1) left the patient on a bedpan for unnecessarily long periods, (2) refused to answer the patient's call lights, (3) wakened the patient in the middle of the night by turning on the room lights when attending to the patient's roommate, and (4) refused to help her get to the bathroom in the middle of the night. The arbitrator found that there was merit in the patient's complaints regarding the overhead lights and the bathroom assistance. Yet, he reduced the discharge to a five-day suspension because the hospital failed to show that the nurse's care of other patients was substandard. The arbitrator also noted that the hospital failed to give this nurse a written notice earlier for a similar complaint. He also said that a nurse aide cannot be expected to perform with the same degree of professionalism required from a nurse.

A physical therapy aide was properly suspended when she and another physical therapy aide began to argue in loud voices concerning the proper procedure for bringing patients to and from the physical therapy department.[11] A patient nearby, becoming fearful, told two other workers in the area that she did not want to cause trouble and could take herself back to her room. The argument continued for another ten minutes as the two protagonists moved down the hall, each pushing a patient in a wheelchair. At this time, another patient asked what was going on. Thus several patients had heard and were affected by the argument. The arbitrator observed:

> Persons, such as the Grievant, who work with and around patients in a hospital setting, must conduct themselves in such a manner so as to maintain conditions conducive to good patient care. They must refrain from acts and words which will upset patients, and make more difficult the work of other employees and physicians.[12]

Physical Abuse

Certainly physical abuse of patients represents a more serious problem to hospitals than verbal abuse or improper attitude. For one thing, the harm to patients is more real, and for another, it exposes the hospital to a potential lawsuit.

In one physical abuse case, a registered nurse working in the Pediatric Care Unit, was alleged to have spanked an eleven-month-old child hospitalized for treatment of anemia and gastroenteritis. Also she was accused of roughly tearing off the dressings covering an infected second-degree burn of a six-year-old child, and pulling another six-year-old concussion patient from a bathtub by one arm. Six other "incidents" over a two-year period had a bearing on the hospital's decision to discharge the nurse.[13] The arbitrator, in sustaining the discharge, observed that while there were three witnesses for the hospital, only the grievant testified in her own behalf. Thus he felt "the balance is tipped heavily against the grievant." Arbitrator Eisenberg concluded that:

> While the grievant may have the technical competence to fill a nursing assignment, it is evident from the circumstances of this case that her temperament is such as to produce bursts of harsh treatment of young children which are totally out of keeping with service as an RN in pediatrics and constitute unacceptable behavior in any such assignment, and justify the penalty of discharge.[14]

In another case, Arbitrator Solomon sustained the discharge of an infirmary "charge nurse" who had been accused of physically and verbally abusing patients. It was alleged that she utilized "unrestrained physical force" in administering medication on certain patients; that she absented herself from her work station without informing other staff members; and that she was guilty of numerous other offenses including neglect of a critically ill patient and refusal to summon a doctor for or administer medication to a patient who was demonstrably suffering great pain. The arbitrator chose to believe the witnesses who testified believably and were unshaken on cross-examination, as opposed to the grievant's "evasive" and "unconvincing" answers.

A hospital was sustained in issuing a second warning notice and a five-day disciplinary suspension to an LVN for "rough handling" of a patient.[15] Though the hospital acknowledged that the grievant did not deliberately "rough handle" or frighten the patient, the grievant did admit to a degree of clumsiness and to having muttered a profanity. These admissions, along with a history of unsatisfactory handling of patients, indicated her performance was not up to "reasonable hospital standards." The arbitrator concluded, "In these days of large malpractice suits, hospitals must be certain that their standards of patient care are kept high and all employees hold to them."[16]

In a closely related case, the arbitrator deemed that discharge was the proper penalty for a nursing home attendant who slapped a patient. Although the facility's delay in firing the attendant indicated that management wasn't certain that the offense had occurred, the evidence and the arbitrator's impressions of the fired worker's personality indicated that the event did indeed occur.[17]

A hospital attendant was suspended for slapping two mentally retarded patients because they sat in the wrong seats before lunch. Two witnesses were believed over the grievant and four kitchen employees who said they had not seen the slapping, because the two witnesses had no motive to lie.[18]

On the other hand, another employee, a nurse aide, had her termination reduced to a 30-day disciplinary suspension.[19] The arbitrator explained:

> However, though the striking of Mrs. D_____ may not have been sufficiently violent or may not have been done with malicious intent to injure, justifying immediate discharge, it certainly was unacceptable conduct and constitutes grounds for discipline. As difficult as it may be to tolerate the involuntary behavior of these old people which results in spitting out of food, an employee working in this field must discipline herself or himself not to react physically. Any touching in anger or in frustration, or to admonish, is gravely unacceptable conduct.[20]

In another physical abuse case, the hospital was reversed in meting out discharge to a male nursing assistant for allegedly abusing a patient.[21] The patient was heard to cry out, "Help, help, murder, murder," and "Help," and "He hit me in the mouth," and "He hit me in the chest." An LPN rushed in to investigate and found the patient sitting on the edge of a chair with the grievant holding his wrists. There was a reddened spot on the patient's chest and a scratch on his wrist.

The arbitrator, in reinstating the grievant with full back pay, took into account that in 27 months of employment the grievant had never before been accused of patient abuse. The arbitrator also noted the patient's mental condition, a condition so substandard that the arbitrator said he was "unable to ascribe normal meanings to words used by the patient." While the patient complained about his mouth and chest, he didn't complain at all about the scratch on his wrist. The arbitrator believed the scratch was accidental and the discoloration on the patient's chest was not due to anything for which the grievant was responsible. Moreover, there were no signs of damage to the patient's mouth, an area he complained about.

Sexual Abuse

A few hospital cases dealt with the sexual abuse of patients, either heterosexual or homosexual.

In one case, a patient accused an attendant aide of forcing him to perform homosexual acts.[22] Another patient accused the aide of other acts while massaging him with lotion. Other patients referred to the grievant as a "queer." The arbitrator, in sustaining the discharge, found that the primary hospital witness, a mental patient testifying through a physician-psychiatrist, would not be able to recall and repeat his story on so many occasions if it were fantasy. Moreover, the patient was not on hallucinatory drugs or medications and was not subject to hallucination or fantasy. The arbitrator also brushed aside the union's contention that the burden of proof used in this type of case had to be the criminal standard—that is, evidence with weight beyond reasonable doubt. He observed:

There is no criminality attached hereto. The moral turpitude is not attached hereto. In today's society even if we found Mr. S＿＿＿＿＿ [the grievant] was a homosexual there is nothing to impugn to him conduct in the framework of our society which would discredit him in its entirety. Homosexuality in our world today is widely accepted when it is between consenting partners. Here the problem arises as to whether or not these patients were capable or even in a position to consent. Medical evidence established the patients involved did not exhibit any homosexual tendencies in any of their conversations, behavior or discussions, nor was it a factor in their treatment. They all appear to have been heterosexual. Thus, the issue in moral turpitude is not involved where a homosexual was involved with another homosexual but here the claim is that sexuality of an alleged homosexual upon the non-consenting heterosexual thereby creating a problem of wrongful conduct justifying discharge and not moral turpitude, since it is not a crime to be homosexual.[23]

In a second case involving homosexual behavior, a mentally retarded patient with the mental age level of a 9- to 14-year-old, accused a transporter of masturbating him in a toilet and attempting fellatio.[24] Again the patient's story was credited over the grievant's because the latter testified he had to help the patient urinate, but it had been established that the patient was capable of performing this function himself. Furthermore, the grievant could not account for his time on the day in question and could not explain why he was even in the area. The arbitrator noted, "Any employee, regardless of length of service, merits discharge for sexual abuse of a patient in violation of the hospital's duty of care."[25]

In another discharge case for sexual abuse, an Operating Room Transporter was accused of touching the vaginal and rectal areas of a female patient he was supposed to transport to an operating room for a surgical procedure on the larynx.[26] Though the transporter testified that he had been alone with the patient for no more than "a few seconds," the clinical supervisor in the area the morning in question testified that she had seen the patient get into the stretcher by herself and that she had left the patient's room for a long enough time to be "surprised" upon her return that the grievant was only then wheeling the patient out of the room. Though this testimony impugned the grievant's credibility, it did not corroborate the charge that the transporter molested her. Though the arbitrator reinstated the grievant (without back pay), he warned:

He should be on clear notice that any future incident which gives rise to any similar complaint against him will surely expose him to summary dismissal. The Hospital's patients are entitled to protection of their persons from staff improprieties of any kind, even those which may be casual or which were admittedly not physically hurtful. The grievant had an obligation, in common with all who tend the sick, scrupulously to avoid any act which could be remotely construed to amount to abusing or taking advantage of helpless individuals entrusted to staff care.[27]

SLEEPING ON THE JOB

Like any other 24-hour-a-day operation, hospitals have their share of disciplinary problems involving sleeping on the job. Usually these incidents occur on the second or third shifts. During these late night and early morning hours, the hospital is normally at its quietest. Thus, there can be a great temptation to take a brief or prolonged nap. Even though a hospital may have a rule forbidding sleeping on the job, individual supervisors may covertly, or even explicitly, approve the practice during times of virtual inactivity. Such practices can subject a hospital to a possible charge of discriminatory treatment or favoritism when one supervisor approves of catnaps, while others do not.

Of course, in hospital work medical emergencies can develop at any time, and an employee who is sleeping may be unavailable to form a vital link in a chain of needed medical aid. This contingency is compounded when the napping employee is the sole employee in that job classification working on that shift.

Such a situation occurred in a Nebraska hospital. The only respiratory therapy technician was fired for sleeping on the 11 p.m. to 7 a.m. shift.[28] The technician was found in the respiratory therapy department office reclining on three chairs that had been drawn together and arranged for resting. A security guard noticed the lights were off in the department, and hearing snoring, discovered the grievant about 3:10 a.m. The guard went to the grievant, shook him awake, and told him he should not be sleeping on the job.

In sustaining the technician's discharge, the arbitrator noted that the hospital had a ten-year-old rule prohibiting "sleeping on duty," listing it as one of four grounds for immediate termination. He noted that: "The duties of a respiratory therapy technician demand alertness to medical requests for the immediate delivery of equipment and services essential in the care and preservation of the life of patients."[29] Moreover, the arbitrator gave greater weight to the testimony of the guard, since the guard had no reason to lie or misstate the incident.

A related case involved the discharge of a watch engineer for sleeping on the job and other misconduct.[30] The grievant was seen sleeping by four eyewitnesses, including a Pinkerton guard, a hospital supervisor, and fellow employees. The arbitrator found that his sleeping was of a "flagrant, extensive, and highly consistent quality."[31] He also noted that the grievant's job was important to the hospital, stating, "It is obviously one thing for a clerk to sleep on the job, and it is another for a watch engineer in a Hospital where life may be held in the balance to sleep at his post."[32]

Though the arbitrator sustained the discharge, he gave the grievant back pay because of extenuating circumstances. For one, the hospital had condoned the practice of sleeping on the job until another hospital employee was discharged for that offense, shortly before the grievant was dismissed. Second, guards testified they would regularly awaken engineers who were sleeping. Third, there was a suggestion that even the assistant engineer was aware that sleeping on the job was not a cause for immediate dismissal and that such practice was tolerated. Finally, the chief engineer failed to warn the grievant directly after the incident in question, and even on the next day did not criticize the grievant. These extenuating circumstances might have invalidated the discharge had it not been for the fact that the grievant's untrustworthiness had been established by a series of other examples of misconduct.

In another case, an arbitrator sustained the discharge of a nurse's assistant who allegedly slept in a patient's bed.[33] Arbitrator Kelliher noted that there was a valid hospital rule prohibiting sleeping in a patient's room while on duty, and the grievant admitted she was aware of this rule. The grievant stated she had spent the time in question in the solarium and even had talked to a guard who was in the area. But the guard could not remember her or anyone else in the solarium at that time.The arbitrator chose not to believe the grievant, whose testimony he found inconsistent.

In another case, a porter was discharged for sleeping on the job on New Year's Day. While the grievant didn't deny he had been sleeping, he claimed it was during his nonwork time. This employee had been warned orally and in writing for sleeping before the January 1 incident. Once more the case revolved around credibility. The arbitrator found the grievant's story implausible. The latter could not explain the time that he was not seen in his work area, namely from 9 a.m. until 11:45 a.m. (the latter time he was found sleeping). Moreover, when he was awakened, he did not protest that he had been napping on his own free time (as he contended), but instead merely got up and went to work until his normal lunch period at noon.[34]

DISCHARGE FOR DRUG USE

Drug use and abuse, while certainly not an issue unique to hospital employees, can present major problems because of the quantity and ready availability of various drugs found in a hospital. This can lead to theft of drugs for street resale purposes or direct and unauthorized use of drugs by various hospital employees. Normally a hospital will discharge any employee involved in such activities.

In one case, a nursing attendant was discharged when it was discovered that he had been convicted of a felony charge for selling one ounce of cocaine.[35] Although the grievant's work record had been good, the hospital noted that because of his job classification, he would have access to narcotics. Management stated also that it had to take into consideration the public confidence and was concerned about potential lawsuits for knowingly retaining an individual who had been convicted of this type of felony. Moreover, the hospital contended that not only would its accreditation be in jeopardy, there was a possibility the grievant might sell drugs to others.

The arbitrator acknowledged that consideration must be given when a dischargeable offense occurs away from the work place and on an employee's own time. However, he noted also that when conduct affects the business, the employer has a right to be concerned about its public image and its responsibilities in the care and treatment of the ill. The arbitrator dismissed the union's argument that the hospital's fears were unfounded, commenting:

> A hospital owes a duty toward its patients and toward the public to avoid unnecessary risks that may cause harm to itself or its patients. A significant part of the Employer's activities consists in the responsible dispensing of prescribed drugs in the treatment of ill patients. When the Grievant pleaded guilty to a felony conspiracy to sell cocaine, he admitted to conduct which reflects gross irresponsibility in the handling of drugs.[36]

Another drug case involved a staff nurse at a Veterans Administration hospital who was employed on a three-year probationary period. Before taking this job, he had been under a physician's care for hypertension and was taking the drug, Valium, to control this condition.[37] The grievant asked a nurse whether he could get the drug from the hospital without cost since he was a qualified veteran. The conversation was reported to the Chief of Nursing Services, who became alarmed because the grievant was due to be reassigned to the Intensive Care Unit where nurses had to react instantly to emergencies. In that unit Valium was readily available in the medicine cabinet and there were no controls (at that time) on its being issued to nurses. At a subsequent meeting in the hospital Chief of Staff's office, the grievant was told he must resign, and if he did not the matter would be turned over the Nurse Professional Standards Board for review. The grievant asked for a day to think it over. But when he did not report to work the following day, the Hospital Director put him on an involuntary leave.

Subsequently, the union filed a grievance. In part, the arbitrator found:

> The recommendation by the Chief of Staff that the Grievant be placed on leave was simply based on the belief that it would be a potential

hazard to patient care for a nurse to have a "drug dependence problem." It was no different from a situation where an employee with no
accrued sick leave might be sent home if found to be a carrier of a
communicable disease.[38]

However, a contract provision required that "Supervisors will disregard remarks
or reports of a derogatory nature regarding an employee or group of employees
unless such remarks or reports are discussed with the employees affected." In the
instant case, the Chief of Staff did not call the grievant in to discuss the nurse's
charges prior to recommending that the grievant be placed on involuntary leave.
This contract violation invalidated the decision to place the grievant on leave, and
accordingly the arbitrator ordered that the grievant be reimbursed for loss of
income. However, because the employee was on probation, the hospital did not
have to hire him back. Had the grievant wished to reverse this decision, he would
have had to seek regulatory or statutory relief.

DISCHARGE FOR COMPLAINTS ABOUT UNDERSTAFFING

Because hospital work frequently involves life and death struggles, professional
staff may disagree about established hospital procedures or the adequacy of
hospital staffing. When these disagreements lead some staffers to take a situation
into their own hands, discipline or even discharge may follow. A few cases
illustrate some of the possible situations.

In a case "Collyerized"[39] by the NLRB,* Arbitrator Leo Killion reversed the
discharge of a registered nurse who had complained about inadequate staffing in
the intensive care unit/cardiac care unit (ICU/CCU), but denied her back pay
because she had left her work station without permission on her last night at
work.[40] The arbitrator's decision sustained two grievances filed by the California
Nurses Association and decided unfair labor practice charges in which the NLRB
deferred to the arbitration award.

The RN had been in charge of the ICU/CCU on the night shift. She complained
to the Professional Performance Committee—a committee established under the
contract to make recommendations concerning professional standards—about
understaffing in the intensive care unit. Accordingly, either another RN or an LVN
was assigned to that unit on a regular basis. This additional nurse was to be
"floated out" to other areas of the hospital only when an emergency arose
elsewhere and when there was no critical need for her services in the intensive care
unit.

---

*I.e., when the NLRB deferred to the arbitration award (see Chapter 1).

Subsequently, the RN complained that her assistant was being floated out of the unit every morning between 5 a.m. and 7 a.m. She asked the head nurse to raise the problem with the unit's director. However, the head nurse interpreted the RN's remarks as a threat and reported the entire conversation to the supervisor on her shift. The supervisor told the head nurse to take the matter up directly with the grievant's supervisor. That same evening a meeting was held at which the supervisor, two relief supervisors, and the grievant were present. The entire staffing matter was discussed. Subsequently, an "understanding" was reached, and the grievant was ordered to never again discuss staffing with the head nurse.

The supervisor reported the results of the meeting in writing to the Director of Nurses. The supervisor also informed the grievant orally that a notice for improvement had been written on the report and that she was thereby put on a 90-day probation. The grievant was not given a copy of the notice. Thereafter the grievant kept her word and did not discuss staffing with the head nurse.

She later decided to protest her probationary notice through a grievance. The Director of Nurses told the grievant that the probationary report would be removed only if she submitted her "written resignation." The grievant refused. Later the supervisor complained in a written memo that the grievant was continuing to harass the head nurse through "gossip" and "insinuations." The memo concluded that the grievant had ignored the terms of the probation report and therefore should be terminated.

The grievant was then informed she would be discharged for ignoring the warning and continuing to harass the head nurse, and for her "chronic complaining and gossiping and also because she left her work station the last night of work."

The arbitrator reinstated the grievant, but without back pay because she had left her work station. He observed that no patient or doctor had ever complained about her work, manners, or demeanor. The grievant had raised the issue of inadequate staffing in the unit on the night shift. When she complained about the hospital's consistent use of the assistant she was provided, she was warned not to protest again to the head nurse. The evidence showed that she kept her word. But when the Director of Nursing raised the penalty from probationary notice to discharge— without new facts or events occurring to reopen the case—the arbitrator regarded it as a double jeopardy. Arbitrator Killion remarked:

> It is now an established tenet of industrial jurisprudence that once a penalty has been assessed and accepted it cannot be increased. This principle is based on concepts of double jeopardy borrowed from the criminal law and on those of due process and fair-play.[41]
>
> Although it may well be true that not all rules applicable to industrial job holders should be applied to job occupants in health care institutions, and especially to professional nurses engaged in direct patient care, the proven fairness of a rule such as this "double jeopardy rule"

should have no work-place boundaries in its scope or in its application. And a professional nurse is to be accorded the highest possible degree of due process in all matters relating to her job security.[42]

Further, the arbitrator observed that the contract recognized the rights of registered nurses to engage in reasonable discussions about staffing. "This is a right arising from and inherent in the purpose of the Professional Performance Committee, namely, to 'make recommendations on . . . subjects that are relevant to the . . . maintenance of the highest levels of patient care. . . .' "

Finally, the arbitrator pointed to the fact that the hospital was unable to cite any rule violation committed when the grievant discussed the staffing problem with the head nurse. He said that discipline could not be supported if management had not first called the grievant's attention to some rule she had violated.

In a case involving the same issue, but where no discipline was involved, the union contended that the hospital failed to live up to contractual commitments in maintaining adequate staffing as set forth in the Seniority Clause.[43] That clause provided: "The Hospital agrees and certifies that it is not its intention to operate any patient care unit with inadequate employee staffing and will use all means at its command to avoid any such department understaffed."

The union contended that the hospital failed to maintain an adequate staff when the hospital went from 157 to 118 full-time employees in the period 1968 to 1972. Despite an increase in the number of patients and doctors, there had been a decline in the number of LPNs, dropping the patient-per-nursing-employee ratio from six to eight patients. The union also contended that temporary transfers were being used to cover patient needs in violation of the agreement that such transfers "shall not terminate an employee's seniority."

In dismissing the grievance the arbitrator put great weight on employer exhibits that showed that the nursing-employee-to-patient ratio, over the years in question, ranged from one to five, to one to seven, with an average over a two-month period of one to 6.23 patients. He said the figures did not "bear out any allegation of the overuse of part time employees as the documents indicate an increase in the number of full time employees and a decrease in the number of part time employees. . . ."[44] He added: "There are no specific guidelines as to the proportion of staff to patient load. However, in comparison with general averages and the experience testified to by the Director of Nursing, the Hospital appears to fall within the general guidelines."[45]

DEMANDS FOR PURCHASE OF EQUIPMENT

An arbitrator ordered the County of Los Angeles to purchase additional emergency equipment for use by the housestaff of Harbor General Hospital, upholding a grievance filed by the Joint Council of Interns and Residents.[46] The council contended there were too few "crash" carts containing monitoring and defibrillating equipment for use on heart attack patients outside the intensive care units. The council asked for 13 additional carts, with an absolute minimum of seven carts.[47] A fund had been established under the parties' 1975 collective bargaining agreement, and a portion of interns' and residents' salaries was diverted into this fund to improve patient care. The council suggested using this fund to buy the equipment.

The arbitrator sustained the grievance, noting that the county had requested 13 carts from the Department of Health Services, which reduced the number to six in its budget request for the hospital. The budget request indicated to the arbitrator that the county shared the council's opinion that additional equipment was necessary. Moreover, he observed, "There can be no greater priority in the patient care area than the prevention of a loss of life and the record substantiates a mutual agreement between the parties in this regard and no discussion is necessary."[48]

In answer to the county's contention that the current equipment was "adequate," the arbitrator noted:

> Although the standard dictionary meaning of the term "adequate" is "barely satisfactory" which the county appears to be arguing in relationship to the existing crash carts, it would appear to be a dangerous if not callous argument where the threat of a loss of life is involved, and the arbitrator on the basis of need reflected in the record rejects this argument. Evidence tends to establish that the optimal number of crash carts is 13 and that a smaller number though not ideal would be sufficient.[49]

Noting that the county had purchased an additional crash cart and that the record indicated that there was "a source of funds available," the arbitrator ordered the county to purchase six additional crash carts.[50]

DISCHARGE FOR BREACH OF HOSPITAL ETHICS

Though hospitals do not have a monopoly on ethical issues, there seems to be a greater chance of possible breach of ethics in such institutions. Disclosing confidential information to patients, or disclosing medical records or information about a patient's condition to the public without authorization are but two of the possibilities.

A California hospital violated its collective bargaining agreement when it discharged a psychiatric technician for "unethical" conduct.[51] In 1976 the grievant attended a hospital staff meeting during which the subject of ethical conduct of hospital employees was discussed. The Medical Director told employees that all "confidential communications" should come from his office and not from them. He also disclosed that an unidentified physician had backdated medical records, and that he was devising a system to avoid that problem in the future. After the meeting a staff psychiatrist asked the grievant if he knew anything about the backdating. The grievant said he had heard rumors and then disclosed the name of the physician alluded to in the rumors. When the Medical Director learned that the grievant had divulged the contents of the rumors, he was discharged for violating the hospital's code of ethical conduct, which contained the following contract provision:

> The employer shall have the right to discharge any employee without notice for proven dishonesty, insubordination, insobriety, incompetence, willful negligence, failure to perform work as required, or for violation of hospital house rules, which must be conspicuously posted.[52]

The union argued that the grievant had not violated hospital rules, because he merely answered a question from a physician about a rumor he had heard. The union also contended the rules had not been "conspicuously posted" as the contract required.

The arbitrator noted that the hospital did not introduce its code of conduct into evidence at the arbitration hearing, and that "the medical director conceded that staff members have never been directed to refuse to answer questions put to them by doctors about other doctors."[53] Thus the hospital "failed to carry the burden of proving that the grievant's conduct violated any established and existing hospital code of conduct." Because the manual was not introduced, the hospital also failed to prove that it posted house rules as required by the contract.[54] The grievant was thus reinstated with back pay and no loss of seniority.

In a similar case,[55] a methadone counselor at the outpatient clinic of the Beth Israel Medical Center was discharged based on her poor work record, her failure to follow clinic procedures and instructions, and an incident in which she divulged an unauthorized and improper disclosure made by a methadone patient.

The arbitrator, in sustaining the discharge, made the following cogent remarks:

> For a hospital employee to divulge the confidentiality of the counselor-patient relationship inadvertently or otherwise is a major violation of the professional ethic and the sensitive and essential role a hospital, and especially a methadone clinic, plays in our society. In and of itself such unauthorized and improper disclosure is cause for discharge. The circumstances in which the disclosure was made were, indeed, inadvertent or as perhaps more accurately described by the grievant herself in her letter to the Personnel Director, an indiscretion. There is no question or even hint of maliciousness, arrogance, defiance or vin-

dictiveness in the grievant's action in this incident. But however inadvertent, her indiscretion was a serious violation of a cardinal rule and the damage in terms of the disclosure being made on the phone in the patient's presence was, from a clinical standpoint, far reaching, highly disturbing to the patient, and irrevocable.[56]

The arbitrator found that her prior record precluded any leniency in the case.

DISCHARGE FOR LOSS OF CERTIFICATION AND/OR LICENSURE

The medical field has widespread requirements for either certification or licensure. Physicians and nurses are required to be registered, while technicians in various hospitals frequently must have state certification in order to work. When an employee loses certification or registration, a hospital may discharge the individual.

In one case, the grievant was hired by a hospital as an Emergency Room Attendant/Ambulance Attendant. This position required that he have an "Emergency Medical Technician" card issued by the New York State Department of Health, certifying that he did "meet the requirements of an Emergency Medical Technician."[57] Although the grievant had possessed this card, the state subsequently suspended it after discovering that the card had been issued to him based on "fraudulent documents and untrue statements regarding his medical background."

Arbitrator Eisenberg stated that the grievant's fraudulent acquisition of the certificate and his subsequent loss of state certification could by themselves constitute a valid basis for discharge. But beyond that, the arbitrator also found additional grounds to sustain this employee's dismissal—such as neglecting prescribed tasks; wearing a hospital jacket other than the one prescribed for his job, a practice that led to his being mistaken for a medical intern or resident; and numerous inaccuracies in his employment application.

EMPLOYER'S OBLIGATION TO PAY FOR UNIFORMS

Though the wearing of uniforms is certainly not limited to employees of hospitals and other health care facilities, these organizations do have a high percentage of personnel in uniform. Sometimes disputes arise over whether hospitals are obligated to either furnish uniforms or pay for them. The answer usually turns on the language of the collective agreement or on past practice.

In the *Pacific Medical Center* case, nurse aides contended that the hospital had the obligation to pay the cost of laundering and furnishing the green dresses they wore.[58] The contract contained the following clause:

> When employees are required to wear uniforms or special type work clothes while in the employ of the Hospital, the cost of laundering and furnishing same shall be borne by the Hospital; provided that the Hospital not be required to furnish or launder apparel traditionally worn by such employees in hospitals generally. The term "uniform" includes wearing apparel and accessories of distinctive design or color.

The union argued that the nurse aides' dresses were not "traditionally" worn and therefore should be furnished by the hospital; and second, that these green dresses were "uniforms" within the meaning of the clause above. The hospital refused to pay for furnishing and laundering the dresses on the grounds that they were not "uniforms."

However, the arbitrator observed that the definition of uniforms found in this clause was not controlling because the parties had executed a subsequent letter of understanding that required them to adopt the definition of "uniform" supplied by the state Industrial Welfare Commission. According to that definition, a uniform had to be of a given color and had to feature some other common element, such as style, cut, or material. Because the nurse aides were required only to wear green dresses, with no other stipulation, these garments did not fall under the furnish and launder provision.[59]

In another case, both parties agreed that the clause that required the hospital to provide and maintain uniforms had been violated. The arbitrator held that the hospital, from the date of the award, must provide and maintain the uniforms it required employees to wear.[60] The arbitrator awarded a uniform allowance rate dating back to the date of the grievance, over the objection of the hospital. He reasoned, "To deny a monetary equivalent which is readily calculable would be grossly unfair to the employees and would allow the employer a windfall to which it was not entitled under the contract."[61] However, the hospital's liability (uniform allowance rate) was limited to the time the union filed the grievance, because the union had numerous opportunities to bring the violation to the attention of the hospital prior to then.

RELIGIOUS OBJECTION TO A UNIFORM

Though not a case with widespread precedential value, an arbitration award involving an operating room technician's refusal to wear scrub gown pants has attracted a great deal of attention from the various arbitration reporting services.[62]

The grievant, a member of the Christian Fellowship Missionary Baptist Church, believed she was bound by the following passage from Deuteronomy not to wear male apparel, such as pants: ". . . the woman shall not wear that which pertaineth unto a man, neither shall a man put on a woman's garment; for all that do so are an abomination unto the Lord thy God" (Deut. 22:5).

This woman had been employed as an operating room technician at Hurley Hospital for nearly 20 years when the hospital began a new program to control the risk of infections in operating areas. In addition to making certain changes in the operating suite, all operating room personnel were required to wear pants. When the grievant refused to comply with the requirement to wear the uniform, she was transferred to another job at the same rate of pay.

The arbitrator said that under the collective bargaining agreement the hospital had the right to require all operating room personnel to wear the new uniform, because of the following contract language: "The Hospital will retain all rights, responsibilities and prerogatives normally exercised by the Hospital in the past, subject only to such restrictions of those rights as are expressly provided in this agreement." The arbitrator noted that

> . . . when a particular uniform is indicated in the interest of patient care, the Hospital is free to require that such uniform be worn by its employees so long as the Hospital provides the uniform. . . . Furthermore, the arbitrator finds that the rationale for requiring the pants uniform is based on a bona fide job qualification. It is directly connected to the patient's health, insofar as the uniform is one means of reducing infections which originate in the operating room.[63]

Regarding the grievant's religious objections, the arbitrator found that the contract prohibited religious discrimination. He found that under Title VII of the Civil Rights Act, the hospital had to show that it could not accommodate her religious conviction without "undue hardship on the conduct of its business." Concluding that the burden of proof fell to the hospital, he also conceded that a job transfer was another way to resolve the problem. The arbitrator concluded that the grievant should design a scrub gown that would meet her objections and should submit it to the hospital's Infection Control Committee for their approval.[64]

A review of the published awards in this chapter shows that there is only one arbitration issue that is unique to hospitals: alleged abuse of patients. No other industry, of course, has patients. Patient abuse was found to take the form of physical, verbal, or even sexual abuse. These cases posed great dilemmas for hospitals, as they have a responsibility to protect the patients entrusted to their care. Of course, unions were concerned about the discipline/discharge of members who might be punished erroneously for offenses that would adversely affect their future job possibilities. Hospital environments also seem to exacerbate the chances of other types of grievances reaching arbitration, such as drug abuse.

NOTES

1. Kaiser Foundation Hospitals, The Permanente Medical Group and Kaiser Foundation Health Plan and Hospital and Institutional Workers, Local 250, February 8, 1973. 72-2 ARB 8673.
2. *Ibid.*, p. 5387.
3. Children's Hospital, Inc. (St. Paul, Minn.) and Minnesota Licensed Practical Nurses Association, June 27, 1974. HMMM-2.
4. *Ibid.*, p. 4.
5. Little Forest Medical Center and Retail Clerks, Local 698, October 7, 1977. 69 LA 671.
6. Jackson County Medical Care Facility and American Federation of State, County and Municipal Employees, Council 55, Local 139, September 9, 1975. 65 LA 389.
7. Oil City Hospital and American Federation of State, County and Municipal Employees, Local 801, January 25, 1978. 78-1 ARB 8082.
8. New York University Medical Center and Drug and Hospital Union, Local 1199, April 13, 1973. LVH.
9. Elizabeth Horton Memorial Hospital and Licensed Practical Nurses of New York, Inc. Employees Association, December 18, 1974. 74-2 ARB 8588. Same case reported at 64 LA 96.
10. Hillhaven of California, Inc., Hospital and Hospital and Institutional Workers Union, Local 399, SEIU, June 24, 1976. BAHA-27.
11. Ralph K. Davies Medical Center and Hospital and Institutional Workers Union, Local 250, October 25, 1977. BAHA-36.
12. *Ibid.*, pp. 10, 11.
13. St. John's Episcopal Hospital and New York State Nurses Association, March 20, 1978. LVH.
14. *Ibid.*, p. 15.
15. Salinas Valley (Calif.) Memorial Hospital District and Hospital and Institutional Workers Union, Local 250, February 10, 1977. LAIG 1803.
16. *Ibid.*
17. Oak Pavilion Nursing Home and Rehabilitation Center and National Union of Hospital and Nursing Home Employees, July 6, 1973. 73-1 ARB 8198.
18. Fort Wayne State Hospital and American Federation of State, County and Municipal Employees, February 26, 1975. 74-2 ARB 8706.
19. Menorah Home and Hospital and Service Employees International Union, Local 144, June 2, 1978. LVH.
20. *Ibid.*, p. 4.
21. Greater Harlem Nursing Home and RWDSU, District 1199, May 7, 1979. LVH.
22. South Oaks Hospital and National Union of Hospital and Health Care Employees, District 1199, January 8, 1976. LVH.
23. *Ibid.*, pp. 6-7.
24. Mount Sinai Hospital and National Union of Hospital and Health Care Employees, RWDSU, District 1199, August 25, 1977. LVH.
25. *Ibid.*, p. 6.
26. Mount Sinai Hospital and National Union of Hospital and Health Care Employees, RWDSU, District 1199, November 19, 1976. LVH.
27. *Ibid.*, p. 9.

28. Douglas County Hospital, Nebraska, and American Federation of State, County and Municipal Employees, Local 2845, January 5, 1976. 650 GERR:B-2.

29. *Ibid.*, p. B-3.

30. Peralta Hospital and International Union of Operating Engineers, Local 39, December 29, 1964. BAHA-4.

31. *Ibid.*, p. 19.

32. *Ibid.*

33. Northwestern Memorial Hospital and Hospital Employees Labor Program (HELP) of Metropolitan Chicago, March 22, 1979. CHC.

34. Hospital of the Albert Einstein College of Medicine and Drug and Hospital Union, Local 1199, October 26, 1972. LVH.

35. Providence Hospital and Hospital and Institutional Workers Union, Local 250, April 13, 1976. BAHA-25.

36. *Ibid.*, p. 11.

37. Veterans Administration Hospital (Kerrville, Texas) and American Federation of Government Employees, Local 2281, November 5, 1977. 740 GERR:29.

38. *Ibid.*, p. 32.

39. See Chapter 1 for a further discussion of the Collyer doctrine.

40. Auburn Faith Community Hospital, Inc. (Auburn, Calif.) and California Nurses Association, May 4, 1976. 66 LA 882. Same case reported at 1000 WCR:A-11.

41. *Ibid.*, p. 893.

42. *Ibid.*

43. Alpena General Hospital and United Steelworkers of America, Local 206-A, July 26, 1973. 73-1 ARB 8226.

44. *Ibid.*, p. 3825.

45. *Ibid.*

46. County of Los Angeles, Harbor General Hospital and Joint Council of Interns and Resident Physicians of Los Angeles County, May 10, 1976. 1004 WCR:A-3.

47. *Ibid.*

48. *Ibid.*, p. A-4.

49. *Ibid.*

50. *Ibid.*

51. Mission Terrace Hospital and Service Employees International Union, Local 250, July 11, 1977. 1060 WCR:A-7. Same case reported at LAIG 1934.

52. *Ibid.*, p. A-7.

53. *Ibid.*

54. *Ibid.*

55. Beth Israel Medical Center at St. Vincent's Staten Island, and Drug and Hospital Union, District 1199, June 8, 1975. LVH.

56. *Ibid.*, p. 3.

57. Long Island Jewish Medical Center and Drug and Hospital Union, Local 1199, August 3, 1973. LVH.

58. Pacific Medical Center and Hospital and Institutional Workers Union, Local 250, February 10, 1970. 70-1 ARB 8426.

59. *Ibid.*

60. Metropolitan Hospital (Philadelphia, Pa.) and National Union of Hospital and Health Care Employees, District 1199C, November 18, 1976. LAIG 1767.

61. *Ibid.*

62. Hurley Hospital and American Federation of State, County and Municipal Employees, Local 1603, May 25, 1978. Reported at 70 LA 1061; 78-1 ARB 8266; 769 GERR:13; and LAIG 2109.

63. *Ibid.*, 70 LA 1063.

64. Subsequently, the Infection Control Committee decided that the grievant's proposed design change did not meet their specifications. Another hearing was therefore held on the matter, and the hospital was permitted to transfer her. Hurley Hospital and American Federation of State, County and Municipal Employees, Local 1603, November 7, 1978. 71 LA 1013.

Federal Mediation and Conciliation Service: Assistance in the Health Care Industry

PART 1420—FEDERAL MEDIATION AND CONCILIATION SERVICE—ASSISTANCE IN THE HEALTH CARE INDUSTRY

Sec.

1420.1 Functions of the Service in Health Care Industry Bargaining under the Labor-Management Relations Act, as amended (hereinafter "the Act").

1420.2—1420.4 [Reserved]

1420.5 Optional Input of Parties to Board of Inquiry Selection.

1420.6—1420.7 [Reserved]

1420.8 FMCS Deferral to Parties' Own Private Factfinding Procedures.

1420.9 FMCS Deferral to Parties' Own Private Interest Arbitration Procedures.

Authority: Secs. 8(d), 201, 203, 204, and 213 of the Labor Management Relations Act, as amended in 1974 (29 U.S.C. 158(d), 171, 173, 174 and 183).

§ 1420.1 Functions of the Service in health care industry bargaining under the Labor-Management Relations Act, as amended (hereinafter "the Act").

(a) *Dispute Mediation.* Whenever a collective bargaining dispute involves employees of a health care institution, either party to such collective bargaining must give certain statutory notices to the Federal Mediation and Conciliation Service (hereinafter "the Service") before resorting to strike or lockout and before terminating or modifying any existing collective bargaining agreement. Thereafter, the Service will promptly communicate with the parties and use its best efforts, by mediation and conciliation, to bring them to agreement. The parties shall participate fully and promptly in such meetings as may be called by the Service for the purpose of aiding in a settlement of the dispute. (29 U.S.C. Sections 158(d) and 158(g).

(b) *Boards of Inquiry.* If, in the opinion of the Director of the Service a threatened or actual strike or lockout affecting a health care institution will substantially interrupt the delivery of health care in the locality concerned, the Director may establish within certain statutory time periods an impartial Board of Inquiry. The Board of Inquiry will investigate the issues involved in the dispute and make a written report, containing the findings of fact and the Board's non-binding recommendations for settling the dispute, to the parties within 15 days after the establishment of such a Board. (29 U.S.C. 183.)

§ 1420.2—1420.4 [Reserved]
§ 1420.5 Optional input of parties to Board of Inquiry selection.

The Act gives the Director of the Service the authority to select the individual(s) who will serve as the Board of Inquiry if the Director decides to establish a Board of Inquiry in a particular health care industry bargaining dispute (29 U.S.C. 183). If the parties to collective bargaining involving a health care institution(s) desire to have some input to the Service's selection of an individual(s) to serve as a Board of Inquiry (hereinafter "BoI"), they may jointly exercise the following optional procedure: (a) At any time at least 90 days prior to the expiration date of a collective bargaining agreement in a contract renewal dispute, or at any time prior to the notice required under clause (B) of Section 8(d) of the Act (29 U.S.C. 158(d)) in an initial contract dispute, the employer(s) and the union(s) in the dispute may jointly submit to the Service a list of arbitrators or other impartial individuals who would be acceptable BoI members both to the employer(s) and to the union(s). Such list submission must identify the dispute(s) involved and must include addresses and telephone numbers of the individuals listed and any information available to the parties as to current and past employment of the individuals listed. The parties may jointly rank the individuals in order of preference if they desire to do so.

(b) The Service will make every effort to select any BoI that might be appointed from that jointly submitted list. However, the Service cannot promise that it will select a BoI from such list. The chances of the Service finding one or more individuals on such list available to serve as the BoI will be increased if the list contains a sufficiently large number of names and if it is submitted at as early a date as possible. Nevertheless, the parties can even preselect and submit jointly to the Service one specific individual if that individual agrees to be available for the particular BoI time period. Again the Service will not be bound to appoint that individual, but will be receptive to such a submission by the parties.

(c) The jointly submitted list may be worked out and agreed to by (1) A particular set of parties in contemplation of a particular upcoming negotiation dispute between them, or (2) a particular set of parties for use in all future disputes between that set of parties, or (3) a group of various health care institutions and unions in a certain community or geographic area for use in all disputes between any two or more of those parties.

(d) Submission or receipt of any such list will not in any way constitute an admission of the appropriateness of appointment of a BoI nor an expression of the desirability of a BoI by any party or by the Service.

(e) This joint submission procedure is a purely optional one to provide the parties with an opportunity to have input into the selection of a BoI if they so desire.

(f) Such jointly submitted lists should be sent jointly by employer(s) and the union(s) to the appropriate regional office of the Service. The regional offices of the Service are as follows:

Region 1, Federal Building, Room 2937, 26 Federal Plaza, New York, NY 10007.
Region 2, Mall Building, Room 401, Fourth and Chestnut Streets, Philadelphia, PA 19106.
Region 3, Suite 400, 1422 West Peachtree Street, N.W., Atlanta, GA 30309.
Region 4, Superior Building, Room 1525, 815 Superior Avenue, N.E., Cleveland, OH 44114.
Region 5, Insurance Exchange Building, 16th Floor, 175 West Jackson Boulevard, Chicago, IL 60604.
Region 6, Chromalloy Plaza Fifth Floor, 120 South Central Street, St. Louis, MO 63105.
Region 7, Francisco Bay Building, Suite 235, 50 Francisco Street, San Francisco, CA 94133.
Region 8, Fourth and Vine Building, Room 444, 2615 Fourth Avenue, Seattle, WA 98121.

§ 1420.6-1420.7 [Reserved]
§ 1420.8 FMCS deferral to parties' own private factfinding procedures.

(a) The Service will defer to the parties' own privately agreed to factfinding procedure and decline to appoint a Board of Inquiry (BoI) as long as the parties' own procedure meets certain conditions so as to satisfy the Service's responsibilities under the Act. The Service will decline to appoint a BoI and leave the selection and appointment of a factfinder to the parties to a dispute if both the parties have agreed in writing to their own factfinding procedure which meets the following conditions:

(1) The factfinding procedure must be invoked automatically at a specified time (for example, at contract expiration if no agreement is reached).

(2) It must provide a fixed and determinate method for selecting the impartial factfinder(s).

(3) It must provide that there can be no strike or lockout and no changes in conditions of employment (except by mutual agreement) prior to or during the factfinding procedure and for a period of at least seven days after the factfinding is completed.

(4) It must provide that the factfinder(s) will make a written report to the parties, containing the findings of fact and the recommendations of the factfinder(s) for settling the dispute, a copy of which is sent to the Service. The parties to a dispute who have agreed to such a factfinding procedure should jointly submit a copy of such agreed upon procedure to the appropriate regional office of the Service at as early a date as possible, but in any event prior to the appointment of a BoI by the Service. See § 1420.5(f) for the addresses of the regional offices.

(b) Since the Service does not appoint the factfinder under paragraph (a) of this section, the Service cannot pay for such factfinder. In this respect, such deferral by the Service to the parties' own factfinding procedure is different from the use of stipulation agreements between the parties which give to the Service the authority to select and appoint a factfinder at a later date than the date by which a BoI would have to be appointed under the Act. Under such stipulation agreements by which the parties give the Service authority to appoint a factfinder at a later date, the Service can pay for the factfinder. However, in the deferral to the parties' own factfinding procedure, the parties choose their own factfinder and they pay for the factfinder.

§ 1420.9 FMCS deferral to parties' own private interest arbitration procedures.

(a) The Service will defer to the parties' own privately agreed to interest arbitration procedure and decline to appoint a Board of Inquiry (BoI) as long as the parties' own procedure meets certain conditions so as to satisfy the Service's responsibilities under the Act. The Service will decline to appoint BoI if the parties to a dispute have agreed in writing to their own interest arbitration procedure which meets the following conditions:

(1) The interest arbitration procedure must provide that there can be no strike or lockout and no changes in conditions of employment (except by mutual agreement) during the contract negotiation covered by the interest arbitration procedure and the period of any subsequent interest arbitration proceedings.

(2) It must provide that the award of the arbitrator(s) under the interest arbitration procedure is final and binding on both parties.

(3) It must provide a fixed and determinate method for selecting the impartial interest arbitrator(s).

(4) The interest arbitration procedure must provide for a written award by the interest arbitrator(s).

(b) The parties to a dispute who have agreed to such an interest arbitration procedure should jointly submit a copy of their agreed upon procedure to the appropriate regional office of the Service at as early a date as possible, but in any event prior to the appointment of BoI by the Service. See § 1420.5(f) for the addresses of regional offices.

These new regulations are a part of the Service's overall approach to implementing the health care amendments of 1974 in a manner consistent with the Congressional intent of promoting peaceful settlements of labor disputes at our vital health care facilities. The Service will work with the parties in every way possible to be flexible and to tailor its approach so as to accommodate the needs of the parties in the interest of settling the dispute. This was the motivating principle behind these new regulations which permit input by the parties to the Board of Inquiry selection and allow the parties to set up their own factfinding or arbitration procedures in lieu of the Board of Inquiry procedure. We encourage the parties, both unions and management, to take advantage of these and other options and to work with the Service to tailor their approach and procedures to fit the needs of their bargaining situations.

Classification of Health Care Arbitration Cases

In the Introduction to Part III of this book we discussed the virtues and pitfalls of the case approach to labor arbitration. Whatever the limitations of this approach, reviewing cases, especially those in health care, can provide practitioners with guidelines by which to assess the strength of their own cases. This approach can also be useful for developing strategies and arguments. Moreover, cases may be referred to the arbitrator for review in the parties' briefs or oral summations, in an attempt to persuade the arbitrator to their respective points of view. While arbitration cases do not have the same precedent value as do court decisions, most practitioners and arbitrators read the cases carefully and take them seriously. Furthermore, both management and labor find it useful to review the awards made by a particular arbitrator to evaluate his or her attitudes, values, and decision-making process. This facilitates the selection of a special arbitrator.

Before now practitioners seeking to research hospital-based arbitrations have found that the reporting services do not classify cases by industry. Thus, the researcher faced the laborious task of reading each citation for each volume of the arbitration reporters—as many as 400 to 500 entries. The task was further complicated by the fact that the reader would often not know what the issue was in a given case until he looked it up.

In this appendix we have attempted to save the busy practitioner some time—not only by identifying hospital/health care cases, but also by classifying them by issue and source. This kind of organization should greatly facilitate necessary research. For an explanation of our sources for these cases and the abbreviations used in these listings, see the Introduction to Part III.

ARBITRABILITY—PROCEDURAL

Associated Hospitals of San Francisco on behalf of Ralph K. Davies Medical Center and Hospital and Institutional Workers, Local 250, October 18, 1976. BAHA-30.

City of Memphis (Tenn.) Hospital Authority and American Federation of State, County and Municipal Employees, Local 1733, November 12, 1974. LAIG 1211.

Community Health Care Center (New Haven, Conn.) and Office and Professional Employees International Union, Local 466, December 2, 1975. LAIG 1500.

Hurley Medical Center (Flint, Mich.) and American Federation of State, County and Municipal Employees, Local 1603, December 12, 1975. LAIG 1521.

Pontiac (Mich.) General Hospital and American Federation of State, County and Municipal Employees, Local 100, June 27, 1975. LAIG 1419.

ARBITRABILITY—SUBSTANTIVE

Brookdale Hospital and Medical Center and District 1199 National Union of Hospital and Health Care Employees, RWDSU, May 24, 1977. 68 LA 908.

City of Detroit (Mich.) and Registered Nurses Organization, Unit I, October 25, 1977. LAIG 2012.

Peralta Hospital and Hospital and Institutional Workers Union, Local 250, June 5, 1969. BAHA-10.

EMPLOYEE BENEFITS

Educational Leave

Carney Hospital (Boston, Mass.) and Massachusetts Nurses Association, August 25, 1978. LAIG 2184.

Free Beverages

South Oaks Hospital and Broadlawn Manor Nursing Home, and District 1199, National Union of Hospital and Health Care Employees, RWDSU, December 6, 1977. LVH.

Free Parking

Kingsbrook Jewish Medical Center and District 1199 National Union of Hospital and Health Care Employees, RWDSU, July 1, 1974. LVH.

Free Prescription Plan

Mount Sinai Hospital and Drug and Hospital Union, Local 1199, April 19, 1972. 72-2 ARB 8595.

Mount Sinai Hospital and Retail, Wholesale and Department Store Union, Local 1199, July 1, 1972. 72-2 ARB 8512.

Funeral Leave

Gratiot Community Hospital (Alma, Mich.) and American Federation of State, County and Municipal Employees, Local 1511, November 27, 1975. LAIG 1523.

Mt. Sinai Hospital of Cleveland and Northeast Ohio Public Employees, American Federation of State, County and Municipal Employees, District Council 78, Local 2679, March 12, 1976. 76-1 ARB 8250.

Presbyterian Hospital and New York State Nurses Association, May 19, 1976. LVH.

Holiday Pay

Akron (Ohio) General Medical Center and Akron General Medical Center Employees Union, September 2, 1975. LAIG 1464.

Appalachian Regional Hospitals, Inc. and United Steelworkers of America, Local 14491, July 20, 1977. 77-2 ARB 8354.

Grant Hospital of Chicago and Hospital Employees Labor Program of Metropolitan Chicago, May 4, 1978. CHC-14.

Hillsdale Community Health Center and Retail Store Employees' Union, Local No. 36, September 27, 1978. 1128 WCR A-5.

Metropolitan Hospital and District 1199, National Union of Hospital and Health Care Employees, December 3, 1976. LVH.

Park Community Hospital and Service Employees International Union, Local 70, April 5, 1975. 1975 ARB 8037.

Leaves of Absence

Cook County Hospital (Ill.) and Building Service Municipal Employees Union, Local 46, October 31, 1975. LAIG 1473.

East Liverpool City Hospital and International Brotherhood of Pottery and Allied Workers, Local Union 333, August 25, 1975. 1975 ARB 8295.

St. Ann's Hospital of Columbus, Inc. and Ohio Nurses Association, September 25, 1976. 1021 WCR A-16.

Veterans Administration Hospital and American Federation of Government Employees, Local 2080, May 6, 1975. 1975 ARB 8144.

Visiting Nurse Association of Reading and Berks County and Pennsylvania Nurses Association, July 28, 1978. 78-2 ARB 8404. Same case reported at LAIG 2178.

Overtime

Associated Hospitals of the East Bay and ILWU, Local 6, December 30, 1975. BAHA-23.

Brooklyn Cumberland Medical Centers and National Union of Hospital and Health Care Employees, RWDSU, District 1199, December 1, 1975. LVH.

Community Health Care Center Plan, Inc. and Office and Professional Employees International Union, Local 466, April 9, 1974. 62 LA 1134.

Hurley Hospital and Hurley Hospital Head Nurses Staff Council, September 6, 1972. 59 LA 487.

State of Rhode Island and Hospital Employees Local Union 1134, March 10, 1976. LAIG 1581.

Western Psychiatric Institute and Clinic and Hospital and Health Care Employees, RWDSU, District 1199P, September 29, 1977. 1072 WCR A-11.

Youngstown Hospital Association and Ohio Nurses Association, May 15, 1978. 78-1 ARB 8243.

Youngstown Hospital Association and Ohio Nurses Association, January 4, 1979. 71 LA 1269. See also LAIG 2258.

Pension

Little Forest Medical Center and American Federation of State, County and Municipal Employees, District Council 78, Local 2028, December 31, 1974. 74-2 ARB 8628.

Retirement, Mandatory

City of Hope National Medical Center and International Union of Operating Engineers, Local 501, September 23, 1976. 67 LA 518.

McGee-Women's Hospital and International Union of Operating Engineers, Local 95-95A, May 15, 1974. 62 LA 987. See same case reported at 74-1 ARB 8174.

Waterbury (Conn.) Hospital and Drug and Hospital Union, Local 119, January 3, 1974. 62 LA 113. See same case reported at 73-2 ARB 8572.

Sick Leave and Sick Pay

Kaiser-Permanente Medical Care Program and Hospital and Institutional Workers Union, Local 250, SEIU, January 16, 1975. 64 LA 245.

Nantucket (Mass.) Cottage Hospital and Massachusetts Nurses Association, April 27, 1979. LAIG 2342.

Sunny Acres Cuyahoga County Tuberculosis Hospital and American Federation of State, County and Municipal Employees, District Council 78, Local 1746, June 7, 1972. 72-1 ARB 8305.

Westchester County (N.Y.) and New York State Nurses Association, May 7, 1976. LAIG 1707.

Youngstown (Ohio) Osteopathic Hospital Association and Ohio Nurses Association, June 10, 1977. LAIG 1931. Same case reported at 9 Indus. Rel. Report 3.4.

Uniforms

Associated Hospitals of San Francisco, Pacific Medical Center and Hospital and Institutional Workers Union, Local 250, February 10, 1970. 70-1 ARB 8426.

Metropolitan Hospital (Philadelphia, Pa.) and National Union of Hospital and Health Care Employees, District 1199C, November 8, 1976. LAIG 1767.

Vacations

Akron (Ohio) General Medical Center and Akron General Medical Center Employees Union, December 6, 1974. LAIG 1220.

Association of Hospitals of Santa Clara County and the California Nurses' Association, March 8, 1974. 74-1 ARB 8035. Same case reported at LAIG 1062.

Beth Israel Medical Center and District 1199, National Union of Hospital and Health Care Employees, RWDSU, March 23, 1976. LVH.

Community Health Care Center Plan, Inc. and Office and Professional Employees International Union, Local 466, April 9, 1974. 62 LA 1134.

Community Hospital of San Gabriel, Calif. and Service Employees International Union, SEIU, Local 399, Hospital and Service Employees Union, January 19, 1978. 78-1 ARB 8061.

W.A. Foote Memorial Hospital and International Union of Operating Engineers, Local 547, March 26, 1974. 74-1 ARB 8076.

Morningside Nursing Home and Local 150 Service and Hospital Employees International Union, AFL-CIO, April 19, 1974. 74-1 ARB 8118.

Providence Medical Center and International Union of Operating Engineers, Local 286, March 31, 1977. 77-1 ARB 8191. Same case reported at 68 LA 663.

St. Joseph Hospital and Pennsylvania Nurses Association, October 12, 1976. 1031 WCR A-8.

St. Luke's Hospital Center and Drug and Hospital Union, Local 1199, November 16, 1973. 63 LA 71.

St. Patrick Hospital and St. Patrick Local Unit, Montana Nurses' Association, November 14, 1977. 77-2 ARB 8575.

Sunshine Convalescent Hospital and Service and Hospital Employees Union, Local 399, February 27, 1974. 62 LA 276.

Wash-Up Time

Akron (Ohio) City Hospital and American Federation of State, County and Municipal Employees, Local 684, January 5, 1976. LAIG 1497.

DISCIPLINE AND DISCHARGE

Absenteeism

Appalachian Regional Hospitals, Inc. and International Union of District 50, United Mine Workers of America, Local 14585, April 21, 1970. 70-2 ARB 8515.

Barberton (Ohio) Citizens Hospital, Inc. and American Federation of State, County and Municipal Employees, District Council 11, October 24, 1975. LAIG 1487.

Bon Secours Hospital Inc. and Hospital Employees Local 1273, Laborers International, October 22, 1976. 77-1 ARB 8129.

Brooklyn Methodist Hospital and District 1199, December 6, 1977. LVH.

Dameron Hospital and California Nurses Association, December 30, 1975. 76-1 ARB 8102. Same case reported at LAIG 1506 and BAHA-24.

Franklin Hospital and Hospital and Institutional Workers Union, Local 250, February 14, 1968. BAHA-9.

Franklin Hospital and Hospital and Institutional Workers Union, Local 250, April 26, 1973. BAHA-17.

Merritt Hospital and Hospital and Institutional Workers' Union, Local 250, July 12, 1977. BAHA-33.

Michael Reese Hospital and Medical Center and Hospital Employees Labor Program of Metropolitan Chicago, July 15, 1975. CHC-3.

Michael Reese Hospital and Medical Center and Hospital Employees Labor Program of Metropolitan Chicago, February 21, 1976. CHC-7.

New York University Institute of Rehabilitation Medicine and Drug and Hospital Union, March 6, 1974. LVH.

Providence Hospital and X-ray Technologists' Unit of ILWU, Local 6, January 19, 1977. BAHA.

Rush-Presbyterian-St. Luke's Medical Center (Chicago, Ill.) and Hospital Employees Labor Program, August 10, 1976. CHC-10.

St. Joseph Hospital and Pennsylvania Nurses Association, December 21, 1976. 77-1 ARB 8016.

Veterans Administration Hospital (Ill.) and American Federation of Government Employees, Local 2107, March 27, 1978. 758 GERR:37.

Veterans Administration Hospital (Pittsburgh, Pa.) and American Federation of Government Employees, Local 2028, January 24, 1975. 74-2 ARB 8611.

Abuse of Patients (Physical)

Bethesda Lutheran Infirmary and Minnesota Licensed Practical Nurses Association, October 23, 1978. HMMM-6.

Fort Wayne State Hospital and American Federation of State, County and Municipal Employees, February 26, 1975. 74-2 ARB 8706.

Greater Harlem Nursing Home and RWDSU, District 1199, May 7, 1979. LVH.

Menorah Home and Hospital and Service Employees International Union, Local 144, June 2, 1978. LVH.

Oak Pavilion Nursing Home and Rehabilitation Center and National Union of Hospital and Nursing Home Employees, AFL-CIO July 6, 1973. 73-1 ARB 8198.

Salinas Valley (Calif.) Memorial Hospital District and Hospital and Institutional Workers Union, Local 250, February 10, 1977. LAIG 1803.

St. John's Episcopal Hospital and New York State Nurses Association, March 20, 1978. LVH.

Abuse of Patients (Poor Attitude toward Patients)

Ralph K. Davies Medical Center and Hospital and Institutional Workers Union, Local 250, October 25, 1977. BAHA-36.

Hillhaven of California, Inc. Hospital and Hospital and Institutional Workers Union, Local 399, June 24, 1976. BAHA-27.

Elizabeth Horton Memorial Hospital and Licensed Practical Nurses of New York, Inc. Employees Association, December 18, 1974. 74-2 ARB 8588. Same case reported at 64 LA 96.

Abuse of Patients (Sexual)

Mount Sinai Hospital and National Union of Hospital and Health Care Employees, RWDSU, District 1199, November 19, 1976. LVH.

Mount Sinai Hospital and National Union of Hospital and Health Care Employees, RWDSU, District 1199, August 25, 1977. LVH.

South Oaks Hospital and National Union of Hospital and Health Care Employees, RWDSU, District 1199, January 8, 1976. LVH.

Abuse of Patients (Verbal)

Bronx Lebanon Hospital Center and National Union of Hospital and Health Care Employees, RWDSU, District 1199, June 3, 1975. LVH.

Children's Hospital, Inc., St. Paul, Minnesota and Minnesota Licensed Practical Nurses Association, June 27, 1974. HMMM-2.

Jackson County Medical Care Facility and American Federation of State, County and Municipal Employees, September 9, 1975. 65 LA 389.

Kaiser Foundation Hospitals, The Permanent Medical Group, Kaiser Foundation Health Plan and Hospital and Institutional Workers, Local 250, February 8, 1973. 72-2 ARB 8673.

Little Forest Medical Center and Retail Clerks, Local 698, October 7, 1977. 69 LA 671.

New York University Medical Center and Drug and Hospital Union, Local 1199, December 10, 1975. LVH.

Oil City Hospital and American Federation of State, County and Municipal Employees, Local 801, January 25, 1978. 78-1 ARB 8082.

Southside Hospital, Bay Shore, New York and National Union of Hospital and Health Care Employees, RWDSU, District 1199, December 10, 1975. LVH.

Southside Hospital, Bay Shore, New York, and National Union of Hospital and Health Care Employees, RWDSU, District 1199, October 11, 1976. LVH.

Alcoholism

Children's Hospital of the East Bay and Hospital and Institutional Workers Union, Local 250, August 28, 1971. 71-2 ARB 8527. Same case reported at BAHA-16.

Dearborn Medical Centre Hospital, Inc., and SEIU Local 79, January 3, 1973, 493 GERR:B-7.

Evansville State Hospital and American Federation of State, County and Municipal Employees, April 14, 1969. 69-2 ARB 8585.

French Hospital and Hospital and Institutional Workers, Local 250, March 5, 1975. BAHA-20.

Home and Hospital of the Daughters of Jacob and Hospital Employees, Local 1199, May 6, 1974. LVH. Same case reported at 74-1 ARB 8234.

Maimonides Medical Center and District 1199, July 15, 1975. LVH.

Constructive Discharge

Mount Sinai Division of Cedars-Sinai Medical Center and Building Service Employees International Union, Local 399, May 30, 1967. 67-1 ARB 8315.

Oak Ridge Hospital of the United Methodist Church and Service Employees International Union, Local 150-T, April 25, 1978. 78-1 ARB 8207.

Denial of Promotion for Disciplinary Reasons

Chippewa County (Mich.) War Memorial Hospital and American Federation of State, County and Municipal Employees, Local 301, August 8, 1974. LAIG 1171.

Disrespect to Fellow Employees

Akron (Ohio) City Hospital and American Federation of State, County and Municipal Employees, Local 684, February 15, 1974. LAIG 1049.

Akron (Ohio) City Hospital and American Federation of State, County and Municipal Employees, Local 684, July 1, 1975. LAIG 1399.

Alta Bates Hospital and Service Employees International Union, Local 250, September 28, 1977. BAHA-35.

Memorial Hospital (South Bend, Ind.) and International Brotherhood of Teamsters, Chauffeurs, Warehousemen and Helpers of America, Local 364, December 18, 1978. 71 LA 1252. Same case reported at LAIG 2248.

Audie L. Murphy Memorial Veterans Hospital and American Federation of Government Employees, Local 3511, July 22, 1978. 776 GERR:32.

Drug Abuse

Providence Hospital and Hospital and Institutional Workers Union, Local 250, April 13, 1976. BAHA-25.

Veterans Administration Hospital (Kerrville, Texas) and American Federation of Government Employees, Local 2281, November 5, 1977. 740 GERR:29.

Exceeding Job Authority

Beekman Hospital and RWDSU, District 1199, January 15, 1979. LVH.

Beth Israel Medical Center and National Union of Hospital and Health Care Employees, District 1199, March 29, 1978. LVH.

Albert Einstein College of Medicine and District 1199, April 14, 1976. LVH.

Grace Hospital, Northwest Unit (Detroit, Mich.) and Service Employees International Union, Local 79, November 10, 1971. 71-2 ARB 8676.

Arthur C. Logan Memorial Hospital and New York State Nurses Association, September 1, 1977. LVH.

Mount Sinai Hospital and National Union of Hospital and Health Care Employees, District 1199, February 7, 1979. LVH.

Providence Hospital (Holyoke, Mass.) and Massachusetts Nurses Association, February 10, 1976. LAIG 1544.

Falsification of Application

Long Island Jewish Medical Center and Drug and Hospital Union, RWDSU, District 1199, October 3, 1972. LVH.

Memphis and Shelby County (Tenn.) Hospital Authority and American Federation of State, County and Municipal Employees, Local 1733, May 10, 1977. LAIG 1846.

Southwest Detroit Hospital Association and Service Employees International Union, Local 79. July 29, 1976. 1018 WCR A-8.

Fighting

Flower Fifth Avenue Hospital and Drug and Hospital Union, Local 1199, May 17, 1973. LVH.

Methodist Hospital of Brooklyn and National Union of Hospital and Health Care Employees, District 1199, June 9, 1977. LVH.

Michael Reese Hospital and Medical Center and Hospital Employees Labor Program of Metropolitan Chicago, January 28, 1976. CHC-5.

Michael Reese Hospital and Medical Center and Hospital Employees Labor Program of Metropolitan Chicago, May 13, 1977. 1057 WCR A-8.

New York City (N.Y.) Health and Hospitals Corporation and Individual Grievant, September 20, 1977. LAIG 1950.

Rush-Presbyterian-St. Luke's Medical Center and Hospital Employees Labor Program of Metropolitan Chicago, February 7, 1974. CHC-1.

Saint Francis Memorial Hospital and Hospital and Institutional Workers Union, Local 250, January 18, 1975. 64 LA 29.

Women's General Hospital (Cleveland, Ohio) and Service, Hospital, Nursing Home and Public Employees Union, Local 47, November 30, 1973. LAIG 1028.

Garnishments

Clearfield (Pa.) Hospital and American Federation of State, County and Municipal Employees, Council 85, undated. LAIG 1758.

Honoring Picket Line

Association of Hospitals of Santa Clara County and California Nurses Association, March 6, 1974. 74-1 ARB 8004.

San Jose Hospital and Health Center, Inc. and California Nurses Association, March 6, 1974. 892 WCR A-2.

Incompetence

Barberton Citizens Hospital and American Federation of State, County and Municipal Employees, Local 684, March 9, 1973. 72-2 ARB 8694.

Cabell Huntington Hospital and National Union of Hospital and Health Care Employees, West Virginia Local 1199, April 6, 1978. 70 LA 976.

Chicago (Ill.) Osteopathic Hospital and Chicago Osteopathic Nursing Association, March 17, 1976. LAIG 1610.

Kaiser Foundation Hospitals and Building Service Employees' International Union, Local 250, January 13, 1967. 67-1 ARB 8055.

Kaiser Permanente Medical Care Program and Office and Professional Employees Union, Local 29, April 24, 1978. 70 LA 799.

Puget Sound Hospital and Washington State Nurses Association, November 9, 1977. 77-2 ARB 8540.

Schuylkill County (Pa.) Commissioners and American Federation of State, County and Municipal Employees, April 18, 1979. LAIG 2328.

Youngstown Hospital Association and Ohio Nurses Association, March 31, 1972. 72-1 ARB 8129.

Insubordination

Akron (Ohio) City Hospital and American Federation of State, County and Municipal Employees, Local 684, September 15, 1976. LAIG 1719.

Akron (Ohio) City Hospital and American Federation of State, County and Municipal Employees, Local 684, December 30, 1976. LAIG 1763.

Barberton Citizens Hospital and American Federation of State, County and Municipal Employees, District Council 11, March 30, 1972. 72-1 ARB 8089.

Barberton Citizens Hospital Company, Inc. and American Federation of State, County and Municipal Employees, District Council 11, Local 684, August 18, 1972. 59 LA 277.

Berton Kutnick and University Hospitals of Cleveland, March 22, 1978. 733 GERR:30.

Carney Hospital (Boston, Mass.) and Massachusetts Nurses Association, April 2, 1979. LAIG 2330.

Children's Hospital of Michigan and American Federation of State, County and Municipal Employees, Local 140, June 24, 1974. LAIG 1135.

City of Memphis (Tenn.) Hospital and American Federation of State, County and Municipal Employees, Local 1733, September 21, 1977. LAIG 1935. Same case reported at 4 PSAA 774154.

Dameron Hospital Association and Hospital and Institutional Workers Union, Local 250, September 27, 1976. BAHA-29.

Hillhaven of California and Hospital and Institutional Workers' Union, Local 250, November 8, 1978. BAHA-41.

Marin General Hospital and Freight Checkers, Clerical Employees and Helpers, Local 856, IBT, May 28, 1975. BAHA-21.

Memphis and Shelby County (Tenn.) Hospital Authority and American Federation of State, County and Municipal Employees, Local 1733, March 11, 1976. LAIG 1645.

Memphis and Shelby County (Tenn.) Hospital Authority and American Federation of State, County and Municipal Employees, Local 1733, September 27, 1977. LAIG 1965.

Metropolitan Hospital (Detroit, Mich.) and Michigan Nurses Economic Security Organization, December 14, 1970. 71-1 ARB 8197.

Metropolitan Hospital (Detroit, Mich.) and Office and Professional Employees International Union, Local 42, September 3, 1975. LAIG 1466.

Metropolitan Hospital and Health Centers (Detroit, Mich.) and Office and Professional Employees International Union, Local 42, April 29, 1975. LAIG 1376.

Michael Reese Hospital and Medical Center and Hospital Employees Labor Program of Metropolitan Chicago, February 13, 1976. CHC-6.

Mount Sinai Hospital and National Union of Hospital and Health Care Employees, District 1199, July 18, 1977. LVH.

New York University Medical Center and National Union of Hospital and Health Care Employees, District 1199, March 29, 1978. LVH.

Providence Hospital and Hospital and Institutional Workers' Union, Local 250, May 31, 1973. BAHA-18.

Roosevelt Memorial Hospital (Chicago, Ill.) and Hospital Employees Labor Program, June 30, 1976. LAIG 1657.

St. Joseph's Hospital (Providence, R.I.) and Rhode Island State Nurses Association, April 26, 1976. LAIG 1641.

St. Mary's Hospital (Brooklyn, N.Y.) and Service Employees International Union, Local 144, June 27, 1977. 68 LA 1199.

Samuel Merritt Hospital and Hospital and Institutional Workers' Union, Local 250, March 2, 1976. BAHA-22.

University Hospitals of Cleveland (Ohio) and Individual Grievant, September 29, 1977. LAIG 1992.

Women's General Hospital (Cleveland, Ohio) and Service, Hospital, Nursing Home and Public Employees Union, Local 47, November 21, 1973. LAIG 1034.

Leaves of Absence

Carney Hospital (Dorchester, Mass.) and Massachusetts Nurses Association, undated. LAIG 1632.

Dameron Hospital and Hospital and Institutional Workers, Local 250, March 12, 1976. BAHA-23.

Grace Hospital (Detroit, Mich.) and Service Employees International Union, Local 79, February 20, 1976. LAIG 1583.

Harrisburg (Pa.) Polyclinic Hospital and Pennsylvania Nurses Association, September 28, 1977. LAIG 1963.

Michael Reese Hospital and General Service Employees Union, Local No. 73, March 25, 1976. CHC-8.

Rush-Presbyterian-St. Luke's Medical Center and Hospital Employees Labor Program of Metropolitan Chicago, October 8, 1976. CHC-11.

Veterans Administration Hospital (Asheville, N.C.) and American Federation of Government Employees, Local 446, May 28, 1977. LAIG 1817.

Veterans Administration Hospital (Baltimore, Md.) and American Federation of Government Employees, July 3, 1972. 475 GERR:247.

Leaving Work Station

French Hospital and California Nurses Association, December 18, 1978. BAHA-42.

Merritt Hospital and Hospital and Institutional Workers' Union, Local 250, October 26, 1960. BAHA-1.

Pacific Medical Center and Hospital and Institutional Workers Union, Local 250, December 17, 1976. BAHA-31.

Veterans Administration Hospital (Canandaigua, N.Y.) and Service Employees International Union, Local 200, May 19, 1978. 767 GERR:25.

Loss of Certification/Licensure

Long Island Jewish Medical Center and Drug and Hospital Union, District 1199, August 8, 1973. LVH.

Negligence

Booth Memorial Medical Center and Drug and Hospital Union, Local 1199, March 17, 1972. LVH.

City of Detroit (Mich.) Emergency Medical Services and Emergency Mobile Medical Technicians Association, April 2, 1979. LAIG 2325.

Cook County (Ill.) Health and Hospitals Governing Commission and Illinois Nurses Association, February 2, 1977. LAIG 1819.

Harrisburg (Pa.) Polyclinic Hospital and Pennsylvania Nurses Association, November 23, 1976. LAIG 1748.

Montefiore Hospital and Medical Center and District 1199, November 14, 1975. LVH.

Mount Sinai Medical Center and Drug and Hospital Union, District 1199, March 26, 1971. LVH.

Ross Nursing Home, Inc. and Drug and Hospital Union, District 1199, May 19, 1975. LVH.

Samuel Merritt Hospital and Hospital and Institutional Workers Union, Local 250, September 17, 1963. BAHA-2.

Outside Activity

Abbott-Northwestern Hospital (Minneapolis, Minn.) and Hospital and Nursing Home Employees Union, Local 113, April 29, 1974. HMMM-1.

Fairmont General Hospital and Retail, Wholesale, and Department Store Union, June 20, 1972. 58 LA 1293.

Personal Appearance

St. Mary's Hospital and Medical Center (San Francisco, Calif.) and Hospital and Institutional Workers Union, Local 250, June 28, 1973. 60 LA 1141.

Veterans Administration Hospital (Marion, Ind.) and American Federation of Government Employees, Local 1020, May 23, 1977. 716 GERR:31.

Personal Conduct

Akron General Medical Center and United Rubber, Cork, Linoleum and Plastic Workers of America, Local 1014, June 16, 1977. 77-2 ARB 8336.

Douglas County, Middle River Sanatorium and General Hospital and American Federation of State, County and Municipal Employees, Local 1146, July 1970. 70-2 ARB 8731.

Kaiser Foundation Hospitals and Hospital and Institutional Workers Union, February 22, 1971. 733 WCR A-5.

Kaiser Hospital (Redwood City, Calif.) and Hospital and Institutional Workers, Local 250, September 8, 1975. LAIG 1514.

University Hospitals of Cleveland and Claimant, January 7, 1977. 77-1 ARB 8053. Same case reported at 700 GERR:15.

Youngstown Hospital Assn. and Service Employees International Union, Local 627, June 4, 1976. 76-2 ARB 8409.

Poor Job Attitude

Franklin Hospital and Building Service Employees International Union, Local 250, February 14, 1968. 68-1 ARB 8276.

Kaiser-Permanente Medical Center, San Rafael Facility, and Service Employees International Union, Hospital and Institutional Workers Union, Local 250, SEIU, February 1, 1978. 78-1 ARB 8174.

Permanente Medical Group and Hospital and Institutional Workers' Union, Local 250, undated. 69-1 ARB 8199.

Providence Nursing Home and Building Service Employees International Union, Local 79, November 29, 1968. 69-1 ARB 8250.

Probationary Employee

Bernalillo County (N. Mex.) Medical Center and Bernalillo County Medical Center Employees Association, December 18, 1978. LAIG 2234.

Jackson County (Mich.) Medical Care Facility and American Federation of State, County and Municipal Employees, Local 139, December 19, 1973. LAIG 1014.

New York City (N.Y.) Health and Hospital Corp. and Individual Grievant, September 11, 1978. LAIG 2186.

Veterans Administration Hospital (Perry Point, Md.) and American Federation of Government Employees, Local 331, February 7, 1977. 750 GERR:27.

Punching Another's Time Card

Palm Harbor General Hospital and United Nurses' Associations of California (Palm Harbor Registered Nurses Association), July 30, 1976. 76-2 ARB 8479.

Rush-Presbyterian-St. Luke's Medical Center and Hospital Employees Labor Program of Metropolitan Chicago, July 29, 1975. CHC-4.

Right of Union Representation during Discipline

Veterans Administration Hospital (Palo Alto, Calif.) and American Federation of Government Employees, Local 2110, December 15, 1978. LAIG 2265.

Sex Discrimination

Kaiser Foundation Hospitals and Medical Centers, Kaiser Foundation Health Plan, Southern California Permanente Medical Group, Southern Permanente Services, Inc. and Building Service Employees International Union, Local 399, June 26, 1967. 67-2 ARB 8471.

Sleeping on the Job

Bronx Lebanon Hospital and Drug and Hospital Union, Local 1199, July 11, 1973. LVH.

Douglas County, Nebraska, Douglas County Hospital and American Federation of State, County and Municipal Employees, Local 2845, January 5, 1976. 650 GERR:B-2.

The Hospital of the Albert Einstein College of Medicine and Drug and Hospital Union, Local 1199, March 22, 1979. LVH.

Jewish Hospital and Medical Center of Brooklyn and Drug and Hospital Union, Local 1199, March 21, 1973. LVH.

Peralta Hospital and International Union of Operating Engineers, Local 39, December 29, 1964. BAHA-4.

Youngstown (Ohio) Hospital Association and Ohio Nurses Association, January 4, 1979. 71 LA 1266.

Stealing

Alta Bates Hospital and Hospital and Institutional Workers Union, Local 250, February 16, 1978. BAHA-38.

Morris J. Bernstein Institute of Beth Israel Medical Center and Hotel, Home and Allied Health Services Union, January 2, 1975. LVH.

Bixby Hospital (Adrian, Mich.) and Michigan Licensed Practical Nurses Association, June 3, 1976. LAIG 1633.

Bronx-Lebanon Hospital and National Union of Hospital and Health Care Employees, RWDSU, District 1199, February 15, 1979. LVH.

Michael Reese Hospital and Medical Center and Hospital Employees Labor Program of Metropolitan Chicago, November 11, 1974. CHC-2.

New York City Health and Hospitals Corporation and Individual Grievant, March 22, 1976. LAIG 1611.

Northwest General Hospital (Wis.) and Service and Hospital Employees International Union, Local 150, March 3, 1975. LAIG 1288.

Pacific Medical Center and International Union of Operating Engineers, Stationary Local No. 39, September 6, 1974. BAHA-19.

Roosevelt Hospital and District 1199, March 24, 1978. LVH.

Saint Joseph's Hospital (St. Paul, Minn.) and Professional Employee Pharmacists of Minnesota, May 7, 1978. HMMM-8.

Strike Activity

Ballard Community Hospital and Washington State Nurses Association, undated. 1056 WCR A-2.

Montefiore Hospital and Medical Center (New York City, N.Y.) and Committee of Interns and Residents, May 23, 1977. LAIG 1875.

INTEREST ARBITRATION

Associated Hospitals of the East Bay, Inc. and Hospital and Institutional Workers' Union, Local 250, February 16, 1966. BAHA-7.

Associated Hospitals of the East Bay and International Longshoremen and Warehousemen's Union, Local 6, X-Ray Technologists Unit, July 1, 1971. 71-2 ARB 8479.

Associated Hospitals of the East Bay, Inc. and X-Ray Technologists Unit of ILWU, Local 6, July 1, 1971. BAHA-16.

Baptist Hospital of Gadsden, Inc. and Laborers' International Union, Local 1333, July 5, 1975. 65 LA 248.

Brookhaven Medical Care Facility (Muskegon County, Mich.) and Michigan Licensed Practical Nurses Association, May 13, 1975. LAIG 1342.

East Liverpool (Ohio) City Hospital and Service Employees International Union, Local 257, December 6, 1972. 60 LA 242.

Grace Hospital and International Union of Operating Engineers, Local 547, A, B and C, June 23, 1972. 58 LA 1363.

Jordan Hospital (Plymouth, Mass.) and Massachusetts Nurses Association, August 5, 1975. 1457 LAIG.

Kent Nursing Home and Medical and Health Employees, Local 4 (OPEIU), October 14, 1977. 69 LA 771.

League of Volunteer Hospitals and Homes of New York, Inc. and District 1199, National Union of Hospital and Health Care Employees, RWDSU, June 29, 1977. 1055 WCR C-1.

League of Voluntary Hospitals of New York and District 1199, Hospital and Health Care Employees, RWDSU, September 10, 1976. 67 LA 293.

Michael Reese Hospital and Medical Center and Hospital Employees Labor Program of Metropolitan Chicago, May 3, 1978. CHC-13.

Saginaw County (Mich.) and Michigan Nurses Association, March 14, 1975. LAIG 1353.

University of Chicago Hospitals and Clinics and Licensed Practical Nurse Association of Illinois, Division I, October 30, 1974. 63 LA 824.

MANAGEMENT RIGHTS

Assignment of Overtime

Veterans Administration Hospital (Lincoln, Nebr.) and American Federation of Government Employees, Local 2219, February 24, 1978. 754 GERR:40.

Job Assignments

Akron (Ohio) City Hospital and American Federation of State, County and Municipal Employees, Local 684, September 30, 1978. LAIG 2175.

Barberton (Ohio) Citizens Hospital and American Federation of State, County and Municipal Employees, January 6, 1977. LAIG 1801.

Easton (Penn.) Hospital and Pennsylvania Nurses Association, April 3, 1978. LAIG 2097.

Metropolitan Medical Center and Minnesota Licensed Practical Nurses Association, October 9, 1978. HMMM-5.
Northwestern Memorial Hospital and Hospital Employees Labor Program, April 26, 1976. CHC-9.
Peralta Hospital and Hospital and Institutional Workers' Union, Local 250, January 19, 1971. BAHA-15.
Saginaw (Mich.) Osteopathic Hospital and Hospital Employees Division, Service Employees International Union, Local 79, June 16, 1976. LAIG 1669.
Saginaw (Mich.) Osteopathic Hospital and Service Employees International Union, Local 79, April 29, 1977. LAIG 1865.
Studebaker Community Hospital (Calif.) and Hospital and Service Employees Union, Local 399, September 23, 1976. LAIG 1735.
Veterans Administration Hospital (Long Beach, Calif.) and California Nurses' Association, November 25, 1969. 328 GERR:65.
Veterans Administration Hospital (Murfreesboro, Tenn.) and American Federation of Government Employees, Local 1844, August 7, 1972. 479 GERR:279.
Veterans Administration Hospital (Palo Alto, Calif.) and American Federation of Government Employees, Local 2110, undated. 588 GERR:A-1.
Women's General Hospital and Service, Hospital, Nursing Home and Public Employees Union, Local 47, March 4, 1976. Ohio Hospital Association OHA-1.
Youngstown (Ohio) Hospital Association and Service Employees International Union, Local 627, September 17, 1975. LAIG 1431.

Subcontracting

Akron City Hospital and American Federation of State, County and Municipal Employees, Local 684, District Council No. 11, March 27, 1974. 74-1 ARB 8098.
Greater Pennsylvania Avenue Nursing Center and National Union of Hospital and Health Care Employees, District 1199E, June 6, 1977. 77-2 ARB 8343.
Hospital for Joint Diseases and Medical Center and District 1199, National Union of Hospital and Health Care Employees, RWDSU, November 3, 1978. LVH.
Kaiser Foundation Hospitals and Hospital and Institutional Workers' Union, Local 250, November 9, 1973. 61 LA 1008.
League of Voluntary Hospitals and Homes of New York and Drug and Hospital Union, Local 1199, May 6, 1969. 52 LA 971.
Metropolitan Hospital and Office and Professional Employees International Union, Local 42, July 8, 1974. 74-1 ARB 8261.
Monongahela Valley Hospital, Inc. and United Steelworkers of America, Local 8041, May 11, 1976. 76-2 ARB 8368.

Rochester Methodist Hospital and Hotel, Hospital, Restaurant and Tavern Employees Union, Local 21, November 22, 1976. 67 LA 927.
Roosevelt Hospital and International Brotherhood of Teamsters, Local 810, March 8, 1976. LVH.

Work Scheduling

Grant Hospital of Chicago and International Brotherhood of Teamsters, Local 743, Hospital Employees Labor Program of Metropolitan Chicago (HELP), August 11, 1977. CHC-12.
Herrick Memorial Hospital and Hospital and Institutional Workers Union, Local 250, September 29, 1970. BAHA-14.
Herrick Memorial Hospital and Service Employees International Union, Local 250, September 29, 1970. 70-2 ARB 8866.
Marinette General Hospital and Marinette General Hospital Employees Union, Local 1752, AFSCME, February 19, 1974. 73-2 ARB 8616. Same case reported at LAIG 1023.
Marshal Hale Memorial Hospital and International Union of Operating Engineers, Stationary Local No. 39, June 7, 1978. 78-2 ARB 8281.
Merritt Hospital and Hospital and Institutional Workers' Union, Local 250, June 8, 1965. BAHA-2.
Miami Inspiration Hospital, Inc. and United Steelworkers of America, April 26, 1977. 68 LA 898.
Quincy (Mass.) City Hospital and Massachusetts Hospital Workers, Service Employees International Union, Local 880, March 8, 1977. LAIG 1804. Same case reported at 4 PSAA 77480.

SENIORITY

Bumping

St. Joseph's Hospital (Hazelton, Pa.) and Pennsylvania Nurses' Association, January 10, 1977. 68 LA 658.
Toronto General Hospital and Canadian Union of Public Employees, Local 2001, July 31, 1978. 71 LA 295.

Denial of Promotion for Disciplinary Reasons

Chippewa County (Mich.) War Memorial Hospital and American Federation of State, County and Municipal Employees, Local 301, August 8, 1974. LAIG 1171.

Downward Bidding

Veterans Administration Hospital (Danville, Ill.) and American Federation of Government Employees, Local 1963, November 4, 1977. 69 LA 822.

Failure to Post Job Assignment

Benzie Medical Care Facility (Benzie County, Mich.) and Benzie Medical Employees Chapter, American Federation of State, County and Municipal Employees, Local 1804, January 18, 1975. LAIG 1277.
Children's Hospital Medical Center and Hospital and Institutional Workers Union, Local No. 250, May 1, 1978. BAHA-39.
Health and Hospitals Governing Commission (Cook County, Ill.) and Illinois Nurses Association, November 10, 1975. LAIG 1499.
Veterans Administration Hospital (Big Spring, Texas) and American Federation of Government Employees, Local 1934, March 15, 1978. 758 GERR:36.
Veterans Administration Hospital (Salisbury, N.C.) and American Federation of Government Employees, Local 1738, August 16, 1977. LAIG 1944. Same case reported at 4 PSAA 774152.

Layoffs

Brooklyn Cumberland Medical Center and District 1199, National Union of Hospital and Health Care Employees, RWDSU, December 1, 1975. LVH.
Dameron Hospital Association and Hospital and Institutional Workers Union, Local 250, SEIU, September 16, 1977. BAHA-34.
The Oak Ridge Hospital of The Methodist Church and Building Service Employees International Union, Local 150-T, June 6, 1967. 67-1 ARB 8317.
Peralta Hospital and California Nurses' Association, July 15, 1976. BAHA-28.
Southwest Virginia Community Health Services, Inc. and United Steelworkers of America, Local 15220, February 3, 1978. 1089 WCR A-4.

Promotions

Alta Bates Hospital and Hospital and Institutional Workers' Union, Local 250, June 19, 1976. BAHA-26.
Brown County Mental Health Center and Brown County Employees Union, Local 1901, July 7, 1977. 68 LA 1363.
Clinch Valley Clinic Hospital (Bluefield, W. Va.) and Hospital and Nursing Home Employees, Local 1199, February 26, 1975. 64 LA 542.

Evansville (Ind.) State Hospital, State of Indiana, and State, County and Municipal Employees, Indiana Council 62, September 12, 1977. 77-2 ARB 8418.

Herrick Memorial Hospital and Hospital and Institutional Workers' Union, Local 250, September 6, 1969. BAHA-11.

Jewish Institute for Geriatric Care and RWDSU, District 1199, April 30, 1975. LVH.

Kingsbrook Jewish Medical Center and Drug and Hospital Union, Local 1199, March 23, 1973. LVH.

Long Island Jewish-Hillside Medical Center and District 1199, July 30, 1975. LVH.

Michael Reese Hospital and Medical Center and Hospital Employees Labor Program of Metropolitan Chicago, April 24, 1979. CHC-15.

Miners Clinics, Inc. and United Steelworkers of America, Local 14077, November 18, 1975. 986 WCR A-1.

Plymouth County (Mass.) Hospital and Massachusetts Nurses Association, April 8, 1977. LAIG 1849.

Veterans Administration Hospital, Muskogee, Oklahoma, and American Federation of Government Employees, Local 2250, September 20, 1976. 682 GERR:C-13.

Veterans Administration Hospital, Perry Point, Maryland, and American Federation of Government Employees, Local 331, January 28, 1977. Same case reported at 699 GERR:28.

Veterans Administration Hospital (Roseburg, Oregon) and American Federation of Government Employees, Local 1042, January 16, 1978. 70 LA 491. Same case reported at 754 GERR:38.

Warm Springs (Mont.) State Hospital and Warm Springs State Hospital Independent Union, January 6, 1977. 699 GERR:10. Same case reported at LAIG 1787.

Recalls

Centerville Clinics, Inc. and Office and Professional Employees International Union, Local 457, May 1, 1973. 60 LA 691.

Mary's Help Hospital and Hospital and Institutional Workers, Local 250, January 14, 1976. 76-1 ARB 8140.

Merritt Hospital and Hospital and Institutional Workers Union, Local 250, November 17, 1964. BAHA-3.

Youngstown Hospital Association and Ohio State Nurses Association, January 23, 1968. 68-1 ARB 8327.

Transfer of Seniority

Isabella Geriatrics Center and National Union of Hospital and Health Care Employees, RWDSU, November 10, 1975. LVH.

Rome Hospital and Murphy Memorial Hospital and American Federation of State, County and Municipal Employees, Local 1088, December 18, 1970. 386 GERR:B-12.

United Hospitals, Inc. and Hospital and Nursing Home Employees Union No. 113, April 17, 1979. HMMM-7.

SPECIAL HOSPITAL ISSUES

Abuse of Patients (Physical)

Bethesda Lutheran Infirmary and Minnesota Licensed Practical Nurses Association, October 23, 1978. HMMM-6.

Fort Wayne State Hospital and American Federation of State, County and Municipal Employees, February 26, 1975. 74-2 ARB 8706.

Greater Harlem Nursing Home and RWDSU, District 1199, May 7, 1979. LVH.

Menorah Home and Hospital and Service Employees International Union, Local 144, June 2, 1978. LVH.

Oak Pavilion Nursing Home and Rehabilitation Center and National Union of Hospital and Nursing Home Employees, July 6, 1973. 73-1 ARB 8198.

Salinas Valley (Calif.) Memorial Hospital District and Hospital and Institutional Workers Union, Local 250, February 10, 1977. LAIG 1803.

St. John's Episcopal Hospital and New York State Nurses Association, March 20, 1978. LVH.

Abuse of Patients (Poor Attitude toward Patients)

Ralph K. Davies Medical Center and Hospital and Institutional Workers Union, Local 250, October 25, 1977. BAHA-36.

Hillhaven of California, Inc. Hospital and Hospital and Institutional Workers Union, Local 399, June 24, 1976. BAHA-27.

Elizabeth Horton Memorial Hospital and Licensed Practical Nurses of New York, Inc. Employees Association, December 18, 1974. 74-2 ARB 8588. Same case reported at 64 LA 96.

Abuse of Patients (Sexual)

Mount Sinai Hospital and National Union of Hospital and Health Care Employees, RWDSU, District 1199, November 19, 1976. LVH.

Mount Sinai Hospital and National Union of Hospital and Health Care Employees, RWDSU, District 1199, August 25, 1977. LVH.

South Oaks Hospital and National Union of Hospital and Health Care Employees, RWDSU, District 1199, January 8, 1976. LVH.

Abuse of Patients (Verbal)

Bronx Lebanon Hospital Center and National Union of Hospital and Health Care
Employees, RWDSU, District 1199, June 3, 1975. LVH.
Children's Hospital, Inc., St. Paul, Minnesota and Minnesota Licensed Practical
Nurses Association, June 27, 1974. HMMM-2.
Jackson County Medical Care Facility and American Federation of State, County
and Municipal Employees, September 9, 1975. 65 LA 389.
Kaiser Foundation Hospitals, The Permanente Medical Group, Kaiser Foundation
Health Plan and Hospital and Institutional Workers, Local 250, February 8,
1973. 72-2 ARB 8673.
Little Forest Medical Center and Retail Clerks, Local 698, October 7, 1977. 69 LA
671.
New York University Medical Center and Drug and Hospital Union, Local 1199,
December 10, 1975. LVH.
Oil City Hospital and American Federation of State, County and Municipal
Employees, Local 801, January 25, 1978. 78-1 ARB 8082.
Southside Hospital, Bay Shore, New York and National Union of Hospital and
Health Care Employees, RWDSU, District 1199, December 10, 1975. LVH.
Southside Hospital, Bay Shore, New York, and National Union of Hospital and
Health Care Employees, RWDSU, District 1199, October 11, 1976. LVH.

Discharge for Loss of Certification/Licensure

Long Island Jewish Medical Center and Drug and Hospital Union, District 1199,
August 8, 1973. LVH.

Drug Abuse

Providence Hospital and Hospital and Institutional Workers Union, Local 250,
April 13, 1976. BAHA-25.
Veterans Administration Hospital (Kerrville, Texas) and American Federation of
Government Employees, Local 2281, November 5, 1977. 740 GERR:29.

Hospital Ethics

Beth Israel Medical Center at St. Vincent's, Staten Island District 1199, June 8,
1975. LVH.
Mission Terrace Hospital and Service Employees International Union, July 11,
1977. 1060 WCR A-7. Same case reported at LAIG 1934.

Hospital Understaffing

Alpena General Hospital and United Steelworkers of America, Local 206-A, July 26, 1973. 73-1 ARB 8226.

Auburn Faith Community Hospital, Inc. and California Nurses Association, May 4, 1976. 66 LA 882. Same case reported at 1000 WCR A-11.

Purchase of Equipment

County of Los Angeles, Harbor General Hospital and Joint Council of Interns and Resident Physicians Association of Los Angeles County, May 10, 1976. 1004 WCR A-3.

Religious Objection to Uniform

Hurley Hospital and American Federation of State, County and Municipal Employees, Local 1603, May 25, 1978. 70 LA 1061. Same case reported at: 78-1 ARB 8266, 769 GERR:13, LAIG 2109. The follow-up to this case is reported at 71 LA 1013, November 7, 1978.

Sleeping on the Job

Bronx Lebanon Hospital and Drug and Hospital Union, Local 1199, July 11, 1973. LVH.

Douglas County, Nebraska, Douglas County Hospital and American Federation of State, County and Municipal Employees, Local 2845, January 5, 1976. 650 GERR:B-2.

The Hospital of Albert Einstein College of Medicine and Drug and Hospital Union, Local 1199, March 22, 1979. LVH.

Jewish Hospital and Medical Center of Brooklyn and Drug and Hospital Union, Local 1199, March 21, 1973. LVH.

Peralta Hospital and International Union of Operating Engineers, Local 39, December 29, 1964. BAHA-4.

Youngstown (Ohio) Hospital Association and Ohio Nurses Association, January 4, 1979. 71 LA 1266.

UNION SECURITY

Bargaining Unit

Baltimore City Hospitals and Maryland Licensed Practical Nurses Association and American Federation of State, County and Municipal Employees, Local 44, February 17, 1971. 393 GERR:B-11.

W. A. Foote Memorial Hospital, Inc. and Operating Engineers, Local 547, January 19, 1976. 66 LA 24.

Group Health Association (Washington, D.C.) and Registered Nurses and Physical Therapists Association, July 5, 1976. 67 LA 72.

Marinette General Hospital and Marinette General Hospital Employees, Local 1752, October 21, 1976. 67 LA 785.

Drs. Sakai, Simms, Simon, Sugiyama and Green, a Dental Partnership, and Hospital and Service Employees Union, Local 399, Service Employees International Union, May 25, 1978. 70 LA 1264.

Discrimination against Union Officers or Members

William Beaumont Army Medical Center (El Paso, Texas) and American Federation of Government Employees, Local 2516, January 30, 1978. 750 GERR:27.

William Beaumont Army Medical Center (El Paso, Texas) and American Federation of Government Employees, Local 2516, February 23, 1978. 758 GERR:35.

Hurley Hospital and Hurley Hospital Head Nurses Staff Council, September 6, 1972. 72-1 ARB 8366.

Veterans Administration Hospital (Fayetteville, N.C.) and American Federation of Government Employees, Local 2080, June 21, 1976. 682 GERR:C-11.

General

Associated Hospitals of San Francisco (on behalf of Franklin Medical Center) and Hospital and Institutional Workers Union, Local 250, August 16, 1976. 67 LA 323. Same case reported at 76-2 ARB 8495.

Board of Mental Retardation, Lucas County, and American Federation of State, County and Municipal Employees, Council 46, Local 544, November 10, 1977. 69 LA 862.

Doctors Memorial Hospital and National Union of Hospital and Nursing Home Employees, RWDSU, Local 1199, May 23, 1973. 73-1 ARB 8167.

Levine Hospital of Hayward, Inc. and Hospital and Institutional Workers' Union, Local 250, December 1, 1966. BAHA-8.

St. Luke's Hospital Center and District 1199, National Union of Hospital and Health Care Employees, May 27, 1975. 64 LA 1034. Same case reported at 1975 ARB 8170.

St. Luke's Hospital Center and District 1199, National Union of Hospital and Health Care Employees, October 14, 1975. 65 LA 862. Same case reported at 1975 ARB 8338.

Veterans Administration Hospital (Salt Lake City, Utah) and American Federation of Government Employees, Local 2199, September 15, 1977. 69 LA 364. Same case reported at 77-2 ARB 8455.

Inter-Union (Jurisdictional) Disputes

Gila County General Hospital, Laborers International Union of North America and American Federation of State, County and Municipal Employees, May 15, 1974. 64 LA 1055.

Lansing General Hospital, Service Employees International Union and American Federation of State, County and Municipal Employees, October 15, 1974. 64 LA 795.

Miles Square Health Center, Service Employees International Union and American Federation of State, County and Municipal Employees, February 17, 1975. 64 LA 1014.

New York City Health and Hospitals Corp., American Federation of State, County and Municipal Employees and Retail, Wholesale and Department Store Union, December 19, 1973. 62 LA 740.

Plaza Nursing Home, Service Employees International Union and Retail, Wholesale and Department Store Union, December 20, 1973. 62 LA 580.

Rules Regarding Distribution of Union Literature

Metropolitan Hospital and Health Centers and Office and Professional Employees International Union, Local 42, August 26, 1974. 63 LA 378. Same case reported at 74-2 ARB 8280.

Subcontracting

Akron City Hospital and American Federation of State, County and Municipal Employees, Local 684, District Council No. 111, March 27, 1974. 74-1 ARB 8098.

Greater Pennsylvania Avenue Nursing Center and National Union of Hospital and Health Care Employees, District 1199E, June 6, 1977. 77-2 ARB 8343.

Hospital for Joint Diseases and Medical Center and District 1199, National Union of Hospital and Health Care Employees, RWDSU, November 3, 1978. LVH.

Kaiser Foundation Hospitals and Hospital and Institutional Workers' Union, Local 250, November 9, 1973. 61 LA 1008.

League of Voluntary Hospital and Homes of New York and Drug and Hospital Union, Local 1199, May 6, 1969. 52 LA 971.

Metropolitan Hospital and Office and Professional Employees International Union, Local 42, July 8, 1974. 74-1 ARB 8261.

Monongahela Valley Hospital, Inc. and United Steelworkers of America, Local 8041, May 11, 1976. 76-2 ARB 8368.

Rochester Methodist Hospital and Hotel, Hospital, Restaurant and Tavern Employees Union, Local 21, November 22, 1976. 67 LA 927.

Roosevelt Hospital and International Brotherhood of Teamsters, Local 810, March 8, 1976. LVH.

Supervisor Performing Bargaining Unit Work

Akron (Ohio) City Hospital and American Federation of State, County and Municipal Employees, Local 684, August 11, 1978. LAIG 2191.

Akron (Ohio) City Hospital and American Federation of State, County and Municipal Employees, Local 684, November 13, 1978. LAIG 2215.

Massachusetts Department of Public Health, Rutland Heights Hospital and American Federation of State, County and Municipal Employees, Local 1170, February 15, 1974. LAIG 1073.

Metropolitan Hospital Center and District 1199, National Union of Hospital and Health Care Employees, RWDSU, May 14, 1979. LVH.

Index

About the Authors

DONALD J. PETERSEN is Professor of Management, School of Business Administration, at Loyola University of Chicago. He received his Ph.D. in industrial relations from the Illinois Institute of Technology. Dr. Petersen has authored numerous articles for scholarly and professional journals on arbitration and other personnel and industrial relations topics.

Dr. Petersen is an arbitrator and is listed on the national panels of the American Arbitration Association and the Federal Mediation and Conciliation Service, as well as the arbitration panels of the Wisconsin Employment Relations Commission, Public Employee Panels of the State of Iowa, and the Board of Governors of State Colleges and Universities (Illinois). A contributor to many AAA arbitration training programs, Professor Petersen is a member of the Industrial Relations Research Association and is listed in *American Men and Women of Science*.

JULIUS REZLER is a full-time labor arbitrator. His name appears on the panels of the American Arbitration Association, the Federal Mediation and Conciliation Service, the U.S. Postal Service, State of Illinois Personnel Department, and the basic steel industry. He is a member of the National Academy of Arbitrators and the Industrial Relations Research Association.

Dr. Rezler was Professor of Industrial Relations with the Institute of Industrial Relations, a graduate program of Loyola University of Chicago. He has authored numerous books and articles, including *Automation and Industrial Labor* (Random House, 1969). He has coauthored several articles in the area of arbitration. His biographical data are published in *Who's Who in America*.

KEITH A. REED has practiced labor law with the firm of Seyfarth, Shaw, Fairweather & Geraldson, Chicago, Illinois, since 1963. He received an undergraduate business degree from the University of Iowa in 1960 and a law degree from the same school in 1963.